CORPORATE DEBT CAPACITY

CORPORATE
DEBT
CAPACITY

A Study of Corporate Debt Policy
and the Determination of
Corporate Debt Capacity

by

GORDON DONALDSON
Associate Professor of Business Administration

DIVISION OF RESEARCH
GRADUATE SCHOOL OF BUSINESS ADMINISTRATION
HARVARD UNIVERSITY
BOSTON 1961

Library of Congress Catalog Card No. 61–17118

Third Printing 1964

Printed in the United States of America

FOREWORD

The research project whose results are reported in this volume was primarily concerned with the risk element involved in the utilization of debt as a source of permanent capital for business. As a management problem this aspect of debt financing receives principal attention in the determination of the amount of debt that a company may have outstanding at a given time. Professor Donaldson approached the subject with two objectives in mind: (1) to describe management thinking, practice, and policies in a sample of manufacturing corporations with respect to risks of debt in general and the determination of debt limits in particular, and, assuming an opportunity existed for improving on "best business practice," (2) to formulate an independent approach to the analysis of the risks involved in debt and the determination of debt capacity.

The volume itself reports extensively on current business practice but then suggests a significantly different approach which the author intends to be of immediate practical value to managements of companies in need of additional permanent capital. The author views the risk of debt as part of the over-all problem of balancing the amount and timing of cash inflows and cash outflows. Measuring the risk then becomes an aspect of the appraisal of expected variations in total cash inflows and of the controlability of total cash outflows in the individual business. Since the objective has been to develop a framework for decision making by corporate borrowers, no attempt is made to develop refined methods of measurement of risk or to construct a set of generalized standards of debt capacity. Interest in these will inevitably follow to the extent that experience proves the suggested approach to be an important aid to business decision making in the problems of long-term financing.

The financial support for this study came in part from an allocation of research funds made available to the School by The Associates of the Harvard Business School and in part from the income from an endowment fund given to the School for the general support of its research program.

BERTRAND FOX
Director of Research

Soldiers Field
Boston, Massachusetts
August 1961

ACKNOWLEDGMENTS

Financial research at the level of individual company experience has, in the past, often encountered resistance because of the confidential nature traditionally associated with financial data. Fortunately for our understanding of decision making in this area of business policy, this sensitivity has been declining, and the experience of the author clearly reflected the increasing willingness of responsible businessmen to make the record public. The condition of anonymity which was imposed on the corporations and executives participating in the field study, and which I initiated, prevents an adequate acknowledgment of their individual contribution. Nevertheless, I wish to record my sincere appreciation to the officers of the participating corporations and of the associated financial institutions whose participation in terms of interest and time went far beyond the normal requirements of good public relations.

In any work of research and writing, it is impossible to distinguish your own contribution from that of others with whom you have been associated through their writings or through personal contact. I have attempted to acknowledge my obligation to previous authors on this subject through the bibliography at the end of the book. I am, however, especially conscious of how much I owe to my colleagues at the Harvard Business School who in various ways have stimulated my thinking along what I hope have been productive channels. I would like to make particular reference to Professors Pearson Hunt, John Lintner, and James E. Walter who read and offered criticisms on the entire manuscript. I also wish to thank Dr. John E. Bishop for his suggestions on the analytical presentation.

Throughout its development from conception to final manuscript this study has benefited greatly from the support and guidance, not to mention the patience, of Professors Bertrand Fox and Lewis B. Ward of the Division of Research.   My appreciation extends also to Miss Ruth Norton who edited the final manuscript and directed it through publication.

Finally, I wish to express my thanks to Miss Nancy Buckley who prepared the index and to Miss Marie Forte and Miss Carol Adamian who assisted me throughout the slow and at times frustrating process of converting ideas into a typed manuscript.

Responsibility for the interpretation placed on the data generated in the study and for the conclusions drawn therefrom rests, of course, on me.

GORDON DONALDSON

Soldiers Field
Boston, Massachusetts
August 1961

CONTENTS

PART ONE. A FIELD STUDY OF CORPORATE DEBT AND
RELATED FINANCIAL POLICIES

CHAPTER   PAGE
1. INTRODUCTION   3
The Scope and Objectives of the Study . . . The Concept
of Risk . . . The Form of Debt . . . The Field Research
. . . The Characteristics of the Field Sample: *The Industries; The Companies* . . . The Organization of the Study

2. BACKGROUND: A REVIEW OF TWENTY YEARS OF FUNDS
FLOWS   27
The Need for Funds: *Scope and Definition; Determining
the Amount Required* . . . A Classification of Patterns of
Fund Requirements . . . The Sources of Funds: *Current
Internal Generation of Funds; Liquid Reserves; External
Sources of Funds*

3. BACKGROUND: BASIC MANAGEMENT ATTITUDES TO EX-
TERNAL SOURCES OF FUNDS OTHER THAN DEBT   51
General Attitudes Toward the Use of External Sources of
Funds . . . Attitudes Toward Specific External Sources
Other Than Debt: *Common Stock; Preferred Stock* . . .
Summary Statement

4. MANAGEMENT ATTITUDES CONCERNING THE USE OF
LONG-TERM DEBT   68
The Incentive to Borrow . . . The Argument Against Bor-
rowing . . . The Basic Problem of Uncertainty . . . How
Management Looks at Uncertainty (Risk)

5. CORPORATE DEBT POLICY AND THE CONTROL OF RISK ..   93
Restraints on the Amount of Debt . . . Decision Rule
No. 1 — No Long-Term Debt Under Any Circumstances
. . . Decision Rule No. 2 — Borrow the Maximum Avail-

ix

able . . . Decision Rule No. 3 — Borrow the Maximum
Available "At the Prime Rate" . . . Decision Rule No. 4
— Borrow the Maximum Consistent with an "A" Rating
. . . Decision Rule No. 5 — Limit the Principal Amount of
(Long-Term) Debt to "X" Percent of Total Capitalization
. . . Decision Rule No. 6 — A Minimum Earnings Cover-
age Standard . . . Decision Rule No. 7 — The Single-
Project Approach to Debt . . . Decision Rule No. 8 — The
Rapid Payback Approach to Debt . . . The Control of Risk
Other Than by Limiting the Amount of the Debt . . . The
Origin of Standards of Debt Capacity: *The Capital Structure
of Other Companies; The Standards of the Lender; The In-
dependent Standard*

PART TWO.   THE ANALYSIS OF CORPORATE DEBT CAPACITY:
AN APPRAISAL OF PRACTICE AND A PROPOSAL FOR
IMPROVEMENT

6.   AN APPRAISAL OF CORPORATE PRACTICE IN THE USE OF
LONG-TERM DEBT 123

Introduction . . . The Appropriateness of Conventional
Sources from Which Debt Capacity Criteria Are Derived:
*The Purely Subjective Debt Criterion; The Evidence of Gen-
eral Industry Practice; The Risk Standard of the Lender; The
Criterion of Past Experience* . . . The Concept of Continu-
ous Versus Discontinuous Borrowing . . . The Fragmented
Approach to Risk Appraisal . . . The Validity of the Single
Corporate Debt Limit . . . The Quantitative Form of Debt
Capacity Standards: *The Balance Sheet Standard — Percent
of Capitalization; The Income Statement Standard — Earn-
ings Coverage*

7.   A CASH FLOW ANALYSIS FOR THE APPRAISAL OF RISK
AND THE DETERMINATION OF LONG-TERM DEBT
CAPACITY 156

Introduction . . . The Objectives of a Cash Flow Analysis
. . . Cash Flows and the Event of Cash Insolvency . . .
The Determinants of Cash Flow: *The Underlying Causes of
Change in Net Cash Flow* . . . The Recession Behavior of
Individual Determinants of Cash Flow . . . A Comprehen-
sive Method of Risk Analysis . . . An Analysis of the Ad-
verse Limits of Net Cash Flows: *Deriving Data on the*

*Chance of Cash Insolvency; Evaluating Adverse Limits —
Maximum Adverse Versus Most Probable Limits* . . . Assembling the Data on Recession Cash Balances . . . Summary

8. THE APPLICATION OF A RECESSION CASH FLOW ANALYSIS TO THE DEBT-EQUITY CHOICE AND ITS INTEGRATION WITH OTHER LONG-TERM POLICIES 193

Introduction . . . An Example of Recession Cash Flow Analysis . . . Interpreting the Data on Adverse Limits of Recession Cash Balances . . . Cash Inadequacy Versus Cash Insolvency . . . The Determination of Specific Debt Limits . . . The Influence of Management Action on the Risk of Cash Insolvency . . . The Broader Implications of the Cash Flow Analysis . . . The Relation of Debt Capacity Rules to General Corporate Liquidity . . . Summary and Comment

9. A REVIEW OF THE DEBT POLICIES OF FIVE COMPANIES IN THE LIGHT OF THEIR SIMULATED RECESSION CASH FLOWS 223

Introduction . . . Company "A" (The Rubber Industry) . . . Company "B" (The Baking Industry) . . . Company "C" (Chemicals) . . . Company "D" (Ethical Drugs) . . . Company "E" (Machine Tools) . . . Summary and Conclusions

APPENDICES

A. COMPANY-BY-COMPANY RECORD OF THE MEANS BY WHICH FUNDS WERE PROVIDED IN YEARS WHEN TOTAL FUNDS APPLIED EXCEEDED INTERNALLY GENERATED FUNDS PLUS FUNDS RELEASED FROM OTHER ASSETS . . 268

B. A PROBABILITY APPROACH TO THE EVALUATION OF CORPORATE DEBT CAPACITY 274

SELECTED READINGS RELATED TO THE SUBJECT OF CORPORATE DEBT CAPACITY 285

INDEX 289

EXHIBITS

NUMBER   PAGE

1   Classification of Company Experience in the Investment
    of Funds in Terms of Long-Term Rate of Growth and
    Year-to-Year Variability   35

2   Company Data on Internally Generated Funds and Re-
    lated Information   41

3   Company Data on Frequency of Use of External
    Sources of Funds   46

4   Typical Cash Budget Form   73

5   Probability Table of Recession Sales Contractions 172

6   Estimated Net Cash Flows Associated with the Antici-
    pated Adverse Limits of Recession Experience: Com-
    pany "A" 195

7   Results of Cash Flow Analysis as Shown in Exhibit 6,
    Regrouped in Order of Increasing Net Cash Flows:
    Company "A" 197

8   Cash Solvency at the Limits of Adversity: Company
    "A" — Anticipated Recession Cash Balances Asso-
    ciated with the Adverse Recession Cash Flow Assump-
    tions of Exhibit 7 199

9   Cash Adequacy at the Limits of Adversity: Company
    "A" — Revision of Exhibit 8 Showing Maximum Ad-
    verse Recession Cash Position after Provision for All
    Expenditures Considered by Management to be Man-
    datory 205

10 Cash Solvency at the Limits of Adversity: Company
    "A"   (Rubber   Industry) — Anticipated   Recession

Cash Position Associated with Adverse Limits of Behavior of Determinants of Cash Flow: Considering Only Those Expenditures Required to Generate Current Income 226

11 Cash Adequacy at the Limits of Adversity: Company "A" (Rubber Industry) — Anticipated Recession Cash Position Associated with Adverse Limits of Behavior or Determinants of Cash Flow: Considering All Expenditures Given Priority over Debt Servicing 227

12 Cash Solvency at the Limits of Adversity: Company "B" (Baking Industry) 236

13 Cash Adequacy at the Limits of Adversity: Company "B" (Baking Industry) 237

14 Cash Solvency at the Limits of Adversity: Company "C" (Chemical Industry) 244

15 Cash Adequacy at the Limits of Adversity: Company "C" (Chemical Industry) 245

16 Cash Solvency at the Limits of Adversity: Company "D" (Drug Industry) 250

17 Cash Adequacy at the Limits of Adversity: Company "D" (Drug Industry) 251

18 Cash Solvency at the Limits of Adversity: Company "E" (Machine Tools Industry) 256

19 Cash Adequacy at the Limits of Adversity: Company "E" (Machine Tools Industry) 258

B–1 Table Showing All Possible Values for Collection from Sales (C_s) Given Previous Assumptions Regarding S and ACP 278

B–2 Table Indicating Recession Net Cash Flows Associated with All Possible Groupings of Determinants Arranged in Order of Decreasing Adversity 282

CHARTS

NUMBER   PAGE

1. Pattern of Application of Funds No. 1: Low Long-Term
   Growth Rate, High Year-to-Year Variability, Company
   "H", 1939–1958 36

2. Pattern of Application of Funds No. 2: High Long-Term
   Growth Rate, High Year-to-Year Variability, Company
   "C", 1939–1958 36

3. Pattern of Application of Funds No. 3: Low Long-Term
   Growth Rate, Low Year-to-Year Variability, Company
   "E", 1940–1958 37

4. Pattern of Application of Funds No. 4: High Long-Term
   Growth Rate, High Year-to-Year Variability, Company
   "K", 1939–1938 37

5. Graph of Frequency of Sales Contractions in Recession
   Periods 187

PART ONE

A FIELD STUDY
OF CORPORATE DEBT
AND RELATED FINANCIAL POLICIES

CHAPTER 1

Introduction

THE SCOPE AND OBJECTIVES OF THE STUDY

This book is concerned with one of the basic financial choices confronting every established business corporation — the choice between debt and equity as the source of its long-term capital. It is a study both of how this choice is made currently by successful industrial corporations and of how the process of making this decision may be improved. In particular, the book focuses on what is considered to be the most difficult aspect of the problem — the determination of the appropriate limit to the amount of long-term debt outstanding at any point of time. This aspect of debt policy has been chosen because it is considered by the author to be a major challenge to financial management and an area where conventional practice is in need of serious reappraisal. In the process of examining the determination of debt capacity, however, other phases of debt policy will come in for examination and discussion.

It is generally recognized that the particular combination of debt and equity capital achieved by a business at a given point of time has important implications for a variety of considerations of significance to management, particularly those of future solvency and profitability. Debt, because of its fixed commitment as to income and repayment of principal, is normally thought of as contributing at the same time to the opportunity for profit and the possibility of loss. An intelligent appraisal of these and other considerations involved in the debt versus equity decision presents management with a problem that is inherently one of the most difficult it has to face.

The starting point of the problem is that this, like other business

3

decisions affecting the future, is a decision made under conditions of uncertainty. The degree of uncertainty may vary from one industry or company to another, but some uncertainty is always present. Added to this is the fact that a contract providing permanent investment capital for a business necessarily commits the business to certain financial obligations over a period which normally extends well beyond that for which detailed forecasts can be undertaken with any degree of confidence.

Under the circumstances management must make certain assumptions about the future with respect to events of importance to the particular decision and must make the decision in terms of these assumptions, taking into account the degree of confidence it has in them. Considering the most universally important aspects of the debt-equity alternative, these assumptions would be those relating to the relative contribution to earnings, on the one hand, and the relative contribution to the risk of insolvency, on the other.

Before this decision can be made it is necessary to be able to identify what data are relevant to the considerations of profitability and risk, and to develop a method of measurement that enables management to appraise the significance of these data as objectively as possible. In these respects greater progress has been made in the appraisal of profitability than in the appraisal of risk. It has become general practice to make debt-equity comparisons either in terms of the expected effect on earnings per share or in terms of cost as a percentage of the capital provided. Refined comparisons continue to be plagued by the problems of anticipating the ultimate effect on the market value of the basic equity investment, such as the relative importance of earnings and dividends and the allowance for variations in risk resulting from varying amounts of debt. In practice, however, because of the fact that (a) borrowing is usually contemplated only in modest amounts and (b) corporate tax law treats interest as a cost, it is generally assumed that debt will be substantially cheaper than equity so that precise quantitative comparisons of cost are attempted only infrequently.

Thus, although much remains to be done in the measurement of the ultimate effect on investment values of the debt-equity choice, businessmen are generally inclined to take the income advantage of debt as given. In contrast, the measurement of risk associated with debt, including the identification of the significant data, continues to be relatively obscure. Much of the present-day thinking on this subject can be summed up as merely a statement of a point of departure, namely, that under conditions of uncertain cash inflow the creation of additional fixed cash outflows adds a new dimension to the risk associated with business activity and that the risk tends to increase as the relative magnitude of the fixed cash outflows increases.

The reason for the lack of progress in advancing thinking beyond a statement of the problem is apparent to anyone who has considered it. It lies in the great complexity of the variables affecting future cash flows, most of which are subject to uncertainty and a greater or lesser degree of interaction in producing the actual outcome. A comprehensive and systematic attack on the problem of risk measurement in a form applicable to practical business decisions has not yet been provided. At the same time management must continue to make decisions affecting the degree of risk, among which is the decision with respect to the use of debt, and it must continue to make some assumption, explicitly or implicitly, as to the magnitude of the risk involved.

As indicated by the book's title, this study is primarily concerned with the appraisal of risk associated with debt financing as it is brought into focus through the establishment of borrowing limits. In concentrating on this aspect of the debt decision it takes other aspects, such as comparative cost and the effect on control, into account only as they bear on the question of risk. In general it is assumed that the businesses under consideration have investment opportunities with sufficient promise to justify the additional investment and that the relative cost of debt capital is sufficiently low to justify active consideration of debt as a basis for the financing of new investment. The fundamental question for management with which we will be concerned may be simply stated: *Given the need for new permanent capital and the opportunity to borrow, how does a company approach the determination of the "wise and proper" limit to such borrowing?*

Part One of this study approaches this question in terms of what may be learned from current business practice. A carefully selected sample of companies was used as a base for exploring the process of decision making related to debt-equity proportions. Having thus observed and described how this decision is made in practice, the study then proceeds in Part Two to look at the question in terms of possible improvements in current practice. In this part a significantly different approach is proposed which is intended to have immediate practical value. While designed primarily as a contribution to financial practice, it is hoped that this approach not only will be useful to the practitioner but also will have logical appeal to the academic audience seeking a better conceptual framework for analyzing the risk dimension of debt.

It must be emphasized at the outset that this study will *not* answer the question: "How much should the ABC Company borrow now?" There are several reasons for this. One is that the amount of debt a company *should* have at any point of time is a function of a number of considerations, only one of which is that of the risk involved. Further, with respect to the risk consideration, this study is concerned only with the problem of assessing the magnitude of the risk associated with any given amount of debt. The other side of the risk coin is willingness to assume risk — the relative importance attached to the possibility of loss as opposed to the opportunity for gain. This is essentially a subjective decision on the part of those in the position of making the choice and cannot be answered by anyone else.

It must also be emphasized that this study does not pretend to provide a refined and final answer to the problem of measuring the risk associated with debt. In fact there is some hazard that the use of the word "measurement" may imply a degree of precision which will not actually be achieved. It is at best a first approximation. Even in this stage, however, it is believed to represent an advance beyond much present-day thinking on the subject.

THE CONCEPT OF RISK

The word "risk" is used in a variety of contexts to mean many different things. Even when used in a single context, as for example in the phrase "the risk of debt," it will mean different things to different people. Generally speaking the word denotes the possibility of occurrence of an adverse event or effect.

With respect to debt the risk is the chance of adverse effects resulting from a commitment to make cash payments, certain in amount and timing, under uncertain future financial circumstances. These adverse effects may range all the way from a modest increase in the emotional strain of management to the event of bankruptcy. They include such considerations as negative income effects and interference with flexibility in future financing. Some are tangible; some are highly intangible.

In order to examine the problem of the risk of debt in a simple and familiar framework, this study focuses on the limits of adversity — the possibility that debt could lead to cash insolvency. This over-simplification of reality is justified on two grounds. The first is that it is common practice for businessmen to think of debt limits in terms of the ultimate hazard of running out of cash under recession conditions. The second is that the risk of cash insolvency may be viewed as the extreme case of a whole family of risks herein described as the risk of cash inadequacy. It can be argued that an assessment of the risk of cash insolvency will provide a basic reference point to which all risks associated with debt may be related. The approach presented in Part Two, however, is not intended as a comprehensive analysis of risk. Rather it is a partial analysis for operational purposes designed to be logically consistent with the more complex analytical framework necessary for the appraisal of the entire spectrum of risk.

With regard to the threat of cash insolvency, debt is no different from any other contractual obligation to pay fixed amounts at fixed dates in an uncertain future and, indeed, is not essentially different from noncontractual fixed payments which must continue if the business is to continue. An illustration of this fact is seen in the increasing awareness that rental payments under a lease or sale-and-leaseback arrangement contain inherently the same risk element as an equivalent debt service charge.

Thus the risk of debt is seen as a part of the over-all problem of the balancing of the amount and timing of cash inflows and cash outflows. Virtually all businesses face some degree of uncertainty in the amount and timing of cash inflows, and the existence of inflexibility in cash outflows presents the hazard of inability to match outflows and inflows at some point in time. Since all businesses also have some rigidity in their cash outflows, the choice of debt is not a choice between some risk and no risk but rather a choice between more and less. Of course, it is possible that in particular circumstances the threat of insolvency is so remote that for practical purposes it will be considered as nonexistent.

Viewed in this way the measurement of the risk of debt becomes a part of a general appraisal of expected variations in total cash inflow, on the one hand, and of the controllability of total cash outflows, on the other. From this appraisal management can form a judgment as to the probability of the event of insolvency and the extent to which the probability is increased by the substitution of a given amount of debt for equity as a source of permanent financing.

Because the measurement of risk associated with debt is to be considered as a problem of forecasting cash flows, it follows that the analysis must be in terms of the special circumstances of the individual business. It also follows that any conclusions reached can be applied with confidence only to the company under consideration. Thus the contribution of this study must be confined largely to the merits of the method of analysis presented and not to any specific values or quantitative standards which are produced by the method, since they apply only to the companies used for purposes of illustration. This is not to deny that some sort of useful generalized standards for companies in essentially similar circumstances might be developed, but it is not the purpose of this study to produce them. Further it must now be clear that the assessment of the magnitude of the risk is only a part of the debt decision, and since the other part is the subjective willingness to assume risk it is fundamentally impossible to generalize about the quantity of debt which *should* be used by any group of businesses.

In considering the individual business the point of view taken in this study is that of the borrower or potential borrower. The risk decision could also be approached from the point of view of the lender with different conclusions being reached as to the appropriate debt limits. It is quite possible, and in fact likely, that an informed and rational borrower and an informed and rational lender dealing with the same situation and the same set of data will reach significantly different conclusions. It is also possible that the borrower will turn out to be more conservative than the lender though the general impression is that the reverse is the case.

It should be added that in identifying the study with the viewpoint of the borrower the other side of the contract is not ignored. It is obvious that in the process of negotiating the terms of a loan, which includes consideration of the appropriate amount and basis of repayment, each side must take cognizance of the thinking of the other. In the field studies an attempt was made to discover to what extent the thinking of particular borrowers had been conditioned by the thinking of their principal sources of debt capital.

THE FORM OF DEBT

In considering risk a number of distinctions have been made in theory and in practice among the many forms which debt assumes — short-term and long-term, secured and unsecured, senior and subordinated, revolving credit and term loan — to name a few. It would therefore appear necessary to be specific as to the form or forms of debt under consideration. In specifying the viewpoint as that of the borrowing company, however, and in defining the basic risk as the risk of being "out of cash" at some point of time over the life of the debt agreement, it can be seen that any debt contract can be appraised on a similar basis. The one essential characteristic is that the contract involves a legal obligation to make future cash payments in predetermined dollar amounts and at predetermined times. Important differences among debt forms then reduce to differences in the amount and/or timing of the required payments.

Since measurement of risk will take the form of a total cash flow analysis, it is obvious that *all* debt, outstanding and actively contemplated at the time of the analysis, must be included. As a consequence the question is not which form of debt to include and which to exclude, but rather which is to be taken as "given" for purposes of the analysis and which is to be taken as subject to possible modification by management following the conclusion and interpretation of the analysis.

The basic application of this study is to the financing of the so-called "permanent" capital requirements of the business. Actually, of course, none of the financial requirements of an individual enterprise can be considered permanent in any absolute sense and the term is used to denote a need of indefinite duration, not necessarily fixed in amount. It excludes the short-term financial requirements commonly defined as those having a duration of less than one year and so excludes a category of debt financing concerned with purely seasonal working capital needs. It must be emphasized, however, that it includes the financing of permanent working capital as well as the so-called fixed assets of land, buildings, and equipment. It also includes cyclical variations in financial requirements as well as secular trends.

The debt contracts which are commonly used to finance permanent needs are usually referred to as being intermediate term or long term. This distinction is not a useful one for purposes of this study and all such debt will be loosely referred to as "long term." Although we exclude capital needs that have a known duration of less than one year, we do not necessarily exclude debt contracts with a similar maturity since on occasion permanent needs are financed in this way. It may happen that due to uncertainty as to the amount and/or duration of the need or the future course of interest rates, a business may choose a revolving short-term credit form as an interim device to be replaced later when the situation becomes clarified. Normally, however, the debt contract used for permanent needs has a definite maturity several years hence.

A comment is necessary at this point on what will be called in this study "spontaneous" credit. This term covers those continuing current liabilities that arise in the normal course of business because of a customary lag of short duration between the incurring of an obligation and the date of cash payment. These are normally described as accounts payable and accruals. While such sources are also of a revolving nature and are often a major continuing source of funds, they are not included in our definition of long-term debt capital. The significant contrast between this source and long-term debt is that spontaneous credit is normally subject to gradual and automatic modification in direct relation to the volume of business and profitability whereas the debt with which we will be concerned is negotiated and renegotiated at long intervals and involves relatively sharp and irregular upward adjustments in the obligatory cash outflows. To exclude spontaneous credit from the definition, however, does not mean that its effects are ignored since this is to be a comprehensive cash flow analysis.

Among the sample of companies which form the experience base of this study the most common form of long-term debt was the term loan privately placed with one or a few commercial banks and/or insurance companies. Loans or portions of loans placed with banks generally had a maturity under 10 years and loans placed with insurance companies usually had a maturity in the 20-year to 30-year range. In addition several companies had bond issues publicly sold through the agency of an investment banker and having a final maturity similar to the longer term loans. Finally there were short-term revolving credit arrangements with commercial banks which either proved to be sufficient in themselves or were eventually refunded into a more permanent term loan with the bank or with an insurance company. Virtually all these debt arrangements required substantial or total repayment of the principal amount over the life of the contract.

The reader is undoubtedly aware that debt contracts often contain conditions of default other than the nonpayment of interest or principal on due dates. This is particularly true of privately placed term loans. Perhaps the most common is the "maintenance of working capital provision" — the provision that working capital must not be allowed to fall below some stated level. Since we are concerned with the events of default and solvency, it might be considered necessary to extend the analysis to all provisions of the debt contract which could lead to these events. While these other provisions are noted in the study, they have not been made a part of the basic analysis. The reasoning is that they are subsidiary to the primary basis of solvency which is the capacity to meet cash obligations on time and that from the lender's viewpoint they are designed both as a means of assuring this capacity and as a secondary line of defense if it should not be realized. If desired, a test for such provisions could be added to the cash flow analysis but this will not be done in this study.

In the traditional analysis of debt and equity as sources of capital, certain distinctions with respect to future cash obligations are made on a legal and contractual basis. Thus payments under a debt contract are treated as mandatory whereas payments under an equity contract are treated as discretionary. This is, of course, literally true and of major practical importance. The primary purpose behind this study, however, is to aid decision making in the area of long-term business finance. From a decisional point of view the classification of cash flows as between mandatory and discretionary is not necessarily a legal and contractual one. Thus, *for decision making purposes* management may choose to treat a preferred or even a common dividend as a fixed, nondiscretionary payment — and may do so for perfectly sound and rational reasons. The same may be true for other kinds of cash payments. Obviously this kind of variation in the interpretation of particular cash flows can have major implications for cash flow analysis and its subsequent application.

It is because of these judgmental aspects that it is particularly important for the reader to bear in mind the point of view adopted throughout the study. It is one of the more important factors which can lead to significantly different conclusions as between the internal management, on the one hand, and the lending institution, on the other. Another facet of the point of view is that the debt payment, which the borrower must necessarily treat as absolutely fixed, may for purposes of the lender's analysis be treated as somewhat variable. Thus the lender may cover the eventuality of another Great Depression, taken seriously by some borrowers even though considered only remotely possible, by saying in effect: "Ours is 'patient money' — if that should happen again, we will just 'work it out' with the borrower." These important distinctions in point of view will be developed at length later in the study.

THE FIELD RESEARCH

As an essential part of developing and appraising the usefulness of an approach to the determination of corporate debt capacity, it is necessary to have an awareness of current business thinking and practice with respect to debt. A major portion of the time devoted to this study was taken up with an intensive analysis of the financial experience of 25 carefully selected companies. Five of these companies comprised a pilot group where the primary purpose was to test and improve the research questions and techniques. In the process, however, many useful data were collected.

The field research then proceeded to a core group of 20 companies, 4 companies from each of 5 different industries. All 25 companies were manufacturing companies. The 5 industries were: (1) machine tools, (2) baking and biscuits, (3) rubber, (4) chemicals, (5) ethical drugs. All companies included in the study were consulted in advance and gave active assistance to the project. The individual businesses will remain anonymous and the companies were so advised for the dual purpose of encouraging maximum freedom in the release of information and of enabling the author to report and comment freely on the results obtained.

The collection of data involved three stages. The first was assembly and analysis of all available published data, including annual reports and financial statements, prospectuses, reports to the Securities and Exchange Commission, and the publications of the financial services. This made possible a more efficient utilization of time in the second stage, which consisted of personal interviews with the company's top financial officers and which lasted anywhere from an hour to a day. With the company's permission the process then proceeded to the third stage, which consisted of personal interviews with lending officers of the company's primary source or sources of long-term debt capital. Generally such an interview was held with the man who was the lender's principal representative in dealings with the borrower. In the case of public issues of bonds the person interviewed was the representative of the principal investment banker concerned with the issue.

The basic purposes of the field research as well as other aspects of the field sample data will be developed at length later in this work. At this point it will be sufficient to summarize the desired information as follows:

(1) A factual history of the debt and cash flow experience of the company.

(2) A description of basic attitudes toward the use of long-term debt as an alternative to other primary sources of permanent capital.

(3) An outline of individual approaches to the measurement and appraisal of risk associated with corporate borrowing.

(4) An indication of willingness to assume the risks of debt financing as expressed in established debt policies and concepts of debt limits.

From this information it has been possible to generalize about current concepts, attitudes, and practices with respect to long-term debt within this sample of companies. Since the sample was selected on a basis other than that which would provide a statistical measure of confidence as to the broader application of the conclusions, they must be taken as suggestive rather than conclusive with respect to behavior in manufacturing companies and business in general. The objectives of the study and the confidential nature of much of the desired information ruled out the possibility of a pre-

dictive sample. At the same time, however, every effort was made
to keep the sample free from bias and it is hoped that the conclusions will have a usefulness as a point of departure for debt studies
providing greater statistical confidence for describing business in
general.

In addition to the field research goals already mentioned, the
further step of testing the implications of the debt criteria in use in
particular companies was desired. This testing required the collection of a considerable amount of detailed historical financial data
for the individual business and management comment on this experience. It also required extensive analysis of this experience.
Since it was neither practicable nor essential that this be done for
all companies in the sample, this phase of the field work was confined to one company in each of the five industries. The significance of the specific observations in the individual case was secondary to the exemplification of the approach involved.

THE CHARACTERISTICS OF THE FIELD SAMPLE

The Industries

The primary consideration in the selection of the sample of companies used in the field study of debt policy was to provide the best
possible opportunity to examine the risks associated with debt
against individual characteristics of cash flow. As indicated previously, one of the purposes of the study has been to obtain a detailed firsthand report of management thinking regarding risk in
general and the risk of debt in particular. A second and equally
important objective has been to provide a basis for assessing the
meaning and significance of management attitudes and operating
criteria. It is a comparatively easy task to report on a series of
decisions with respect to long-term finance in a sample of companies and what the responsible executives have to say about their
reasons for these decisions. The more challenging assignment is to
provide a common basis for appraisal which is at the same time
logically defensible and practical. Given the decision to undertake
the appraisal in terms of cash flows, this became the governing consideration in the selection of the sample. Since the study is viewed
as exploratory and suggestive rather than conclusive as far as industry as a whole is concerned, it is not represented as having broad

statistical validity. On the other hand, every effort was made to avoid situations where important characteristics were so unique as to rule out the possibility of representativeness.

In selecting an area of business activity for examination it was decided to confine the sample to manufacturing companies. The reason for this was the desire to have the general structure of cash inflows and outflows roughly the same for all units in the sample. Thus all companies in the sample had cash inflows that were subject to continuous modification, that were largely uncontrollable, at least in the short run, and that involved considerable uncertainty. All companies had the same basic categories of expenditures and the common characteristic of major obstructions to the rapid circulation of funds in the form of specialized productive plant and equipment, inventory in process of transformation, and a lag in the collection of cash for goods delivered. Likewise all companies relied to a significant extent on spontaneous credit in the form of payables and accruals as a continuing offset to cash outflow.

Given a similar general structure of cash flows within the manufacturing group, there are at the same time important variations in the pattern of actual cash flows among industries and companies within this group, and it is these variations with which we will be primarily concerned. We shall return to this point in a moment.

A second and important reason for confining the study to manufacturing is that there is a widespread tendency on the part of investors to treat this group as an identifiable risk category distinct from such other groups as public utilities, transportation, and retailing. This is evidenced in such ways as the grouping of statistical and financial information, the organization of investment and research departments, and, of particular significance here, the acceptance of standardized criteria of risk capacity. Specific reference to these standards will be made later in the study. One of the purposes of the study is to examine the validity and usefulness of such generalized standards.

It should be added, however, that although the study is confined to this area of business activity, the method of analyzing the risks of debt in terms of individual patterns of cash flow is considered as equally applicable to businesses in other areas.

In selecting the specific industries to be represented within the manufacturing group, the primary objective was to obtain sharp contrasts in the characteristic behavior of the principal determinants of cash flow. Thus, for example, the machine tool industry approaches one extreme in the degree of variation of cash inflow over time, while the baking and biscuit industry approaches the other. In this way the significance of differences in these determinants of cash flow among companies and industries could be observed without the necessity for precise measurement. It is recognized that differences in the variability and uncertainty of cash flows and hence in debt-bearing capacity are relative rather than absolute and are a matter of degree. Unless a precise technique is available, small differences are not observable. The method to be used is an approximate one (though susceptible of further refinement) and is best illustrated by situations where the possibility of significant differences exists.

In view of the objectives of the study it has not been considered necessary to provide significant contrasts with respect to *all* principal determinants of cash flow. To do so would have greatly increased the volume of analysis without significantly increasing the value of the results. In Chapter 9 where the details of cash flow of one company in each of the five industries are examined, the significant contrasts among the industries selected — machine tools, baking and biscuits, rubber, chemicals, and ethical drugs — will be described. At this point it will be sufficient to summarize the outstanding characteristics of each industry. It will be recognized that because there is no such thing as a completely homogeneous "industry" the statements that follow are an oversimplification in the interests of brevity. They must be qualified in the individual case.

The machine tool industry is often cited as a classic example of extreme cyclical variation in sales. The nature of the product — a durable capital good of relatively high unit value — is such that it reflects in exaggerated form the fluctuations in the general economy. This has meant that the companies in this industry have experienced a series of periods of sharp and prolonged contractions in cash inflow. It is possible in this industry for annual sales to contract to a level that is only 20% of the sales of the previous peak year. In most industries such a prospect would be unthinkable and yet at least some of the machine tool companies survive. Three of the four companies included in this study were organized prior to 1900 and the fourth prior to 1920.

Part of the reason for their survival lies in certain compensating characteristics. One of these is that the industry usually has some advance warning of a downswing. Rigidities in capacity to produce a product made to order over an extended production period typically result in a substantial backlog of orders the downward trend of which can be observed as much as a year in advance of the actual decline in cash inflow from shipments of finished units. This is of considerable significance to orderly conservation of cash. In addition, the production against firm orders from highly reliable accounts means that a substantial cash inflow from declining inventories and accounts receivable can be expected to follow any major sales decline. The result is that in a well-managed machine tool company a recession of short duration, far from producing a major hazard of insolvency, creates a condition of unusual cash liquidity — so much so that the primary problem of the treasurer becomes a question of what to do with his idle cash.

This is not to suggest that the industry is free from risks. It does illustrate, however, that a closer examination of the determinants of cash flow may reveal a picture significantly different from what might be assumed from the behavior of sales or earnings.

In contrast to the machine tool industry, the baking and biscuit industry appears to enjoy great stability of sales and of cash inflow over time. The recession contraction of dollar sales is more of the order of 5% to 10% from the peak level as contrasted with the 60% to 80% contraction in machine tools. Stability of inflow would normally be assumed as favorable to a relatively high proportion of stable or fixed outflow. Stability in this industry, however, is associated with sharp competition in a period of secular stagnation (which some would say contains elements of secular decline). This is particularly true of the production of bread. Price consciousness and relatively narrow margins between cash inflows and the cash outflows necessary to generate the inflows means that small declines in dollar volume can present real problems in cash management.

Other features of the industry are also significant to cash flows. The inventory and accounts receivable picture is very different from machine tools. Here the product is rapidly moving and highly perishable, and thus daily production is closely tied to daily sales. Further, when contraction in dollar sales comes — in the form of price rather than volume declines — little can be expected in the way of cash throw-off from declining inventories. A substantial portion of sales made to retailers and ultimate consumers is on a cash or near-cash basis.

Another governing feature in the baking and biscuit industry in recent years has been the necessity for substantial plant and equipment expenditures in order to have the protection of the most recent ideas in cost-cutting equipment and plant layout. Although new investment in plant is often thought of as discretionary, this type of competitive replacement can become for practical reasons nondiscretionary as to both amount and timing.

In contrast to the baking industry, the chemical industry has been characterized by a sustained period of substantial growth. Steadily mounting sales have necessitated a major investment program in plant and equipment. Because of the nature of the productive process this expansion typically requires "big bites" of cash at irregularly spaced intervals. The industry generally has enjoyed favorable profit margins which, coupled with amortization charges that at times are almost equal to net profit in dollar amount, provide a relatively large cash throw-off from operations, serving as both a source of funds for expansion and an important cushion against the effects of a decline.

The ethical drug industry presents an interesting contrast to the other four industries in the study in regard to the nature of the uncertainty of cash inflow. The other four industries, including rubber which is to be described later, fluctuate in greater or lesser degree with general business conditions. The ethical drug industry is largely recession-resistant so that it does not tend to move in harmony with industry in general but has its own set of fluctuations based on very different factors. The major uncertainties in the magnitude and timing of change in cash flow are those associated with product development and product obsolescence. Such changes are inherently difficult to forecast and can have major consequences for the individual firm.

Offsetting these uncertainties, however, is the fact that the industry is in a period of rapid growth and the larger and older firms have considerable product diversification. In this respect there is a similarity to the chemical industry and associated with this growth has been one of the most dramatic profit records in business generally.

In contrast to chemicals, however, the investment in plant and equipment is less important in amount and the facilities are more flexible in use and susceptible of more gradual expansion. The major items of cash outflow here with respect to growth are the expenditures on research and on sales development and promotion.

It is one of the underlying premises of this study that in any industry with a considerable degree of homogeneity there are certain observable characteristics of cash flow which have a degree of stability over time and which therefore can be of value in predicting the probable limits of behavior of cash flows in future periods of sales contraction. The characteristics of cash flow illustrated in the four industries cited above have persisted over extended periods of time and within these periods of time have had an important bearing on cyclical behavior of cash flow.

It is recognized, however, that even these fundamental aspects are themselves subject to change — though the change is usually gradual and therefore more easily predictable. Thus, for example, while the volume of accounts receivable will fluctuate with sales from month to month, the range of its effects on cash flow are circumscribed by conventional credit terms, customer credit practices, proportions of cash and credit sales — factors which result from basic business conventions, the nature of demand, the structure of the market, and the like. Within short periods of time these do not change but over longer periods they can and do change, and these secular changes in fundamental practices and habits can have a profound effect on the problem of cash solvency.

An outstanding example of this is found in the rubber industry, though examples may be found in any industry. In the period following World War II it became generally recognized that basic changes had taken place which had radically altered the riskiness of the rubber industry as an investment. Investors began to talk in terms of certain rubber stocks as "blue chips" whereas formerly this had been considered a highly cyclical industry tied to the new car market. The changes were twofold and were working in the direction of more stable cash flows. On the one hand, inflow from sales was being stabilized by the development of the replacement market for tires and new industrial rubber products. On the other, the demoralizing effect of sharp price fluctuations in the market for natural rubber and natural fiber was substantially reduced by the widespread use of synthetic rubber and fiber.   These changes were the basis of expectations that future fluctuations in earnings and in cash flows would be less severe.   It is of particular interest to this study to observe whether and to what extent these changes affected attitudes of management toward debt and concepts of debt capacity.

The Companies

The number of companies to be studied in each of the five industries was set at four for a total of twenty.   This number was arbitrary and was primarily determined by time considerations and the objective of studying each company as closely and in as much detail as the opportunity afforded.   In addition five other companies were used as a preliminary test sample; they were in industries other than the five previously mentioned.   The additional industries represented in this preliminary group were electronics, textiles, mining, and retail food distribution.

In order to qualify for the study all companies were required to have two major characteristics in common.   One of these was the requirement that each company must have had a long period of experience in dealing with the ups and downs of economic activity in a given industry.   This firsthand experience was an essential foundation upon which management could form an informed judgment as to the nature of the risk involved and, equally important for this study, would provide a factual base upon which a description of the behavior of cash flows could be built, thus providing some objectivity in appraising the attitudes of management.

This obviously restricted the study to a consideration of "mature" companies.   All companies in the study were organized prior to 1935.   A tabulation of approximate dates of origin follows.   (Unless otherwise indicated, this tabulation and others which follow refer only to the core group of twenty):

Date Organized	No. of Companies
Prior to 1910	10
1910–1920	5
1920–1930	3
1930–1935	2

Thus virtually all these companies passed through the hazardous experience of the Great Depression of the early 1930's, and all through the sharp recession of 1937–1938 and the fluctuations of war and peace which have followed. Of course over such an extended period of time many of the companies have changed in various ways as the industry or company policy was modified. Likewise there have been the inevitable changes in the personnel of those who have been making financial decisions. With a very few exceptions, however, there have been no changes of direction so sharp as to invalidate the usefulness of past experience for future planning.

The requirement of extended experience naturally tends to restrict the study to the larger and more profitable companies in any given industry since profitability and growth would be essential to survival for 30 or more years. The second prerequisite for each company which was laid down also tends to work in this direction. This was that each company should give evidence of having had access to both debt and equity sources of capital over the period in question. In other words, there should be evidence that management had a degree of freedom in making its choice as between debt and equity and that one source or the other was not precluded by market or other circumstances. Of course this does not mean that all sources were available without limit at all times.

This second requirement was considered to apply both to internally generated equity capital and to external acquisition through the sale of stock. Thus basic profitability was a prerequisite. It also meant that each company should have an established public market for its common stock. This excluded privately held companies but did not exclude substantial holdings by a few key shareholders. In fact, three of the companies were privately held until the last ten years and several of the companies continue to have large family holdings. The common stock of all but three of the companies in the study was listed on the New York Stock Exchange and in the case of eight of the companies, on two or more of the organized exchanges. The three issues not listed were actively traded over the counter.

The requirement of public ownership of stock was of obvious value in assuring the maximum availability of financial information. All companies were to be found in the manuals of the investment services and were subject to the disclosure rules of the organized exchanges and the Securities and Exchange Commission.

Further, management was prepared by experience to respond without resentment to the prying questions of outsiders and this attitude tended to reduce time-consuming preliminaries to a productive field interview. It may be of interest to note here that out of all the interviews requested for purposes of the study there were only two refusals.

It is to be expected that by confining the study in this way to larger, more successful companies the sample would include a disproportionate share of competent management. Whether this was true in fact, there is no way of knowing but it was a result to be desired. It was hoped that the study would have the benefit of some of the most experienced and perceptive business judgment on this question. Subjective impressions during the interviews and objective evidence in the record of performance appeared to confirm that this hope had been realized at least in part.

The impression of a bias of "bigness" in the sample should not be allowed to go completely unqualified. There were in fact substantial variations in size among the companies within each industry group and over all. The following data for the year 1957 show assets and sales in terms of the arithmetic mean and the range from the largest to the smallest company included:

Industry	Total Assets		Annual Sales	
	Mean	Range	Mean	Range
		(in millions of dollars)		
Machine Tools	$ 45	$ 95	$ 65	$ 145
Baking and Biscuits	110	175	260	285
Chemicals	630	285	590	455
Drugs	145	145	145	120
Rubber	620	650	935	1,000

Thus there is considerable room for variation in competitive strength among the companies in each industry and in their standing in the eyes of the investing institutions.

While no particular attention was given to the geographic location of the borrowers or lenders included in the study, it evolved that for practical purposes the area was limited to the northeastern quarter of the United States. This refers only to head office locations since the majority had national and international operations. The study included businesses with head office locations in Connecticut, Illinois, Indiana, Massachusetts, Michigan, New Jersey, New York, Ohio, Rhode Island, and Vermont. The principal financial centers concerned were New York City, Chicago, Detroit, and Boston.

Given the characteristics of extensive economic and financial experience and the opportunity to choose among debt and equity sources, the next objective for the sample was to have in each industry a representation of companies which had a history of being "heavy" borrowers and a representation of "light" borrowers. These of course are purely relative terms. In any company the amount of debt varies significantly over time, and what might be classed as heavy in one industry, say, ethical drugs, might be considered light in another, say, chemicals. The objective, however, was to sample the thinking of those who were not borrowing, for one reason or another, as well as the thinking of those who had by experience become accustomed to using this source of funds. While the sample does not necessarily include the heaviest and the lightest borrower in each industry, it was desired to have relatively sharp contrasts in the debt experience.

The majority of the companies included had done some long-term borrowing at some time during the past 20 years. Very few of the companies included were prepared to assert that it was their firm policy never to borrow permanent capital. The larger number of the light and spasmodic borrowers were on record not as being opposed to debt but merely as not having need of this source of capital. This concept will be examined in detail later in the study.

Among the borrowing companies all primary forms of long-term debt are included in the experience — revolving bank credit, term loans privately placed with banks and insurance companies, and public bond offerings. It has been mentioned before that the study included interviews with the principal recent sources of debt capital for each company. These interviews were set up following the interviews with officials of the borrowing company and with their consent. These interviews had two purposes. One was to further confirm the facts concerning particular debt negotiations and the considerations which were involved. On this score the interviews tended to be useful but less significant than those with the borrower because of the fact that the particular loan, from the lender's viewpoint, was merely one of many in a continuing stream of negotiations whereas for the borrower it stood out very sharply in memory. The second purpose was to gain an understanding of the underlying attitudes toward corporate debt capacity in that specific segment of the capital market with which an individual business was negotiating and, if possible, to observe whether and to what extent these had a bearing on the viewpoint adopted by the borrower.

It should be understood that the interviews with lending institutions and agencies were not intended in any sense as a comprehensive study of the lending practices and policies of these institutions with respect to long-term debt. It was confined to the sixteen lenders who had been associated with the core sample of borrowers, and the purposes as outlined above were subsidiary to a consideration of debt policy with the borrowers' circumstances and objectives in mind. As a consequence lender attitudes were not considered independently in the light of lender circumstances and objectives. This was considered beyond the scope of this study.

THE ORGANIZATION OF THE STUDY

The study is divided into two main parts. The first part, called *A Field Study of Corporate Debt and Related Financial Policies,* is largely descriptive of business attitudes, practices, and policies with respect to long-term debt as observed in the sample of industrial companies previously described. The first step is to provide certain background information which will help the reader to keep the observations on debt in perspective. This background, which is provided in Chapters 2 and 3, consists of:

(1) A review of the record of funds flow in the sample of companies for the past twenty years and a commentary on similarities and contrasts. This includes the nature, magnitudes, and timing of the application of funds and the sources of these funds, the amounts provided by each source, and the sequence and frequency of use.

(2) A review of the available evidence on basic management attitudes toward uses and sources of funds with the purpose of reconciling these attitudes with the historical record of the acquisition and disposition of funds. While it was not a major objective of the study to observe and re-

port on financial policy as a whole, it is obvious that debt policy cannot be fully understood without some appreciation of management thinking on the alternatives.

With these observations on the over-all financial picture in mind the study then proceeds to consider the record with respect to the use of long-term debt and the concepts and attitudes which underlay management decisions (Chapter 4). Following the emphasis of the study, the primary concern is with the risks associated with debt, management's concept of these risks, and its methods of dealing with them. The basic philosophy of debt is observed in relation to the various aspects of the debt negotiation and contract. In the process of considering why management thought and acted as it did, the information is extended to include observations on the thinking of the principal creditors with which debt contracts were negotiated.

The subject of management's methods of dealing with the risks of debt constitutes the focal point of the study. In Chapter 5 there is a detailed examination of the means by which management sought to limit the potential disadvantages of debt, the most obvious of which is a limit on the amount of debt itself. Given acceptance of the amount of the debt, the process then becomes one of minimizing the hazards associated with various aspects of the contract. Interest here centers both on operational rules which governed management's decisions, where they existed, and on the method by which management reached a decision in the individual case.

Part Two of the study, called *The Analysis of Corporate Debt Capacity: An Appraisal of Practice and a Proposal for Improvement,* is largely analytical as contrasted with the largely descriptive material of Part One. It begins by examining the debt policies and decision rules which were observed to be in current use by the managements of industrial corporations in terms of the validity of the underlying assumptions, their logical consistency, and their usefulness and reliability in producing the desired decisions (Chapter 6). Particular attention is given to practices with respect to restraints on the risks associated with fixed-charge sources of funds.

This appraisal of business practice with regard to the determination of debt limits is followed by a description of what the author considers to be an improved approach to the problem (Chapters 7 and 8). As previously indicated this approach does not provide specific answers as to the appropriate amount of debt since this decision is in essence a subjective one, to be made by those whose equity guarantees the sanctity of the debt contract (or by their representatives). Rather, the approach provides a way of thinking about the problem in terms of the circumstances of the individual firm which should make for a more informed decision. Drawing on intensive company and industry experience in the pattern and limits of variation of the primary determinants of cash flow, the analysis produces a set of values of the probable lower limits of cash flow from operations under varying recession assumptions. These values represent a specific framework which can be of direct assistance to management in deciding whether and to what extent incremental fixed cash outflows for debt servicing should be assumed.

This approach is then illustrated in the concluding chapter by reference to the past experience of five companies, one in each of the five industries included in the study. With a set of values expressive of the expected limits of variation of cash flow in each company, the study proceeds to interpret the implications of the actual debt experience, management thinking, and operating rules in use in each of these companies. Also, on a more general level, the approach to debt and debt capacity found in the sample of companies and described in earlier chapters is appraised in terms of this cash flow approach.

CHAPTER 2

Background:
A Review of Twenty Years
of Funds Flows

THE NEED FOR FUNDS

Scope and Definition

As a first step in acquiring the necessary background for a consideration of debt policy, an examination of the need for funds in each of the twenty companies was undertaken. By the word "funds" is meant the financial means by which a private enterprise conducts its transactions and takes title to the assets essential to the conduct of its business. Most business transactions involve a cash payment before the cycle is completed but this is not universally true. For example, in the acquisition of assets by the purchase of an existing business a cash transaction is often deliberately avoided by the vendor for tax reasons and the financial vehicle is an exchange of stock. Thus the phrase "need for funds" encompasses the need for cash but at this stage does not exclude alternative bases for the attainment of financial objectives.

The financing decisions with which the field interviews were concerned were necessarily those made in the recent past, generally within the past ten years. Accurate recollection of circumstances and particularly of reasons and motives beyond that point is difficult to obtain. Thus the study of the need for funds which generated the need for external financing might be confined to the same period. It was considered desirable, however, to extend the examination of needs beyond this period to gain a better perspective on the basic character of these needs. For most companies studied the publication of detailed financial information, particularly on costs and revenues, did not start until the late thirties and the availability of data became the primary limiting factor. It was therefore decided to undertake a study of needs and sources of funds for each company in the sample for the period 1939 to 1958 inclusive. (Because of private ownership for a portion of this period, three of the companies were studied for a shorter period of time.) The conclusions derived from the results of this study follow.

In examining the need for funds a basic classification of needs was made which seemed best suited to the purposes of the study. The reader should have this clearly in mind in reviewing the statements in the following pages. The Total Funds Applied have been broken down and identified as follows:

(1) net working capital needs,
(2) plant and equipment expenditures,
(3) investment in other assets,
(4) dividend payments.

It will be noted that this list excludes any funds devoted to the servicing of debt or any form of refinancing or recapitalization. It was the intention to focus on the basic operating requirements of the business — the investment essential to the generation of future income — independently of the means by which these funds had been obtained in the past.

In this respect it could be argued that dividend payments would be better treated as a deduction from sources rather than as a use of funds. It was considered more informative, however, to show the total of funds generated internally from operations as a source and the dividend payments as one of the continuing needs or uses. In this way the effect of managements' decisions on dividend payout are more apparent.

The item "net working capital needs" is defined as the need for a continuing investment in current assets, exclusive of liquid reserves and over and above that which is supplied through spontaneous credit:

{Current Assets − [Cash + Marketable Securities] − Current Liabilities}

Thus these are the working capital needs which must be supplied from permanent sources. While it is recognized that cash can be just as much a working capital need as inventory, cash and marketable securities are excluded because they act as a key part of the balancing mechanism, rising and falling as the needs and sources fluctuate from year to year. As such the Cash plus Securities items must be examined separately when needs and sources are brought together.

The item "plant and equipment expenditures" represents the total of funds expended for these purposes regardless of whether the expenditure is considered as a replacement or a new addition. This is not an accounting concept but a total of actual expenditures other than maintenance and repairs, and while it normally involves cash expenditures it may from time to time include additions to assets made possible by an exchange of stock. While in most cases the figures for actual expenditures were available from the company, in some instances and for certain years, particularly earlier years, this item had to be approximated from the balance sheet and the income statement.

The item "investment in other assets" for most companies is a minor item and could have been ignored for purposes of the study. Because there were some instances where it did become significant, however, at least for periods of time, the item was included. The most common reason for its significance in certain cases was because of investments in and advances to subsidiaries not consolidated. In general, our primary concern has been with the first, second, and fourth items listed above.

Determining the Amount Required

In considering the year-to-year variations in the financial requirements of the companies under study no systematic attempt has been made to identify the limiting considerations which determined the actual sums added to invested capital each year. For the purposes of this study the financial needs must essentially be taken as given. Thus the historical study of needs with which this section is concerned observes only those needs which were actually satisfied during the period in question. It does not reveal any needs, perhaps more properly described as investment opportunities, which went unsatisfied for one reason or another. This distinction is of particular significance in periods of advanced prosperity when annual needs outstrip the internal resources of the business.

At the same time, however, the field study has touched on the determinants of the need for funds from time to time, and some observations on this subject may be made in passing. Many of those theorists who have given consideration to the investment decisions of individual firms think of a business as having at any given time a range of investment opportunities which may be ranked both as to expected return on investment and as to risk. Taking into account the available sources of capital and the costs associated with each, the individual or group making the decision is considered to arrive at a cutoff point on the list of opportunities such that the approved investments can be financed and will give the maximum return at any given level of risk.

The observations of this study do not coincide with this image of the investment decision at all points. A significant difference appears to be that in practice there is an important distinction between the "known" or familiar investment and the unknown or unfamiliar investment. There is a tendency in business to treat the familiar investment — the investment in the traditional business activity of the firm — as a mandatory investment without regard to rate of return or risk. This is particularly true of the additional investment in working capital in response to an increase in sales. It is also true of plant and equipment expenditures identified with the traditional products, particularly those which are a direct replacement of existing capacity. The businessman is likely to think of money for such investments as money he has "got to have" — in a sense regardless of the cost or the source or the risk involved.

By contrast the investment in an unfamiliar area which constitutes a clear departure from the traditional area of activity is more likely to be examined in minute detail along the lines which theory suggests. The uncertainty that is associated with the unfamiliar makes the businessman look closely at the anticipated return and associated risk. There is a chance that in the process he will set his payback or return-on-investment standard so high as virtually to exclude all investment opportunities outside the familiar area (unless the risk is clearly and substantially less than that associated with the existing business). Thus the standard does not necessarily reflect the relative risk associated with the opportunity so much as it reflects the businessman's unwillingness to depart from what he knows best.

This distinction between the traditional or familiar and the unfamiliar is part of a broader "fact of life" in business investment: that is, the average businessman approaches his investment opportunities with a number of built-in limits which may be so much a part of him that he does not even think of them as such. These self-imposed limits may relate to a variety of things — the industry, the product line, the sales area, the size of the plant, the "proper" rate of growth, to name the more obvious. Such limits may or may not be the result of what we might consider as "rational" decisions based on profit-motivated analysis. Taken together they act to give relatively precise limits to corporate needs at any point of time.

Another way of presenting these constraints is to say that it is not necessarily true in practice, as we sometimes assume in theory, that the businessman views his business essentially as an investment opportunity which will be modified according to the dictates of purely financial objectives, and in the longer run as relatively independent of the specific activity in which it is engaged at the moment. Rather he is more likely, at least for purposes of year-to-year budgeting, to consider the investment opportunity as subsidiary to and dependent upon the fortunes of a specific industry, product line, sales territory, productive facility, work force, and management team. Business conceived as a finite entity will have finite needs.

It follows that these needs may for extended periods of time be well within the capacity of internally generated resources of the business to supply. Thus when the nonborrowing business is confronted with the question, "Why do you not use debt as a source of permanent capital?" the frequent response is "Because we don't need the money." What is implicit in this statement, whether recognized or not, is that the company does not need the money *to achieve the limited investment goals which it has set for itself.* Unfortunately it is not possible to ascertain directly the extent to which these limits have been influenced by a desire to avoid dependence on particular sources of capital. Not all businessmen would care to admit this interpretation even if it were the case.

A CLASSIFICATION OF PATTERNS OF FUND REQUIREMENTS

Turning now to the specific experience of the 20 companies in this study, it is helpful to characterize their individual financial requirements over the 20-year period in two major respects. First we would like to know whether the average rate at which new funds were invested by each company over the period would be classified as "High" or "Low," using the group experience as the standard. Second, we would like to know whether the management of the individual company was required to cope with substantial short-term variations (increases) in the need for funds. In this latter respect individual experience may be classified as having a "High" or "Low" degree of variability from year to year, again using the group experience as the standard.

Classified in this way each company may fall into one of four sets of investment characteristics:

(1) A *Low* long-term average growth rate coupled with *High* year-to-year variability in required funds.

(2) A *High* long-term growth rate coupled with *High* year-to-year variability.

(3) A *Low* long-term growth rate coupled with *Low* year-to-year variability.

(4) A *High* long-term growth rate coupled with *Low* year-to-year variability.

It will be apparent that these categories are described in relative terms, and as a result the lines drawn between them are somewhat subjective and arbitrary. Not all companies fit perfectly within one group or another. Nevertheless, for the large majority the contrast was significant. For this group the term "Low long-term growth rate" meant that *the total funds applied annually as a percentage of the Net Tangible Assets at the beginning of the year* averaged in the 14% to 16% range for the 20-year period. (The reader is reminded of the definition of what is included in "Total Funds Applied" given on page 28.) With a very few exceptions there was a relatively sharp break between this category and those companies having a relatively high long-term rate of growth which ranged from 19% upwards to 27% of Net Tangible Assets. It will be apparent that there were significant variations within these two broad categories, particularly within the "high rate" group.

All but 3 of the 20 companies could be classified as having either a high or a low rate of growth as described above. Two of these were companies for which information was not available for the full period and for which existing evidence was not conclusive. Generally speaking, companies within an industry tended to be consistent as to their rate of investment. Within this sample the companies with a low average rate of funds application were found in machine tools, baking and biscuits, and rubber. This did not mean that individual companies did not depart from the pattern or that they did not experience accelerated rates of growth for shorter periods of time. The companies within these industries with a substantially higher average rate of growth, however, were usually companies which had diversified into other faster growing industries. The two remaining industries, chemicals and drugs, showed clear evidence of having a relatively high rate of growth. In all, of the 17 companies so classified 9 fell within the High rate category and 8 fell within the Low rate category.

The other dimension of this classification relates to the degree of variability in the need for funds from year to year. Here again the classification is relative and somewhat arbitrary, designed to show up sharp differences but not to draw precise dividing lines.

Since the problem of variability in need is primarily that which is presented by sudden and perhaps unexpected *increases* in fund requirements from one year to the next, the criterion of variability focuses on those years in which the dollar amount invested exceeded the previous year. The figures given are an "average" company experience in this respect and *show the amount of such increases as a percentage of the total amount invested in the previous year.* These are the terms in which the businessman would normally view whatever problem is presented by such variations. As in the grouping with respect to long-term growth, the classification was not in terms of preconceived standards but rather had the purpose of dividing the total into two groups having markedly different characteristics in this respect. Here it was found to be even more difficult to find an obvious spot for every company and only 16 were so classified.

Of the 16 companies classified as to year-to-year variability, 9 fell into the "Low" degree of variability class. For these companies increases in need from one year to the next were rarely in excess of 50% of the previous year's requirements. (In this group 70% to 90% of the instances of increased need experienced over the 20-year period were of a magnitude of 50% or less.) The other 7 companies which were classified as having a "High" degree of variability were somewhat less uniform. Speaking generally for this class only 30% to 40% of the instances of increased need fell in the 50% or less category and 40% to 50% of the instances of increase from one year to the next were upwards of 100% of the need of the previous year. Increases of 200% or more were not uncommon.

Particular industries showed less conformity with respect to year-to-year variations than they did with respect to long-term rate of growth. In general the machine tool industry and the rubber industry showed a high degree of variability and the baking and biscuit industry a low degree of variability. The other two industries did not show any particular tendency. Of course with such a small sample size no clear generalization can be made in any case.

Data with respect to the pattern of application of funds for those companies, numbering 12, which could be readily classified in respect both of long-term rate of growth and year-to-year variability are given in Exhibit 1. These data serve to illustrate the significant contrasts in the need for funds occurring within the group. As can be seen from the table, there were only two companies which could be clearly identified as a Low-High pattern, three which could be classified as High-High, four as Low-Low, and three as High-Low. Three of the companies in the Low long-term rate of application and Low variability category were in the baking and biscuit industry. No other industry represented in this sample showed a similar tendency to a common pattern.

These four different patterns are illustrated in the bar charts on pages 36–37. The bars measure the annual total of funds applied expressed in millions of dollars.

All this information tells us something about the character of the need for funds in this sample of companies. It is generally recognized that the character of the need is an important consideration in the determination of sources of permanent capital and the specific contractual forms utilized. While it is not within the scope of this study to attempt to isolate this factor and measure its significance, it is helpful to be aware of the character of the need in the

EXHIBIT 1. CLASSIFICATION OF COMPANY EXPERIENCE IN THE INVESTMENT OF FUNDS IN TERMS OF LONG-TERM RATE OF GROWTH AND YEAR-TO-YEAR VARIABILITY

(1) Characteristics of Fund Requirements*	(2) Company Code Letter	(3) Industry	(4) (5) Long-Term Growth Rate (Average of Annual Funds Invested as % of Net Tangible Assets at Beginning of Year)		(6) (7) Year-to-Year Variability in Need (Average of Annual Increases in Need as % of Total Need in Previous Year)	
			High	Low	High	Low
Pattern No. 1	H	Baking		14.8%	92%	
	S	Rubber		15.6	94	
Pattern No. 2	B	Machine Tools	28.8%		271	
	C	Machine Tools	27.1		192	
	R	Rubber	20.4		122	
Pattern No. 3	A	Machine Tools		14.6		61%
	E	Baking		14.7		34
	F	Baking		15.9		34
	G	Baking		16.6		25
Pattern No. 4	I	Chemicals	19.8			46
	K	Chemicals	19.8			32
	M	Drugs	19.6			34

* See page 32.

individual case when observing debt policy. There is no question but that the environment surrounding the decision to use or not to use debt is different as between the company that operates under conditions of an unusually high and sustained need for funds and the company that has a relatively modest need over the same period. Likewise the environment for decision making will be different between the company with a sharply fluctuating and relatively unpredictable need from year to year and the company where such variations are comparatively modest and uniform.

At this point it seems appropriate to comment that a significant consideration in interpreting the impact of irregular investment expenditures on the character of corporate financing is the question of whether such irregularities are involuntary — in the sense of being the product of basic industry characteristics over which manage-

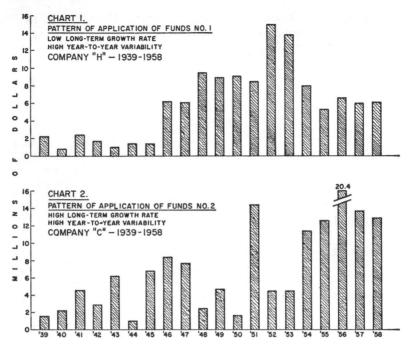

ment has little control — or voluntary in the sense that they are generated by the free choice of management. The distinction may be difficult to draw in practice, but an obvious contrast would be apparent in the plant expansion of a growing chemical company in response to market requirements versus an acquisition for purposes of diversification. In the latter case there may well be considerable freedom in timing if not in the opportunity to accept or reject outright. It is, in a sense, the distinction as to whether the company consciously and deliberately "achieves greatness" or has "greatness thrust upon it."

The Sources of Funds

Now that we have considered the need for additional funds in terms of what was actually applied by these companies in order to add to current assets, cover plant and equipment expenditures, and pay dividends, the obvious next step is to examine the sources from which these funds were obtained. For this purpose sources have been classified into internal and external. Internal sources are

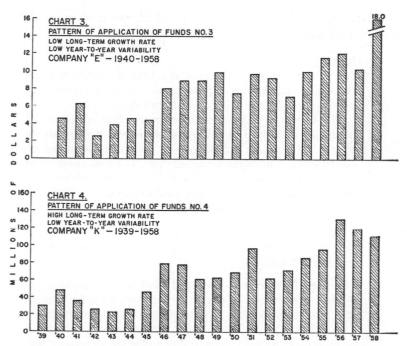

CHART 3.
PATTERN OF APPLICATION OF FUNDS NO.3
LOW LONG-TERM GROWTH RATE
LOW YEAR-TO-YEAR VARIABILITY
COMPANY "E" — 1940-1958

CHART 4.
PATTERN OF APPLICATION OF FUNDS NO. 4
HIGH LONG-TERM GROWTH RATE
LOW YEAR-TO-YEAR VARIABILITY
COMPANY "K" — 1939-1958

those over which management has full and direct control and consist of (1) funds currently generated from operations, (2) funds released by the liquidation of working assets (most commonly, current assets), and (3) liquid reserves (cash and marketable securities) accumulated from the operations of previous periods. Management need not consult anyone in determining the disposition of these sources of funds. It will be recognized that the year-by-year amounts generated by and available from these sources are only partly within the control of management and are in part subject to external conditions over which management has little or no control.

External sources are those which lie outside the corporation, which involve the acquiescence of an independent party, and which therefore are available only if and when the negotiated terms under which the funds will be transferred to the corporation can be made acceptable to both parties. For the purposes of this study these sources have been classified into four contractual forms: debt, straight preferred stock, convertible preferred stock, and common stock.

Given the needs as previously described, we now proceed to match these with sources in the following sequence:

(1) Internal Sources

(a) Funds realized in the normal course of operations from the sale of the company's products and by the conversion of existing working assets from one form into another.

This being the major continuing source of current financial needs, the data have been developed to show the magnitude by which this source exceeds or falls short of total annual required funds. It should be noted that a full consideration of this source includes the question of dividend payout and possible variations in the per share cash dividend as a means of balancing year-to-year fund requirements.

The next step is to observe company by company the extent to which any deficiencies have been provided by the second internal source:

(b) Liquid Reserves — Cash and Marketable Securities.

Most businesses feel that it is necessary to carry enough idle cash to make up any normal intra-month inequality of cash inflow and outflow. Many businesses also consider it good practice to carry enough liquid reserves to balance seasonal inequalities as well, rather than having periodic recourse to short-term bank loans. Some companies, comparatively few if this study is any indication, attempt to go the whole way by having liquid reserves adequate to meet cyclical inequality of cash flows and to take care of normal growth. The ability to insulate the company from external capital sources depends on a number of things, the more obvious being the initial extent of these reserves and the capacity to replenish at intervals, the magnitude of the fluctuations in the need for funds and the extent to which variations in inflows move in harmony with variations in outflow.

(2) External Sources

The large majority of companies in this sample found it necessary to have recourse to one or more of the external sources of funds at least once and usually more frequently over the 20-year period under study. This study focuses on sources involving debt contracts, but to set debt in perspective it is first necessary to look at the whole range of external sources. The contractual forms other than debt which were found in this group of companies included straight preferred stock, convertible preferred stock, and common stock. There were no instances of convertible bonds or other less common variations cutting across debt and equity forms.

Current Internal Generation of Funds

One of the most significant characteristics of the sample of companies under study is the extent to which the need for new capital was supplied by the business itself. The reader is again reminded that the concept of need here includes the incremental investment in net working capital and other assets, plant and equipment expenditures, and dividend payments. Individual company data for the 20-year period are given in Exhibit 2, column 4. This column shows funds internally generated from operations plus conversion of assets as a percentage of the total need. Because this is a single figure for the whole 20 years, it naturally obscures variations from year to year and trends. These will be considered shortly.

The figures show that in 12 of the 20 companies, 96% or more of the total funds required were internally generated. Note that this does not include the alternative of drawing down the cash balance or drawing on marketable securities. Of the remaining 8 companies, 5 generated between 80% and 90% of their need and the remaining 3 generated 77%, 66%, and 46%. Thus it may be said of the majority that during this period, either by chance or by design, they were able to conduct their businesses fundamentally independently of the capital markets and with funds over which management had free and independent jurisdiction. This does not mean, of course, that there were not occasions when they found it necessary to turn to external sources but the need was of a temporary nature which could in time be supplied from within. This point is of considerable significance in reviewing the contractual basis upon which such companies obtained whatever external funds they needed.

The question naturally arises as to the reasons for the overwhelming importance of internally generated funds in a majority of cases and for its deficiency in the remainder. Some observations on this point seem appropriate. The variables which we have been considering in this respect are:

(1) the annual rate at which funds are being invested,
(2) the rate at which funds are thrown off from operations (rate of profit after taxes plus noncash charges),
(3) the dividend payout policy,
(4) the rate of release of funds from working assets.

Item number (4) can be dropped from general consideration as it has not emerged as an item of major long-term importance in most of these companies. The exception to this has been in the machine tool industry where sharp cyclical swings in the working capital investment have been a dominant characteristic. In general, however, this source does not contribute more than 2% to 3% of the 14% to 27% of funds required each year (percentage of Net Tangible Assets). It should be noted, however, that this source can be of great importance over shorter periods of time — specifically, in periods of sharp recession.

With respect to number (1), the rate of investment of funds — and again cautioning the reader against the now familiar limitations of the sample — it is interesting to note some correlation between the capacity to finance internally and the rate of growth of the company. Of the companies falling into the low long-term growth rate category, only 2 of the 9 generated internally less than 96% of the total required funds and 4 generated in excess of 100%. The average percentage internally generated for this group was 99%. Of the companies classed as having a high rate of growth, only 3 of the 8 generated in excess of 83% and the average percentage internally generated was 82%.

Making a similar comparison as between the companies having high and low year-to-year variability there was an evident tendency for the companies having low variability to have a higher percentage of need internally generated (102%, as compared with 89% for the high variability group). The difference, however, is not so great as in the comparison with respect to long-term growth.

Next considering number (2), funds from operations, the key element here is the rate of profit after taxes. Noncash charges are important in the total computation — for some companies being of an amount equal to the after-tax profit — but they tend to be relatively stable over time and are a function primarily of the relative

EXHIBIT 2. COMPANY DATA ON INTERNALLY GENERATED
FUNDS AND RELATED INFORMATION

(1)	(2)	(3) Pattern of Funds Application		(4) % of Total Need	(5) Measure of Profitability Average	(6) Dividend Payout
Company Code Letter	Industry	Average Long-Term Growth Rate	Measure of Year-to-Year Variability	Internally Generated over 20-Year Period	Net EAT* as % of Net Tangible Assets	Common Dividends as % of Available Net EAT*
A	Machine	14.6%	61%	107%	8.0%	54%
B	Tools	28.8	271	89	14.1	55
C		27.1	192	97	16.3	39
D		17.0	105	106	9.2	58
E	Baking &	14.7	34	114	10.0	33
F	Biscuits	15.9	34	103	8.1	72
G		16.6	25	97	11.9	79
H		14.8	92	89	7.5	45
I	Chemicals	19.8	46	83	9.3	70
J		18.8	71	77	8.1	59
K		19.8	32	110	13.9	62
L		19.1	81	46	6.2	55
M	Ethical	19.6	34	97	15.9	62
N	Drugs	17.2	45	108	12.7	59
O		24.0	85	83	13.9	47
P		18.4	62	161	23.2	25
Q	Rubber	16.8	44	96	8.9	32
R		20.4	122	66	8.4	44
S		15.6	94	98	9.6	33
T		16.9	80	84	7.2	36

* Earnings after taxes.

importance of durable assets in the total investment and of the rate
of growth. The main variable element is the margin of profit over
which management exerts some influence and for which it must accept some responsibility. At the same time it is recognized that
the rate of profit cannot be merely budgeted into existence.

In comparing the proportion of needs supplied internally with the rate of profit (columns 4 and 5 of Exhibit 2), the most significant observation is the wide variation in rate of profitability among those companies which generated internally 95% or more of their required funds. It ranged all the way from 8% to 23% of net tangible assets (the lowest was 6.2%). The rates of return below 10% in this group were distributed among three industries — machine tools, baking, and rubber. Since it seems a safe observation that management is likely to have more control over the long-term annual rate of investment than it does over the long-term annual rate of profit, this tends to suggest that the rate of growth in these companies was to an important extent "paced" by the rate of generation of funds from operations. This statement may seem obvious except for the fact that the author was unable to find many companies which would admit that there was a deliberate policy to this end. It is certainly remarkable if this equality was produced by mere coincidence during this 20-year period.

Among the companies which generated less than 95% of their need, the majority had relatively low rates of profit and the lowest rates of profit were to be found here. At the same time two companies in this group had a rate of profit at the 14% level. As might be expected, these were also companies with relatively high rates of application of new funds. (In fact, they were two of the three fastest growing companies.) Based on a knowledge which goes beyond the mere statistics, it can be stated that most of this group showed a gap between need and internal generation not because the rate of earnings lagged behind a minimum competitive rate of growth but rather because they deliberately set a pace for investment which outstripped the known rate of internal generation. Thus it is more accurate to say that these companies created the necessity for going "outside" for funds rather than having circumstances of the industry and the firm force it upon them. This is a highly subjective distinction to draw, but it is significant with respect to the use of debt and the attitude toward the risks associated therewith. The study will return to this point again when debt policy is considered.

The remaining consideration in the list of variables is the dividend payout, and it is one which is naturally associated with the consideration of earnings. Since it is completely within the prerogative of management to vary the dividend rate between the maximum permitted by earnings and zero, such variations could be one of the means whereby management brought sources and needs into balance. If this was the dominant consideration in long-term payout policy, then one would expect to find that in those companies which had a long-term deficit of internally generated sources there would be a downward pressure on payout evidenced by a lower than average percentage.

The evidence on dividend payout for these companies is seen in column 6 of Exhibit 2. For the group as a whole it will be noted that there was a general and basic policy of heavy and sustained retention of earnings for reinvestment. The figures shown are the average percentage of earnings available for common dividends paid as cash dividends to common shareholders over the 20-year period, company by company. It ranges from 25% to 79%, and the average for the group is a 51% payout. Seventy-five percent of the companies paid out less than 60% of available earnings over the 20-year period.

It will also be noted, however, that there is no observable correlation between low payout and deficiencies in internally generated sources (column 4). Within the group with important deficiencies there are as many payout percentages above 50% as there are below. Similarly comparisons within industries (of greater significance to individual management) fail to reveal any such tendency. It will also be noticed that the lowest payout was in a company with a heavy surplus of internally generated funds. It appears that considerations other than the desire to balance current needs and sources internally were governing the payout policy. Of course it is generally recognized that dividend policy is subject to a variety of pressures.[1] It has been seen that these companies were already retaining a substantial fraction of current earnings. Further, a company with a substantial deficit of internally generated funds must always consider the alternative of a further common stock issue which would be adversely affected by a reduction in cash dividends per share.

Another way to approach the role of dividend policy is to ob-

[1] See John V. Lintner, "Distribution of Incomes of Corporations Among Dividends, Retained Earnings, and Taxes," *American Economic Review* (May 1956), pp. 97–113.

serve the extent to which dividends per share were reduced in years of substantial excess needs. (The company-by-company experience is to be found in Appendix A, page 268.) On the average these companies had current needs which exceeded currently generated funds in approximately 10 of the 20 years. Five of the companies did not reduce the dividend per share at all in these years and another nine reduced it either once or twice. Of the remaining, three companies reduced the dividend in such years three times, two companies four times, and one five. The general impression, then, is that this was not commonly used as a means of balancing needs and sources internally.

These, then, are the general observations which can be drawn from the statistical record of needs and internally generated sources of funds for 20 manufacturing companies over a 20-year period. In brief summary the principal observations were:

(1) That with respect to need, there was marked variation among companies and industries both as to the long-term rate of investment of funds (funds required) and as to the variability from year to year.

(2) That internal sources currently generated were overwhelmingly the most important source of these funds and that in a majority of cases the companies had been able to finance long-term fund requirements virtually independently of external negotiated sources.

(3) That this was true of companies with relatively low rates of profit as well as companies with high rates of profit. The inference was drawn that a number of companies deliberately paced long-term expansion to match the normal rate of internal generation of funds. On the other hand, a number of companies were just as deliberately pushing growth in such a manner as to create a substantial continuing deficit of internally generated funds.

(4) That the importance of internal generation was in large part a result of a general long-term policy of maintaining dividends at a relatively low percentage of available earnings. On the other hand, there was no evidence of correlation between internal deficits and unusually low payout or of a widespread use of a reduction in cash dividends per share as a means of balancing year-to-year deficiencies.

Now that these general observations have been made to provide background information, the reader is reminded that our primary concern is with individual decisions under individual circumstances. In this respect the exception can be equally as important as, if not more important than, the rule. The value of the "rule," insofar as a preponderance of evidence suggests one, lies in lending perspective to the individual case. We now turn to a more detailed, case-by-case observation of the means by which these companies financed themselves in those years and through those periods when current internally generated funds proved inadequate to cover the minimum needs. A summary of this experience is given in Exhibit 3 and the detailed evidence in Appendix A, page 268. For purposes of preserving anonymity, these companies are no longer grouped by industries and cannot be identified with the code previously used.

The Appendix shows for each company the record of those years in which there was a deficiency of current internally generated funds relative to the total need for funds, the magnitude of the deficiency as a percentage of the Total Funds Applied, and the sources from which these sums were obtained. In addition to the information given in Exhibit 3 the Appendix gives the years in which the deficiency occurred in each case, its magnitude, and further details on internal sources.

Thus, using Case No. 6 as an example it is seen that there were four years of significant deficiency — 1940, 1946, 1947, and 1951. In the remaining years internal generation was at least adequate to fill the need determined by management. It can also be seen that the company was able to meet these deficiencies out of its previously accumulated reserve of cash and marketable securities. It was not necessary to reduce the cash dividend to do so nor was it necessary to go outside the company for funds during these years. It will be noted later that this was a rather exceptional company.

It is important to point out here that the data for external sources do not necessarily record the dates of *all* security issues and debt contracts. Their purpose is to record only those which were required for purposes of financing current deficiencies in funds (whether they actually occurred in the year of the deficiency or anticipated it). Thus it specifically excludes recapitalization — for example, the retirement of a preferred stock by means of a bond issue, and also the issuance of common stock under an employee in-

EXHIBIT 3. COMPANY DATA ON FREQUENCY OF USE
OF EXTERNAL SOURCES OF FUNDS

Company Code Number	Number of Years of Deficiency*	Number of Years Covered by Internal Sources Alone	Number of Years in which External Sources were Used				
				Preferred Stock		Common Stock	
			Debt	Straight	Convertible	Exchange	Cash
Internal Sources Alone							
1	9	9					
6	5	5					
20	2	2					
Internal Sources & Debt							
3	5	4	1				
4	11	10	1				
10	11	9	2				
12	7	6	1				
13	10	8	2				
18	8	2	6				
19	2	0	2				
Internal Sources, Debt & Straight Preferred							
14	9	5	3	1			
Internal Sources, Debt & Common (Exchange Only)							
2	9	3	5			1	
5	8	5	2			1	
9	12	7	4			1	
Internal Sources & Common Equity (Convertible Preferred and/or Common for Cash)							
7	12	7	0	2			3
8	12	5	2	3	2		3
11	10	6	3				1
15	13	3	7		2	2	
16	14	3	8	2	2	2	
17	13	6	7				1

* Years in which Total Funds Applied exceeded Funds Generated from Operations and Released from other Working Assets.

centive or executive stock option plan. It *does* include securities issued in exchange for assets in a company acquisition.

So far the discussion has centered on internal sources including adjustment in the cash dividend. The remaining internal source to be considered is the accumulated liquid reserve in the form of cash and marketable securities.

Liquid Reserves

Among the group of 20, only one company (number 6) managed to operate throughout the entire 20-year period without recourse to external sources and without dividend cuts. This company had a high average rate of funds application but a low rate of variation in need from year to year (Pattern of Application number 4). Periodic excesses of need over internal generation were financed out of liquid reserves which averaged 30% of net tangible assets (compared to a group average of 23.8%). Two other companies (numbers 1 and 20) were also able to operate without external funds. In Company No. 1, however, several dividend cuts were required to do it and Company No. 2 had an incomplete record. These companies also had relatively high liquid reserves (28.8% and 44.5% of net tangible assets). One of these companies had a low growth rate and a low rate of variability (Pattern number 3). The other had a high rate of growth and low variability (Pattern number 4) coupled with above-average profitability and below-average payout. All three companies had in common a relatively low rate of variation in need from year to year.

This statistic on the importance of liquid reserves in meeting cyclical variations in need, however, substantially underrates the importance of these reserves for this purpose. A perusal of Appendix A shows how frequently cash and security reserves were sufficient to meet the year's deficiency. In many cases the retention of reserves of internally generated funds over then-existing needs was sufficiently large for it to be necessary for the company to go "outside" only occasionally and at extended intervals of time. As an objective measure of this independence Exhibit 3 shows that there were nine companies which did not go outside for funds more often than twice in this 20-year period, and six companies that went outside only once or not at all.

The close proximity of the long-term rate of funds application and the long-term rate of funds retention did not necessarily mean a low long-term application rate compared to the group as a whole. This relatively low growth rate was true of the majority, however, and it was also true of the majority that the year-to-year variability was low. The most common pattern in the above group of nine companies was Pattern number 3 (Low-Low) as given on page 32.

In general, it may be said that these companies carried enough excess liquid reserves to see them through one or two years of moderate deficiency but that any large and/or sustained deficiency forced them into negotiation with external sources in order to replenish these reserves and to anticipate any excess needs in the near future. A significantly large number of companies in the sample were able to come through this period successfully with only infrequent exposure to this experience and the necessity of making the associated decisions, among which is the debt-equity alternative.

External Sources of Funds

A general summary of the character and usage of external sources of funds is shown in Exhibit 3. The previous data on internally generated funds indicated that there were a substantial number of companies which, considering the period as a whole and *on the average,* were operating essentially independently of the external capital markets. This does not mean, however, that there were not occasions when these companies found it necessary to enter into contracts with outside sources to meet the unusual need of the moment. On the other hand, for these companies such occasions were rare.

As previously mentioned there were three companies which were able to develop throughout the entire period without recourse to any external sources. A second group of companies, numbering seven, were able to finance the needs of the period by internal sources supplemented only by debt. In six of the seven cases such borrowings were infrequent — occurring only once or twice in the entire period. In the remaining case there were very frequent borrowings over a short period of time under circumstances of a high rate of growth and low rate of profitability.

In one additional case the company financed its needs by a combination of internal sources, debt, and one issue of straight preferred stock. Three other companies also used straight preferred but this was accompanied by the use of other equity sources as well.

Thus over half of the companies, with or without the assistance of borrowings, were able to operate throughout the period without any action which disturbed the existing distribution of ownership (of common stock) or diluted its claim to future earnings. The remaining group of nine companies did find it necessary or desirable to enlarge the participation in ownership either through the direct issue of common stock or potentially through the issuance of convertible preferred.

Within this group, however, some distinctions must be drawn. One of these is the distinction between common issued in exchange for the stock of a newly acquired subsidiary and common sold on the market for cash. Stock issued in exchange may not involve the potential dilution of a cash offering. This may be true for several reasons: (1) the relatively small amount which may be involved, (2) highly favorable terms of exchange, (3) the impact of the earning capacity of a going concern versus assets which must take time to reach earning capacity, (4) beneficial balance sheet effects, (5) the circumstances of the former owners of the acquired company which cause them to hold the new stock off the market at least for a time (for tax reasons).

For this reason companies may use common stock for favorable acquisitions but not as a source of cash for further investment in earning assets of the parent company. Three of these remaining nine companies were in this category — using internal sources plus debt to carry the basic year-to-year needs and occasionally (for each of these companies, once in 20 years) issuing common in an acquisition.

There were in fact only four companies which could be said to have made frequent use of equity sources (numbers 7, 8, 15, and 16). All four used preferred as well as common stock and two used convertible preferred as well as straight preferred. In general these companies used debt as well and used it more frequently than equity. There was only one company in the entire group which used equity but not debt.

To further emphasize the relatively minor role played by common equity sources in these companies, it can be noted that out of a total of 179 company-years of deficiency in internally generated funds there were only 21 issues of common and convertible preferred stocks, 7 of which were issues in exchange for the stock of subsidiaries. This of course excludes issues which were purely for purposes of recapitalization with no new funds involved. In dollars provided the 21 issues accounted for about 2½% of the total funds applied by the companies during the period.

All but four of these companies used long-term debt *at some time* during the 20-year period. Most used debt as their sole or primary source of external funds *to the extent that they were needed*. On the other hand, as previously pointed out, there were many which used it very sparingly indeed. Only one company by-passed the debt alternative entirely in going outside for necessary funds.

This, then, is the historical record in summary form. With respect to the needs for and sources of funds it has answered the questions "what," "how," and "when" but not "why." We now proceed from information available in the published financial reports of these companies, essentially statistical and factual in character, to information gained in personal interviews with corporate officers in an effort to learn the reasons behind the specific decisions and actions which helped to produce these results. In the next chapter the focus is on matters of financial policy other than debt. With this as background the study then proceeds in the following chapter to the matter of debt policy with particular reference to the element of risk.

CHAPTER 3

Background:
Basic Management Attitudes to
External Sources of Funds Other Than Debt

GENERAL ATTITUDES TOWARD THE USE OF
EXTERNAL SOURCES OF FUNDS

Before turning to a consideration of management attitudes toward long-term debt, attitudes which found expression in the financial record considered in the previous chapter, it is helpful to consider the evidence as to attitudes toward external sources generally. It has been established that a majority of these companies (12 out of 20) had demonstrated the capacity to generate internally virtually all (96%+) of their funds requirements. The balance showed a significant deficiency in this respect, the magnitude varying from 11% to 54% of total need. The question arises: To what extent did the degree of independence from external sources result from the chance happenings of the period from 1939 to 1958 and to what extent was it a deliberate result of management attitudes toward external sources in general? It should be stated at the outset that no categorical answer has been found on this question but there are important pieces of evidence.

Consider first the group of companies which were essentially independent of the external capital market. Circumstantial evidence suggests that it is not just coincidence that internally generated sources worked out to be in the range of 95% to 105% of the required funds for the period.

51

Only a minority (four) of these companies were prepared to state publicly that it was their long-term objective to hold to a rate of growth which was consistent with their capacity to generate the funds internally. Recognizing that temporary deficiencies might arise, two of the companies had accumulated substantial liquid reserves which would be drawn down at such times and later replenished when needs declined below the amount of funds internally generated. Hopefully such reserves would insulate the companies completely from the external capital markets. For these two companies cash and securities averaged approximately 30% of Net Tangible Assets. The other two companies planned to take care of temporary deficiencies in internal generation by drawing on external sources. For these two cash and securities averaged 20% and 10% respectively.

The remainder of these companies did not offer so simple an answer to the financial record of the past 20 years and in general resented any inference that they were attempting to avoid dependence on external sources. There was, however, evidence of a variety of restraints which operated to hold down the annual rate of application of funds. There was the previously mentioned tendency to stay within traditional and familiar boundaries of industry, product line, market area, and to be content with preserving a competitive position therein particularly when the accepted yardsticks of success — dollar sales, net earnings, and earnings per share — showed some progress over the past. For all these companies the two basic benchmarks of financial performance were (1) their own record in the immediate past and (2) the record of their closest competitors in the same industry.

Evidence of general company acceptance of "creeping expansion" was reflected in such statements as:

"Our management is essentially conservative."

"The word which describes our corporate image is 'dignified.'"

"This company is not in the business of squeezing out every last dollar for the shareholders."

"Our management is not expansion minded."

"Our rate of investment was acceptable because we *were able to maintain our competitive position* at this rate. Had we been slipping in this respect we might have stepped it up."

"I suppose in a way we're lazy."

In general this was not just a matter of steering a comfortable course between the Scylla of stockholder complaints and the Charybdis of antitrust action, although this was undoubtedly a factor in some cases. Rather there was evident a basic conviction that management should stick to what it knows best and that its appetite for growth should not exceed its organizational digestive capacity.

This approach tended to produce two financially significant results with regard to the application of funds. Capital budget proposals tended to fall into two categories: (1) those which "we've got to have in order to stay in (the traditional line of) business," and (2) those which were merely opportunities to make a return on an investment. In the former category were the basic replacements necessary to maintain efficient productive capacity and the additions to plant and to working capital needed to handle the normal growth in sales within established market positions. With respect to these fund requirements it was generally true that no real test of expected return on investment was applied. To the observer who thinks of business as an investment process — as a dynamic flow concept with funds constantly seeking their most profitable employment and with little concern for company or industry "loyalty" — this appears as questionable long-term policy. To management which identifies itself with a specific organizational entity within a specific industry it is a highly sensible simplification of decision making.

Those fund expenditure proposals which fell outside the "got to have" category and particularly those which constituted a radical departure from the normal type of investment were subjected to careful screening, including some type of return on investment test. Undoubtedly the intensity of the screening process was strongly influenced by whether the funds could be expected to be available from internal sources or whether the need would require negotiation with outside sources. The most common earnings test appeared to be the rule that any such investment should earn at least as much as that currently being realized in the business. Some businesses would substitute the phrase "substantially more than" in place of "at least as much as" in this statement. It was natural to require some margin to allow for errors of estimate in unfamiliar opportunities.

This earnings performance was usually measured as a simple expected annual return in savings or profits as a percentage of the dollars invested, and the measure of current company performance was commonly profits as a percentage of asset book values. In a period of prosperity and high profits when management was most disposed to consider additional investment, such a standard could be rather prohibitive.

Such absolute and apparently arbitrary rules of capital budgeting are at variance with what is often considered to be in the best interests of the investor — namely, to adopt a marginal or an incremental approach in which management continues to add to the invested funds so long as the expected return exceeds the cost of available funds, external as well as internal. Assuming in theory that the company undertook the most profitable opportunities first so that the remaining opportunities offered steadily declining rates of return, the approach suggested by practice would tend to freeze expansion (except for normal growth in the established investment) whereas the marginal approach would accept a gradual lowering of the average rate of return so long as there was a net gain to the original owners.

There is, of course, no way of objectively measuring the relative importance of what we call rational economic and business considerations, on the one hand, and an unwritten and unspoken policy of taking the line of least resistance, on the other (so long as things are reasonably successful and comfortable). There is no doubt that internal financing is the line of least resistance in most companies. These are funds over which management has complete and independent control. There is no process of negotiation with troublesome outsiders, no regulatory red tape. Further, it avoids the glare of publicity and shareholder attention which accompanies the decisions and actions of management if externally financed, attention which can be particularly disconcerting if the ultimate terms of financing are not as favorable as expected. If the company has any weak spots, they are likely to be picked up.

On the other hand, retained earnings have the obvious disadvantages of being somewhat uncertain as to amount and timing (though not necessarily more so than some forms of external financing) and particularly of not being adaptable to sudden sharp increases in times of unusual need. Thus we have the practice which was typical of the majority of companies in this sample — of using retained earnings as the primary source of new funds with occasional recourse to external sources when the rate of investment showed a temporary increase substantially in excess of the rate of internal generation. The primary cause of such temporary deficiencies among these companies was the need to replace or expand plant facilities, an expenditure which for physical or economic reasons could not be broken down into smaller, internally manageable "packages" of annual expenditure.

So far we have been considering the attitude toward external sources of funds among those companies which over the 20-year period generated internally an amount of funds roughly equivalent to the total need for the period. The question naturally follows: How does this compare with the attitude of those companies that had a substantial deficiency of internal funds? Examining the five companies that had the greatest deficiencies, the author was unable to detect any characteristic differences in concepts of or attitudes toward either external sources in general or specific internal sources. These were companies which had gone outside for funds anywhere from 6 to 14 times over 20 years. It appeared to be not so much a case of disliking external sources less as liking expansion more. These were all companies that were aggressively pushing expansion. The three that had the greatest deficiency were diversifying in fields radically different from their original product group. A fourth, located in a growth industry, had a rate of funds investment substantially in excess of the other three companies in the sample from the same industry and the second highest rate for the sample as a whole. The fifth, the leading producer in its industry as measured by sales volume, did not have an unusual rate of funds application but had a low rate of profitability and an average dividend payout (the lowest profit percentage in the industry sample and the second lowest for the group as a whole). It is apparent that these were companies which were not satisfied with the rewards, financial and non-financial, associated with a growth rate consistent with internal financing and were deliberately forcing themselves into substantial reliance on the external capital market over an extended period of time. It should be noted that without exception these companies had a divided payout which was as low as industry practice would justify.

ATTITUDES TOWARD SPECIFIC EXTERNAL SOURCES
OTHER THAN DEBT

It will have been observed that very few of the company managements interviewed were prepared to make categoric statements about a subject as broad as "the use of external sources of funds." Hence such general observations as seemed worthy of reporting were drawn by inference from the record of action or obliquely from related matters such as the standards for earnings performance of new investment opportunities. It was recognized from the outset that direct questions on matters of over-all policy usually elicit a meaningless or facetious response whereas questions relating to specific aspects of finance, particularly within a framework of specific decisions, almost invariably bring sharp, emphatic answers. It is the job of the researcher, then, to work cautiously from the particular back to the general.

Thus as the discussion turns to more specific aspects of financing the evidence becomes much more clear cut. At this point we may usefully consider the evidence on attitudes toward specific external sources other than debt since this aids in defining attitudes to external sources in general and particularly in viewing debt against other alternatives once the decision to go outside for funds had been made.

Common Stock

It will be apparent that the attitude toward the sale of common stock must be taken in relation to the attitude toward retained earnings since these are alternative ways of adding to the common equity base. The overwhelming importance of retained earnings and the comparatively infrequent use of stock issues suggests that management was avoiding a common issue as much as possible. Was this so and if so, why? Both the statistical and the interview evidence indicates that it was, and for reasons which were believed by management to be in the best interests of the common shareholders.

The quantitative criteria of the "best interests" of the common shareholder both in the stock market and in the minds of management are generally accepted as (1) earnings per share, (2) cash dividends per share, and (3) market price and price-earnings ratio.

If these *absolute values* are improved or at least maintained from period to period, management is considered and considers itself to have successfully fulfilled its responsibilities to its shareholders. Disregarding the obvious exceptions in the case of stock splits and stock dividends, management generally recoils from any voluntary action which would tend to reduce any one of these values.

It is apparent that the issuance of new common stock adds to the number of shares outstanding and thus directly threatens the current performance of these three criteria. This is particularly true of new common sold for cash for the purpose of adding to plant and working capital where there is likely to be a lag in the generation of new earnings. Unless the new money earns *at the same rate* as the existing investment, the Earnings per Share will decline. Undoubtedly one of the reasons for the more frequent use of common stock in acquisitions is the fact that it usually adds directly and immediately to total earnings (and also that the stock is more likely to be held off the market).

If management is preoccupied with the short-run effects of its action as measured by these per share criteria, this standard could inhibit action which would ultimately be distinctly advantageous. The basic measure lies in a comparison between the (expected) inflow of funds resulting from the investment and the outflow of funds which the financing of the investment requires. There is of course a problem in the unequal timing of these flows which is usually handled by comparison at a common point in time (present value). Assuming an excess of inflow, the gain from investment must then be considered in the light of the uncertainty surrounding the flows of funds. Earnings per Share and Market Price do not provide an accurate measure of this gain, particularly in the early stages of investment productivity though it may be expected that they will eventually reflect the improved financial position of the company.

Evidence that an important segment of business may have become unduly preoccupied with current E.P.S. and Market Price is seen in a widespread and persistent reluctance to issue new common stock for cash. In the interviews it was found almost without exception that management made a particular point of its concern to avoid "dilution" of the common stock. This was generally measured in terms of depression of Market Price or E.P.S. though in a few cases book values were mentioned. Though few companies would go so far as to rule out a sale of common under any circumstances, the large majority had not had such a sale in the past 20 years and did not anticipate one in the foreseeable future. This was particularly remarkable in view of the very high Price–Earnings ratios of recent years. Several financial officers showed that they were well aware that this had been a good time to sell common but the reluctance still persisted.

A variety of reasons can be advanced for management's concern for these current market criteria. The most obvious is that the market itself is preoccupied with them and communicates this to management in an increasingly regular fashion through the steady stream of market analysts seeking interviews with top company officials. In these interviews management may tell little or nothing that is not already public information, but in the process it learns what the so-called sophisticated investor is interested in.

Another reason is that while theoretical earnings projections may unconcernedly extend 10 or 15 years into the future, management at its present stage of knowledge cannot see or plan with any degree of assurance more than a year ahead. Some of the companies interviewed had an abbreviated 5-year plan but without exception those managements that had such a plan expressed doubts as to its significance. Under these circumstances the events and performance in the near future are going to be of overwhelming importance in decision making. It is little wonder that a simple payback criterion for new investment which measures cash inflows in the first few years is so widely used.

It has also been suggested that the widespread use of executive stock option plans for senior officers of the company has in an increasing degree caused management to weigh each decision in terms of its short-run impact on the market price of the common stock. This is not to suggest that self interest is the governing factor, but when this appears to coincide with the best interests of the shareholders as a whole it is undoubtedly a persuasive consideration.

Perhaps the most important reason, however, for the avoidance of the real or potential dilution of new common stock issues lies in the fact that most managements have been able to obtain sufficient equity capital to achieve minimum investment goals by means of retained earnings and thereby have avoided the danger of *apparent dilution*. So long as reinvested earnings add *something* to the total earnings of the following years, they serve to increase Earnings per Share *regardless of the rate of return on the investment.* It is here that the E.P.S. standard can become seriously deceptive, and in view of the heavy reliance on retained earnings it is of great importance to recognize the limitations of the standard.

Here a simplified example may be helpful. Assume the following facts about an imaginary company:

(1) Current Net Earnings after Taxes — $1,000,000 per year

(2) Only Common Stock Outstanding, 1,000,000 shares currently selling on the market at $15 a share

(3) Dividend Payout   40%

(4) Resultant E.P.S. $1.00

    Dividend per share $.40

    Retained earnings $600,000

(5) Noncash charges $300,000

(6) Funds required for investment in coming year — $900,000

Assuming that the company has a continued internal generation of $900,000 in the coming year and that its requirements are such that they can be timed to match internal generation, this company can avoid the necessity of going outside for funds. Whatever is earned on the $900,000 reinvested will add something to the current net earnings of $1,000,000 and the E.P.S. will increase. If, for example, it is only 2% after taxes, the new net earnings will be $1,000,000 + $\frac{2}{100}$(900,000) = $1,018,000 or $1.02 a share.

Suppose alternatively that the company had to raise $900,000 by the sale of common stock and that it could be sold at the current market price of $15 a share (a favorable assumption). This would add 60,000 new shares and in order to earn *the same* E.P.S. as before the new level of earnings would have to be $1,060,000. This would mean an incremental return of *6.6%* on the $900,000 investment *just to show a continued E.P.S. of $1.00.* Obviously if management performance is to be measured by the amount of the increase in Earnings and Dividends per Share (and in Market Price which reflects these), the goal of success is much more easily attained if equity capital is supplied by the retained earnings route.

Another way of saying this is that the simple E.P.S. standard implies that retained earnings have no cost. They do not of course add anything to the costs of operation as do bonds, or to cash outlays as do dividend-bearing stocks. If this is extended to mean that they have no cost at all, however, then two conclusions follow: (1) companies should use retained earnings as much as possible before any other source is considered, and (2) their reinvestment is justified so long as *any* positive return is forthcoming. The cutoff point on expected rate of return on proposed investments to be financed from this source would then be just in excess of zero. The 2% in the example above would be acceptable, assuming no better alternatives were available at the time.

Financial theory would argue otherwise. With respect to retained earnings theoretical calculations would apply an "opportunity cost" which is the return that would be realized if the money were invested in the best alternative investment opportunity of comparable risk outside the company. Thus the decision to retain and reinvest depends on an internal investment opportunity which can at least match the opportunity cost, and this becomes the cutoff point. Obviously, investment decisions will be radically different under the two opposing concepts of cost — the actual outlay versus the foregone income.

It is interesting to consider the evidence as to which of these approaches the management of the 20 companies in question appeared to be following. It has already been suggested that the simple market criteria hinging on E.P.S. lead in the "no-cost" direction. Most financial officers appeared to be doing their thinking in these terms. For example, in discussing what he considered to be a weakness in the concept of trading on equity, the treasurer of the second largest company interviewed (over one billion in annual sales) argued as follows: "Most equity capital in a business comes from retained earnings. Suppose a company revised its policy so as to pay out a higher amount in dividends, thereby reducing retained earnings, and it made up the difference with so-called low-cost debt. The result would be a lower E.P.S. because of the interest charges. If the company had used its own money E.P.S. would have been higher." The obvious implication was that retained earnings is the better (cheaper) way to do it. In fairness to this particular treasurer it must be added that he did not appear to be wholly convinced by his own argument but was "hung up" in his mind on the inability to reconcile the obvious appeal of trading on equity with what appeared to him to be a valid criterion of performance — E.P.S.

A number of general practices and attitudes were consistent with a cost-free concept of retained earnings. One of these was the common failure to apply an earnings standard in investment decisions relating to the company's established markets. The implication was that the management had no choice but to invest in and the shareholders no choice but to finance the continuation and expansion of these activities, regardless of the rate of return. It is really not surprising that management which has had a life-long identification with a particular business finds the opportunity cost concept rather vague and unreal except as specific alternative investment opportunities actually exist for their consideration. It is not surprising if management assumes the same identification on the part of the shareholders, so that the idea of withdrawing funds when an internal need exists merely in the hope of a somewhat higher return from an unspecified investment outside the company appears not only somewhat academic but even disloyal. It is not uncommon to hear the statement: "Our investment and payout policies are public information. If the shareholder doesn't agree with them, he should not have bought the stock in the first place and should sell out now. He is not our type of investor."

Among these companies there was no evidence of periodic examination of the dividend payout proportions in the light of expected rate of return and internal investment opportunities. Regardless of considerable variation among companies as to payout percentages, there was practically no disposition to consider departure from traditional payout practice. Invariably the argument was presented that for tax reasons shareholders preferred future capital gains to additional current dividend income, though no company had any statistically valid information on the circumstances and wishes of its shareholders as a whole. On the other hand, it was also generally agreed that the shareholders required some stable current income and that the then current dividend satisfied that need. Thus it was simply a defense of the status quo.

This practical approach to the use of retained earnings makes sense from the investor's point of view if it can be assumed that any gap between the rate of return which can be realized internally and the alternative opportunity outside the company does not exceed the costs, in incremental tax payments and otherwise, of withdrawing the funds and investing elsewhere at comparable risk. Assuming that a majority of shareholders are in a relatively high income tax bracket, this could well be true. It could be argued that in this case all earnings should be retained, except for the assumed need for some current income and possible reactions from federal tax and regulatory authorities who show periodic interest in the payout question.

This approach to investment decisions, however, has the weakness of not in itself providing an "automatic alarm system" when the internal rate of return declines to and below this point. In this connection the reader is reminded of the rate of return standards that most of these companies applied to investment opportunities other than those that were considered mandatory. These were previously described as being typically a rate of return that as a minimum had to be at least equivalent to the current demonstrated earning capacity of the business. Thus such a standard, where applied, acted to prevent the logical extension of the cost-free concept of retained earnings implied in the E.P.S. standard of performance to low level income opportunities. In a sense this rule might be regarded as a practical approximation to the opportunity cost standard for the application of internally generated funds. As such, however, the rule implies that roughly comparable rates of return are being realized outside the company on alternative investment opportunities of comparable risk, and the standard has an upward bias since it is usually stated as a rate of return *at least* as high as that being earned in the company and disregards what may be substantial costs of withdrawal.

The net conclusion is that the common practice of these 20 companies with respect to quantitative guides to investment decisions suggested a cost-free concept of retained earnings for the so-called mandatory investments in maintaining traditional product lines and a rough internal opportunity cost standard for "voluntary" investment opportunities. It is interesting to note however, that in the companies where, at the time of the interview, internally generated funds were running ahead of current needs for funds, the treasurer's first thought was not for a reconsideration of payout but rather for increased activity to find investment opportunities which would drain off the excess cash. It was universally agreed that it was easy to increase a cash dividend but difficult to cut it back, and the inability to foresee future needs caused the traditionally cautious financial officer to act so as to preserve maximum flexibility. A substantial surplus of cash raised questions about the aggressiveness of management, encouraged ideas for increased dividends, and invited "raiders."

Preferred Stock

In using market standards which showed retained earnings in a substantially more favorable light than the sale of common stock as a source of equity capital, management generally sought either to restrain needs so as to avoid reliance on common stock or to find other sources when needs exceeded internal generation. In theory preferred stock offers a means of avoiding dilution of the common stock while at the same time avoiding the fixed obligations of debt. In practice it was not a popular alternative with this group of companies. Preferred stock, both straight and convertible, was used by only five companies and was generally a supplement to more frequent use of debt. Two of the five companies used convertible preferred as well as straight preferred.

Considering the cases involving convertible preferred first, the three companies in question all had fund requirements that were consistently running substantially in excess of internal generation (average generation of 83%, 77%, and 66% of total need), and all three were using debt in amounts that they considered approached appropriate limits. Two of the three (those with the greatest internal need) did not issue common for cash at any time during the 20-year period. Convertible preferred was, in fact, considered as an issue of common at next year's market price. It added to the equity base but avoided the immediate dilution associated with a sale of common for cash and postponed the impact on the market for common, giving the new investment a chance to build up earning power and assuring that the new common would not be issued unless the market was on a strong upward trend.

With regard to straight preferred, the record was that 14 companies had an issue outstanding at some time during the 20-year period. Of these, nine had preferred outstanding at the beginning of the period but did not issue any new preferred during the period.

Of these nine, six either reduced or eliminated their outstanding straight preferred stock during the period. The remaining three all expressed a desire to retire their preferred but had been obstructed from doing so for technical reasons, principally because of the absence of a call provision.

The fact that the large majority did not use straight preferred as a source of funds during the period, and particularly that all those that had a preferred issue outstanding at the outset took steps to eliminate it, is clear indication of the relative unpopularity of this source of equity capital with this group of companies. Although preferred stock is legally ownership capital, it is commonly regarded by management as "outsider" capital and thus management does not identify itself with the interests of this shareholder group as it more commonly does with the common shareholder group. It tends to regard the voice of this group as expressed in restrictive covenants and voting rights as "interference" and bothersome red tape. Since these were companies in which management felt a strong responsibility to pay a regular common dividend, it is inevitable that they would come to regard the preferred dividend as a fixed charge which for planning purposes was just as mandatory as debt servicing.

Viewed in this way, it is not surprising that preferred suffered by comparison with a comparable bond issue with its lower tax-deductible interest charges. The fact that preferred dividends were not deductible for tax purposes appeared to be the primary reason for the drive to get rid of the preferred. One or two companies nibbled away at their preferred through a preferred sinking fund or by open-market purchases. The majority, taking advantage of unused debt capacity, floated a bond issue or arranged a term loan and wiped out the preferred in one or two steps. In most cases the company then proceeded to retire the debt with the ultimate result that the preferred equity was replaced by common equity (retained earnings). There was one instance where the preferred was retired in large part out of the proceeds of a rights offering of common stock.

To an observer who is sensitive to the relative cost of the basic sources of capital, as measured by the dilution of earning power of the investment of the common stockholders, this process appears somewhat inconsistent. Considering only the cost aspect, the first stage in which debt replaces preferred appears advantageous as it increases the residual earnings available to the common shareholder. The second stage in which debt is replaced by retained earnings further increases the dollar amount of the residual earnings by eliminating the interest charge and so may also appear advantageous. It is accomplished, however, only by draining off undistributed earnings of previous years in order to repay the debt — earnings which otherwise might have gone into revenue-producing activity either inside or outside the business. Consequently, from an opportunity cost standpoint, this second stage increases the actual residual earnings but *reduces the potential earnings* from what they would have been had the debt been replaced by further debt issues and the retained earnings productively employed.

From the point of view of the financial interest of the common stockholder the replacement of preferred by debt and then by retained earnings makes good sense only if it can be assumed: (1) that debt presents an excessive risk which the common stockholders are unwilling to assume except for short periods of time when the near future appears unusually promising and then only as a means of anticipating future earnings for use in the present; and/or (2) that there are no currently available internal investment opportunities which yield a return higher than the cost of the preferred or the cost of the debt (which latter on an after-tax basis may be as low as 2%) or external opportunities which, after adequate allowance for the costs of withdrawal, yield a higher return.

This reasoning, it is recognized, ignores the various considerations (which may or may not be identified with the interests of the common shareholder) which inhibit an increased rate of investment within the firm or the withdrawal of funds for investment outside the firm. Some of these have already been raised for consideration in previous discussion, not the least of which is the fact that management may not consider the maximization of the earning power of the common shareholders' investment as the sole criterion in decision making.

Having considered those instances where companies either did not use preferred at all or chose to reduce or eliminate what was then outstanding, we can turn to the minority that did use straight preferred during this period and consider the reasons why. These companies fell into one of two categories. Of the four companies involved, two had an unusually high rate of growth relative to the rate of internal generation of funds and could maintain this gap only by drawing on both debt and equity sources. These companies had generally used debt to a limit considered by themselves or their creditors (or both) as prudent before floating a preferred issue. In one case management had rejected the use of common as an alternative and in the other it had not. The other two companies were also running at a relatively high rate of funds application, which required the use of external sources but were different in that they had rejected debt as a major continuing source of long-term funds. Incidentally both companies in this category found it necessary to sell common on three different occasions during the period. The rejection of debt was made on the grounds that industry characteristics created a degree of risk which they did not care to enlarge by adding further fixed charges.

SUMMARY STATEMENT

This chapter has been concerned with observations and interpretation of the basic attitudes of management toward the application and sources of funds, exclusive of debt, which lay behind the historical record of financial decisions described in the previous chapter. The purpose has been to assist in keeping in perspective the detailed discussion of debt which follows. The reader will be aware that an accurate statement of considerations and motives behind a decision some time after the fact is difficult to obtain. Even when one is dealing directly with the person involved, there may be important differences between what actually happened, what the individual now recollects as having happened, and what he would like you to believe happened. Recognizing all the problems of establishing and interpreting reliable information on the elusive subject of attitudes and points of view, the findings are necessarily tentative. However, the author reported only such evidence as was, in his judgment, beyond any reasonable doubt. Like all efforts at generalization, the statements have their limitations even within the small sample of companies under consideration. Consequently in any instance where there were important exceptions to generalized statements, these were noted.

Having given formal notice that these limitations are recognized, a brief summary of the major observations of this chapter follows:

(1) Managements' quantitative standards for investment favored the established and familiar investment areas over new and unfamiliar opportunities, even to the point of having no minimum earnings standard for the established areas and a prohibitive one for the new opportunity.

(2) Managements' standards for investment tended to set absolute limits on the rate of investment related to the availability of internally generated funds.

(3) Management strongly favored internal generation as a source of new funds even to the exclusion of external sources except for occasional unavoidable "bulges" in the need for funds. Only a small minority were pushing the rate of investment to the point of having a need substantially in excess of internal generation over extended periods of time.

(4) Management considered these policies in the best interests of the common shareholders as reflected in the customary stock market standards. Literally interpreted, these standards show the use of retained earnings as distinctly more beneficial to per share performance than equity issues and even debt. This apparent benefit to earnings, coupled with the apparent advantage of the capital gains tax rate over the personal income tax rate, was taken as adequate justification for continuation of high rates of earnings retention. The opportunity cost concept, particularly as it relates to investment opportunities outside the firm, is not one with which company-oriented management can find much identification. On the other hand, many managements followed a rough internal opportunity cost standard for new investment opportunities.

(5) Management did not follow a single-minded devotion to maximizing the financial goals of the common shareholders. In general it appeared to have fulfilled its responsibilities to its shareholders if earnings and dividends per share were improved over the preceding period, or at least maintained, if market price and the price-earnings ratio were holding firm or improving, and particularly if this record did not reflect unfavorably in comparison with the company's nearest competitors.

CHAPTER 4

Management Attitudes

Concerning the Use of Long-Term Debt

It is generally accepted that the primary incentive to use long-term debt capital in business is the fact that debt is normally a cheaper source than retained earnings or new equity issues. In view of the debt proportions usually considered by business and the tax shield of the interest charge, it is substantially cheaper. Assuming that the primary objective of business is to maximize net revenue, it would appear to be highly desirable to use debt as a source of funds and to use it as continuously as possible. The question arises as to whether the evidence among the group of companies studied supports this reasoning.

There is no doubt that every financial officer interviewed was well aware of the reputed advantage of debt leverage. Whether every member of their respective boards of directors had the precise meaning of this concept clearly in mind is perhaps more open to question. It was quite apparent, however, that there was a general acceptance of debt as a relatively low-cost source of funds. This advantage has been heightened and dramatized in recent years by the high level of federal corporate income taxes. There is evidence to support the observation that some businessmen did not become excited about the income possibilities of debt until the period of high tax rates during and following World War II. In fact, there appears in some instances to be an almost fanatical devotion to the exploration of opportunities for minimizing taxes. One of the most obvious opportunities in this respect and one which was widely acted on in the postwar period was the substitution of bond interest for preferred dividends. Although generally speaking a significant differential has always existed favorable to debt, the primary motivation for recapitalization at this time was the advantage of the tax shield.

For the majority of businesses in this group the income advantage of debt was assumed to hold at any level of debt which they and their creditors would be prepared to consider. Consequently, there was little evidence of precise cost comparisons among financing alternatives prior to a decision on external financing. In a small minority of cases Earning per Share comparisons were made on the basis of varying sales assumptions. Even here, however, the motive was not always to provide critical evidence for the decision but rather to make the consideration explicit in a formal presentation to the Board. Here, as elsewhere in business, there is a tendency to base decisions on abiding convictions about such matters rather than on precise analysis at any point in time. The exception to this was found where a business was considering debt for the first time.

The idea of debt as a low-cost source of funds must be qualified by the distinction which businessmen commonly draw between equity capital generated internally and equity capital from additional issues of stock. It has already been noted that businesses will invariably utilize retained earnings before they will have recourse to debt or outside equity sources. In Chapter 3 it was indicated that this cost-free concept of retained earnings appeared to be supported by the customary standards of financial performance, particularly the Earnings per Share standard. Interpreted literally, a comparison between retained earnings as a source of funds and an equivalent amount of debt capital in terms of the resultant E.P.S. always shows debt as second best. The question of the validity of this evidence again comes back to the point of whether internally generated funds should be considered as available for investment outside the firm when investment decisions are being made.

It should be emphasized that we are talking here only of internally generated funds ("earnings" in the conventional sense plus depreciation and depletion allowances and other noncash charges) which are in excess of the customary cash dividend. The view was widely expressed that the utilization of internally generated funds which cut into the accustomed dividend per share would have a substantial cost in the adverse impact on market price of the common stock. Considering this on an incremental basis — charging the expected loss in market price against the funds made available by the reduction in the customary cash dividend payment (and not against *all* retained earnings) — the cost appears prohibitive. Such a course of action was unthinkable to most managements except as a defensive measure in a period of considerable financial distress.

In considering the choice between retained earnings and debt as a source of funds it must be recognized that there are considerations other than those directly related to the earnings performance of the company. The advantage of using funds already within full control of management, available without delay, uncertainty, negotiation, interference, publicity, explanation, or apparent cost to the shareholder, is undoubtedly of major importance to management. The appeal of these considerations, some of which management might not care to recognize publicly, could lead to rationalization in terms of conventional earnings criteria and the best interests of the shareholders. The validity of management's assumptions are particularly open to question on the point of stockholder preferences for retention rather than distribution of earnings. Invariably management will defend the status quo with respect to dividend policy on the grounds of shareholder preference when in fact it knows very little about the actual composition of its own shareholder group.

Recognizing the priority given to retained earnings as a source of funds in practice, it is apparent that a potential income advantage as an incentive to borrow is operative only when internally generated funds prove inadequate to meet the recognized need for funds. Then the issue lies between debt, on the one hand, and the sale of additional shares of stock, on the other. Here it is generally agreed that debt has a distinct advantage. With ultimate performance being judged largely in terms of the market price of the common stock and Earnings per Share, the disadvantages of financing by means of an increase in the number of shares are apparent. Within the normal range of profitability, interest rates, and price-earnings ratios, an E.P.S. comparison will show debt to be clearly the better alternative. The use of debt relieves the current market of the direct threat of dilution due to more shares being traded. Even on a cash flow comparison and after allowing for sinking fund payments, debt may not show up too unfavorably since management must make allowance for added cash dividends on the new common stock, a payment that is likely to be at a higher rate per dollar of invested funds and that does not have a tax shield.

As brought out in Chapter 3, the survey of management attitudes showed a very strong and persistent reluctance to raise funds through new issues of common stock in the large majority of cases, and this attitude is largely due to the adverse short-run effects on the value of the stockholder's investment directly, or on the market's criteria of investment value indirectly. Consequently when investment opportunities exceeded internal financial capacity there was good reason to consider debt as a source of funds. The minority of companies in the sample which had sold common stock for cash during the past 20 years (numbering four) either had a strong dislike of debt which outweighed the income advantage or had reached what they and/or their creditors considered to be the appropriate limit of their borrowing at the time of further financial need.

The consideration of the potential earnings from an investment financed by debt capital as an incentive to borrow has a meaning only if it is assumed that management has a choice as to whether to make the investment and that profit making is a primary motive in seeking out investment opportunities. In fact, it is generally implicit in investment theory that profit maximization is *the* primary motive in investment decisions. Without denying the widespread validity of these assumptions, it is nevertheless true that there are many occasions on which management does not have (or does not consider itself to have) a choice in making an investment and where the profit motive, in the sense of maximizing the value of the shareholders' investment, is secondary if, indeed, it is important at all. This brings us to a consideration of the need for funds as an incentive separate from the opportunity to make a profit.

Some observations on this point were made in previous chapters. These may be briefly reviewed by considering the conventional form of an over-all cash forecast which is the starting point of the process that ultimately results in the negotiation of a debt or equity contract. In general this forecast is a combination of elements that differ not only as to the degree of certainty of amount and timing but also as to controllability within the forecast period. For those outflows of funds which can be controlled by management, at least in some degree, a further distinction must be drawn between those that management chooses to treat as fixed and those that it considers variable. The extent to which outflows are, or are considered to be, controllable has an obvious bearing on whether and to what extent there is pressure for added investment capital.

A consideration of the customary forecasting procedure sheds some light on the factors and considerations leading up to a plan for adding new debt capital. Exhibit 4 shows a highly condensed version of a cash budget form for one of the companies included in this study. Although no two companies have exactly the same approach, this form is typical in its basic outline. As can be seen, it is a comprehensive forecast of all cash inflows and outflows covering the period of a year, broken down by quarters and within the first quarter by months. The starting point is an estimate of cash to be generated from operations which is based on anticipated sales and collection experience in the established market areas. Offsetting this inflow is the outflow of cash which is necessary to produce and which in large measure precedes this cash inflow. Management may exert some degree of control over the magnitude and timing of this outflow, but in general it is taken as mandatory for continued operations. Although there is no reason why the inflow from operations will necessarily exceed the outflow, even in a profitable company, in the typical mature and successful company this will normally be the case so that the opening balance will be augmented by the net cash flow from operations. It should be noted that implicit in these figures will be any increases in the investment in working capital which may be necessary to support whatever increase in sales is assumed in the forecast.

The next step in the procedure is to deduct payments of cash dividends which, at least in the preliminary budget, will be calculated on the assumption that the most recent dividend rate will be continued. This rate is of course subject to review by the Board in the light of the over-all budget, but as previously noted there is a strong presumption against a reduction except under conditions of serious financial adversity. Consequently this figure is likely to be a mandatory minimum outflow for this purpose. Whether it is increased will depend to a considerable extent on the nature and magnitude of competing uses for Available Cash.

The remaining item, Capital Expenditures, is subdivided into those which have already been approved by the Board and those which are merely in the proposal stage at the time the budget is drawn up. The detail of these expenditures, in this case broken down only for items in excess of $200,000, is commonly shown in a supporting exhibit. It can be reasonably assumed that items in the Approved category will not ordinarily be subject to review and arbitrary reduction by management, particularly once the project is actually under way, except in adversity when conservation of cash becomes the paramount consideration. Under normal circum-

EXHIBIT 4. TYPICAL CASH BUDGET FORM
Cash Forecast for Year Ending ____

		1st Quarter			2nd Q.	3rd Q.	4th Q.	Total for Year
		1st Month	2nd Month	3rd Month	Total			
Opening Balance	(1)	$						
Add Receipts								
Collections on Sales		$						
Other		$						
	(2)	$						
Less Disbursements								
Payroll		$						
Purchases		$						
Tax Payments		$						
Etc.		$						
	(3)	$						
Available Cash								
(1 + 2 − 3)		$						
Less Cash Dividends		$						
	(4)	$						
Less Capital Expenditures								
Approved		$						
Proposed		$						
		$						
Closing Balance (Deficiency)		$						

stances these items would be taken as given although it is possible that the timing might be subject to some variation in the light of the current expectations.

It can be seen that down to this point on the cash budget the items of cash outflow might be open to question by top management on the basis of the accuracy of the underlying assumptions (e.g., the sales forecast) but not as to the necessity of providing for these payments if the assumptions are in fact realized. To do otherwise would be to question whether the business should be continued, a question which management does not ordinarily debate except when confronted by bankruptcy.

It is the remaining item, Proposed Capital Expenditures, which is the primary discretionary aspect of the budget and the point at which the goals and standards of management can have a major bearing on whether and to what extent there will be a need for outside capital. These proposed expenditures are for the most part initiated at the operating level without regard to the current availability of funds or the particular source from which the funds might come. They are of course usually subjected to a screening process in terms of a minimum earnings and/or cash generation standard set by management. Such standards do relate in part to the general availability of funds but are not necessarily applied against all proposals and may or may not reflect management goals as to debt-equity proportions and the current level of costs which must be incurred in order to obtain capital from these sources. In the experience of this sample there was very little evidence of a serious effort to employ an average cost of capital standard in investment selection. Rather, the standard was more typically either a rough internal opportunity cost standard, as previously described, or merely a reflection of top management's willingness or unwillingness to assume the risks of new and untried investment opportunities.

The point has already been made in a previous chapter that management usually draws a distinction between those expenditures that it feels compelled to make now to preserve and provide for the normal growth of the vital functions of the established business, such as those involving plant capacity, and those that are "merely" profitable. The dividing line can, of course, be fuzzy and the distinctions perhaps illogical but they are nonetheless real. In every set of Proposed Capital Expenditures presented for management consideration there are likely to be some that management regards as a "must," *now*. Here the refinements of investment analysis will have little part in the decision.

To the extent that a management group is in an expansive frame of mind and is deliberately encouraging investment opportunities, it is exerting some control over the timing of these opportunities. With regard to the mandatory element of capital expenditure, however, the timing may be largely out of management's control and subject to a variety of random influences. These relate to such considerations as the competitive situation, technological obsolescence, deterioration of physical assets, variations in consumer demand, and so forth. Events may combine to produce irregular peaks in such capital needs which, combined with the other mandatory outflows in the cash budget, may at any point in time substantially exceed the internal resources. This peaking of need is particularly likely to happen in those companies and industries where capital expenditures because of physical or other characteristics cannot be broken down into "bite sized" pieces which over a period of time can be handled internally.

Thus the incentive to use outside funds, including debt, may be very simply an uncontrollable peaking of mandatory expenditures. Under these circumstances the decision to use debt as a source of funds is very different from a decision to use debt where management considers that it has a choice as to whether or not to make the investment. It is quite apparent that several of the companies in this study would have consistently rejected debt (and possibly new equity issues also) if they were convinced that the only penalty from a decision to reject the related investment opportunity was the loss of the earnings from that investment alone.

The significance of the nature and urgency of the need is of particular importance with respect to debt capital. Stock may be sold to the general public with little justification of the need other than that "general purposes" require it. In contrast lenders invariably require detailed evidence that the funds requested are an imminent and unavoidable need. Companies do not normally borrow money for undefined future possibilities or merely to have the benefits of leverage. Consequently debt tends to be associated with the more urgent investment requirements related to the central activities of the business. Incidentally, this characteristic of experience tends to work against the theory that companies should have long-term goals of appropriate debt leverage and time actual issues so as to take advantage of low points in the trend of interest rates.

The concept of a need which is not directly related to the profit motive may be illustrated in terms of one of the companies under consideration. This company, operating in one of the more cyclical industries, had a long-standing practice of purchasing important components of its finished product from other manufacturers. The president had for many years cherished the hope of some day having the entire manufacturing operation within the company, in spite of the fact that the operations in question were generally considered to be of marginal profitability. The productive process involved in producing the components in question was such that the operation could not be broken down and required a substantial investment if it was to be done at all. As the president approached retirement, his sense of urgency increased and the decision to act was finally made. The new plant and equipment required a 25% increase in invested capital. Internal funds were not available in sufficient quantity for this purpose. Approximately one half of the funds was raised by a sale of common stock — the maximum which seemed possible at the time. The balance obviously had to come from long-term debt. In this instance the motivating force was not the potential leverage of a low-cost source of capital — it was rather an incidental result of the necessity to use all available sources of funds.

Another important incentive to use debt as a source of funds relates to the limited duration of the contract and the relative ease of terminating the contract if and when the means to do so become available. If management operates on the premise that internally generated funds are the best (cheapest) source of funds for permanent use, and if, as the data of Chapter 2 show, most businesses can hope in the long run to finance all or a large part of their necessary investment internally but find a temporary peaking of this need due to circumstances beyond their control, then there will be an incentive to finance these peaks from sources which can be repaid rather than from sources which become a permanent part of the capital structure. Debt contracts have a distinct advantage over common equity contracts in this respect. Stock can of course be repurchased but the process is often uncertain and difficult, whereas debt is contracted with this eventuality clearly in mind. In several companies in this study it was apparent that the use of debt was looked on simply as a means of being able to use future retained earnings now.

In a company that accepts these premises and that has distinct limits to its investment goals, the minimization of the cost of external financing and the selection of a contract basis which does the most to achieve this goal makes business sense. Unless the capital supplied through debt is kept actively invested, the leverage concept loses its meaning and the interest charges become an unnecessary drain. This point of view was apparent in a number of the debt negotiations under review. Management on occasion deliberately asked for a shorter maturity than the creditor required in order to force the business to repay as quickly as possible. Great importance was often attached to the prepayment clauses in an effort to minimize or eliminate the penalty involved. Treasurers secretly welcomed onerous dividend restrictions which enabled them to combat the complaints of shareholders while internal funds were being diverted to repay the debt. In general, from the moment the debt contract was signed the goal was to repay it as quickly as possible.

Up to this point we have considered in some detail the incentives inherent in the nature and timing of the recognized need, the effect on earnings and the value of the shareholders' investment, and the relative flexibility of use. These were the incentives that were most in evidence in discussions with management. There were others that were apparent from time to time. Undoubtedly one of these related to relative ease of access to such funds under normal circumstances. Compared with the internal and external processes of arranging for an issue of stock, the arrangement of a loan, particularly a loan privately placed with a single creditor, is usually significantly less time-consuming both with respect to the number of executive hours devoted to it and with respect to the period over which the negotiation extended. As one executive put it, the negotiation of a debt contract "merely involved sitting down for a couple of afternoons" with the creditor's authorized representatives and "working out the details." The relative speed and certainty of debt money are clearly of real importance to companies whose capacity to foresee the future with confidence is generally recognized as limited to a year or less. It is for this reason that many companies preferred to use debt capacity as a reserve against the unexpected rather than as a continuous source.

Another related consideration is that of privacy. An issue of stock by a publicly held company involves the annoyance of public explanations to government agencies, stock exchanges, shareholders, and the industry at large. In the light of the information which must be disclosed, the objection is more apparent than real but to some businessmen it is a significant consideration. Privately placed debt, on the other hand, involves only the management and the lender at the time the decision is made and at the year end a brief word of explanation to the shareholders in the annual report if management considers it necessary.

One factor that was presented from time to time in discussions with management was the question of inflation. Obviously there is some incentive to finance on the basis of fixed dollar commitments if it is expected that there is a trend of deterioration in the purchasing power of the dollar. Although this trend (on a modest scale) is generally recognized by businessmen as being an accepted characteristic of the United States economy, few companies appeared to be significantly influenced in their financial policies by it. A small minority of companies volunteered the information that they were disposed to use debt financing because of anticipated inflation.[1] On the other hand, it was invariably true that those companies that had foreign subsidiaries in countries with a serious inflation problem were borrowing as heavily as they could (abroad) to finance these subsidiaries. This did not appear to be coordinated with the over-all debt policy of the company as a whole, probably because in most instances these subsidiaries involved only a relatively small fraction of the total commitment of funds.

Other considerations which showed up from time to time as possible incentives to borrow were that some companies were used to debt financing, had established channels of communication, and therefore tended to follow a familiar pattern. Expressing this idea negatively, one treasurer pointed out that one reason why he did

[1] There was no evidence that this attitude was based on any precise expectations as to the effect of inflation on the comparative cost of debt and equity capital.

not borrow was that he had never had occasion to do so, did not quite know where to begin, and as a result was under the influence of a certain inertia. He did not say, but it may have been true, that as the chief financial officer of a major corporation he did not care to reveal his inexperience in this area of the capital market.

Somewhat related to the matter of familiarity is the question of the aggressiveness of lenders, particularly of commercial banks. It is generally true that because of the character of the capital market, those who supply debt capital have a greater opportunity to seek out directly investment opportunities among business firms than do the suppliers of equity capital whose changing interests are more likely to be apparent only indirectly through the market's price system. On more than one occasion a financial officer confided that the idea for a bond issue had originated with "the boys on Wall Street" — for example, the idea of substituting debt for an outstanding preferred stock issue. Reference was also made to the fact that from time to time a banking connection would remind a company that it would look with favor on a new or additional loan should the need arise. It was impossible to judge the significance of this on corporate debt-equity balance but the impression was that over all it was not very significant.

In concluding this section on the incentives to borrowing, as contrasted with equity alternatives, it should be noted that in practice formal reasoning may follow rather than precede the debt decision. There is no doubt that debt is one of those aspects of financial policy regarding which deep-seated attitudes on the part of those who make the decision have an important bearing. The question as to whether an individual is fundamentally conservative or venturesome by nature is a matter of far broader implications than the debt-equity choice and yet it can be the determining factor. These personal prejudices are generally the result of the impact of the random events of past experience rather than an intelligent appraisal of the present and the future and can be quite unreasoning and unyielding. On subjects such as debt policy, influential board members need not offer a reason for their point of view; it is enough that they hold it. There is ample evidence that such dogmatic positions on the part of top management seriously inhibited detailed "logical" analysis by financial officers who are quick to note the practical limits of rational decision making. Their job may then be reduced to the task of finding a convincing reason for an unreasoned conviction.

This line of thinking can readily lead to cynicism regarding the usefulness of available evidence on management attitudes. However, doubt as to whether the arguments advanced for or against the use of debt did or did not determine action in particular instances does not detract from the fact that these were the considerations that to the men concerned had the greatest rational appeal — and would govern the decision to the extent that rationality played a part.

THE ARGUMENT AGAINST BORROWING

As has just been suggested, some of the statements of management regarding the use of debt were merely statements of attitude and personal conviction, without any direct appeal to economic considerations. This was particularly true of arguments against debt, particularly where management took an extreme position. Thus, for example, more than one company official expressed the feeling that income from debt leverage was not really "earned" in the same way that income from normal productive effort was. Related to this was the idea that debt was not quite respectable and that a company was somewhat "ashamed" to have it on the balance sheet. Incidentally, this idea usually applied to long-term debt but not to seasonal debt. Another related viewpoint was to be found in the statement that a large and mature company cannot "go for broke" — that is, flirt with bankruptcy. One company treasurer expressed the opinion that one reason why his company did not borrow was because the general public sentiment of the area in which the company was located and from which it drew its ownership group was opposed to the idea of financing on borrowed money.

While these deep-rooted attitudes come to be a force in themselves, needing no support from rational or economic argument, it is undoubtedly true that they often have their origin in economic influences. Obviously past experience plays a big part in shaping such attitudes. The depression of the early thirties still casts its long shadow over debt policy, though it is fading as a new generation gradually replaces those who passed through this harrowing experience. A chance encounter with a cautious or surly banker at a time of need has more than once formed a lifetime distrust of lending institutions. The importance and significance of past experiences to debt policy will be discussed later when specific debt policies will be taken up in detail. It is sufficient to recognize here that to the extent that past experience has shown the adverse potential of debt to be a practical reality the expectation of such adverse effects in the future is given strong support. As will be discussed later, the validity of this line of reasoning is open to question.

Closely related to the attitudes that managements bring to a discussion of debt policy, is their expectation of the influence of debt on the attitudes of others. To the extent that their expectations prove to be accurate this does, of course, have considerable practical significance. This study of corporate practice with respect to debt revealed considerable evidence of conformity in industry thinking and practice and a sensitivity to the reactions of those competitors who were considered to be near rivals. Very frequently a financial officer would preface his remarks on debt policy by saying "The practice in this industry is. . . ." Likewise there was a common tendency to look to other companies for specific guides on such matters as debt capacity. This matter of industry practice and the attitudes of others could of course work both ways — being a justification for some debt as well as a reason for not borrowing — but it appeared to be more commonly a negative rather than a positive influence.

Similarly, management was concerned about the adverse effects of debt on the company's credit standing, on the opinion of its shareholders, and on the market reception to its stock. These could be matters of real, practical significance affecting the capacity of the company to raise both debt and equity capital in the future. However, management did not have any reliable information on these possible effects. From a rational point of view it is possible that some debt could have a favorable instead of an unfavorable influence on these market attitudes, but it was more common to assume that the reverse was the case. There appeared to be few managements who recognized a difference between the effects of a "reasonable" amount of debt and "excessive" debt, and this lack of recognition was undoubtedly due in large part to a general inability to decide the point at which debt became excessive. As a consequence opinions tended to apply to any amount of debt and the varying effect of greater or lesser amounts of debt was merely one of degree.

It is interesting to note that in the management team, the financial officers are commonly the exponents of conservatism. There is here something of the concept of checks and balances whereby the treasurer or financial vice president acts as a balance to the unrestrained enthusiasm of the sales and production executives. One company executive described his company as "a curious combination of extreme risk-taking, product-wise, and financial ultraconservatism." Treasurers are almost invariably conservative in outlook. Very frequently the financial officers of borrowing companies said in effect, "If I had my way we would have no debt, but. . . ." If this is, in fact, the conscious or unconscious role of the financial officer, it is not surprising to find financial policies in which their point of view has particular weight, reflecting a reluctance to add to the uncertainties under which the company operates.

In terms of the job the financial officer has to perform there are several practical reasons for opposition to debt. Although debt is often easily and quickly negotiated, it brings with it certain results which make the job of the treasurer and of management generally less comfortable and more complex. One important matter is that of control. In theoretical discussions of the debt-equity choice the point of control, in the general decision making sense of the word, is usually chalked up in favor of debt because it is assumed that existing management does not wish to run the risk of having the present balance of stock ownership upset by more voting shares on the market. Within the group of companies included in this study this interpretation did not appear to be valid, with the possible exception of one or two privately held companies. For the most part these were companies the stock ownership of which was widely dispersed and the management position well established. Here management appeared to be more concerned with the control or potential control of creditors than they were with that of new shareholders. Many managements openly resented interference by "outsiders," a term which was applied to bankers, insurance companies, and, to a lesser extent, investment bankers. They resented both the formal interference in control via the terms of the debt contract and representation on the Board and informally through requests for information and "suggestions" presented in periodic discussions.

Interestingly enough, such resistance to the influence of creditors over decision making appeared in closely held companies also. Of course in a company that has neither borrowed nor issued common stock for many years it is impossible to tell how this consideration would weigh if a direct choice between the two had to be made. To the outsider, the objection to "interference" by creditors sometimes appeared to be founded on inconsequential matters and was more of an instinctive opposition to anything that might upset the status quo than a reaction to any specific covenant or act. It must be added that there were also some companies that appeared to take the normal intervention of creditors quite casually and to be unconcerned about restrictive covenants and the like. Here again is one of those considerations that gets back to the personal attitudes of the men charged with making the decision which makes "rational" analysis difficult.

In addition to the question of interference in decision making there is also the practical fact that debt tends to make the treasurer's job more demanding. Debt covenants add another set of considerations which have to be taken into account in financial planning and control. More importantly, to the extent that debt servicing adds to the inflexibility of cash outflows, the job of cash management becomes that much more exacting. One fact which the study of corporate practice made abundantly clear was that the "state of the art" of forecasting is not far advanced, with the possible exception of very short periods of time. Consequently for the forecast period with which we are here concerned, the margin of error can be and is very broad. Under such circumstances financial peace of mind is acquired through maintaining maximum flexibility of cash outflows and by having substantial cash reserves (actual and potential). Added debt has the double disadvantage of adding to the rigidity of outflows and of reducing a potential source of cash through future borrowing. Substantial additions to debt invariably mean increased attention to cash flow forecasting and tighter controls over cash flow. The company studies showed some sharp contrasts between the casual approach to cash management in certain debt-free companies and the tight, almost tense approach in other companies with high debt burdens. Since the ability to preserve cash solvency at all times is the ultimate test of a good treasurer, this is of great importance to the man on the job.

Obviously his capacities to do the job and his peace of mind are very much involved here. It is also apparent that the debt-equity balance is an area of decision making where the "cost" of opportunities (to borrow) foregone is not nearly so apparent as the cost of opportunities seized which later prove to have been ill-advised.

So far the effect of a debt issue on future borrowing capacity has been noted incidentally — it will now be discussed more fully as an important argument against the (current) use of debt. In discussions with company executives this argument has been presented in what may be described as both a positive and a negative sense. The positive argument runs that long-term debt capacity should be held in reserve against the time when there may be a major investment opportunity promising an unusual return on investment. It is contended that the timing of this need cannot be forecast and that when the time comes the need may be urgent and the alternative of a common issue inadvisable. Examples of this line of thinking are seen in the possibility of a research "break-through" in chemicals or drugs or the opportunity of recession-generated acquisitions in the machine tool industry.

It is, of course, easy enough to visualize such a possibility and to see the desirability of having a reliable source of funds ready at hand. Reasoning objectively, however, it is apparent that offsetting the superior return from the unusual investment to commence sometime in the uncertain future is the revenue foregone on the more pedestrian investment which could be made now. If the unusual investment opportunity is any distance out in the future, a present value comparison will show that the investment has to be very unusual indeed to warrant this postponement in utilizing debt capacity. It can be assumed that the company's normal investment criteria will assure that any investment will provide a return at least comparable to that realized in past experience.

This line of reasoning assumes that the company has a choice between investment now and investment later. Some managements would argue that the future investment need that they have in mind may not be in fact a free choice but may be a necessity in order to preserve the competitive position of the company. If this expectation is true, then the kind of analysis suggested in the preceding paragraph may not have much impact on management thinking. However, there is good reason to take a hard look at a company policy that is based on an expected event which rarely if ever materializes. More than one company that presented this argument had been operating for many years and were still to experience such an opportunity.

The negative argument for the preservation of debt capacity anticipated the possibility of an unexpected reversal of company fortunes when additional funds might be necessary to carry the company through. At such times an equity issue would appear out of the question and debt would be the only alternative by which the company could lay its hands on outside funds in substantial amounts and in a hurry. Here again, objective analysis raises some doubts as to the substance of the argument. For one thing, it is generally recognized that debt capacity has a habit of evaporating when a business turns unprofitable. More than one businessman remarked rather cynically on this. At best, debt capacity will be subject to an "agonizing reappraisal" if such an eventuality really comes to pass.

A second and perhaps more significant point is that at such times a business is more likely to be drawing on its short-term debt capacity rather than on long-term debt capacity. Obviously the two are interrelated but they are not identical. From the company's point of view the uncertain and hopefully short duration of the need would suggest a short-term bank loan. From the creditor's point of view the closer control and the prospect of better security from current assets associated with short-term loans would also argue in the same direction. If this type of need is in fact of long duration, the creditor is unlikely to want to make the loan, and if the need is of short duration, the credit instrument should conform to it.

These points tend to weaken but not entirely destroy the threat of adversity as an argument against the present use of long-term debt capacity. The basis of the argument is an integral part of the whole problem of uncertainty which will now be considered in detail under a separate heading.

THE BASIC PROBLEM OF UNCERTAINTY

In a very real sense the various arguments against debt presented in the preceding section all reduce to one fundamental problem — uncertainty as to the nature, amount, and timing of future cash flows. Every private enterprise operating in a competitive dynamic economy has a degree of uncertainty associated with expected future income. This risk is inescapable and it must be borne by someone. Of the several distinct groups representing various interests in this future income, however, not all are equally willing to assume the risk. As a consequence and by means of negotiated legal contracts some groups are able to shift "their share" of the risk to another group, giving up something in the process — usually the chance of a larger share of the uncertain future income. Of course, in reality no group ever escapes risk entirely in an absolute sense but the risk is greatly reduced.

One group which achieves this result is that which supplies capital by means of a debt contract. A strict limit on the claim to assets and future earnings is the price that is paid for a "guaranteed" claim — or more accurately, a high priority claim. In the process the risk borne by other groups, notably the shareholders and management, is heightened. Obviously the prime incentive for the shareholders is the claim to the future income foregone by the suppliers of debt capital, the "leverage" as it is often called.

Speaking in practical "cash" terms, the fundamental risk is the chance that at some point of time in the future the company will be confronted with unavoidable cash outflows which it is unable to supply. This risk is obviously not confined to debt service obligations. To the extent that a business voluntarily assumes such obligations, however, it is deliberately increasing and adding to the rigidity of its cash outflows. While the investment of the funds so supplied usually adds as much or more to the expected cash inflows, it rarely has the same certainty of amount and timing so that the chance of cash insolvency is thereby increased. This is of course a matter of degree and, as will be seen later, it is the extent of the change in the risk resulting from new debt which is the crux of the debt-equity decision.

It is from uncertainty regarding future cash solvency that other "risks" associated with debt are largely derived. Thus the concern over the effect of new debt on the future credit standing of the company and its future debt capacity is in part a fear that this potential source of funds from which unexpected cash needs may be supplied will be thereby diminished. This concern is directly related to one of the most universal and enduring of the rules of financial practice, which is: "always have an alternative" — as insurance against the threat of the unexpected.

It may be noted here, however, that such matters as credit standing may become an end in themselves. Clear-cut evidence of success and superiority in business is much sought after but hard to come by. The common criteria are often intangible and transitory. There is, however, an element of unquestionable substance to an "A" rating in Moody's Industrials which has great appeal for some businessmen and tends to become of value in and of itself. Its preservation becomes an important financial objective. The same can be said about a record of financing at the prime rate. Some managements will refuse even to consider any deliberate act which would jeopardize these hard-earned symbols of status. Obviously this is not merely a question of preserving solvency.

There is another dimension to the problem of uncertainty with respect to cash flows that is related to the question of solvency but not included in it. Solvency is a question of legal obligations only. On top of cash outflows which are fixed in amount and time by legal contract are other cash outflows which are fixed because management operating within a given business framework chooses to make them so. In the minds of management such action is vital to the long-term best interests of the business. Examples of such expenditures fixed by executive decision are dividend payments, research expenditures, capital expenditures. *For purposes of planning and decision making* management may act as if these expenditures were as fixed as bond interest payments and may have perfectly sound economic reasons for doing so. Obviously this is of great significance for the debt-equity choice since it serves to increase the risk of being "out of cash" and makes the incremental effect of new debt more hazardous than otherwise. Of course, it is these expenditures which would be first to feel the adverse effects of an excessive debt burden.

How Management Looks at Uncertainty (Risk)

Before discussing the evidence as to how management views uncertainty, it seems advisable to make clear one or two characteristics of the people we are here designating as "management." The debt-equity choice is one of a group of financial decisions which are made at the highest level of the management structure. In contrast to the other basic functional areas of responsibility, finance does not have a broad base of lower-level decision makers who both generate ideas and dispose of a large number of lower-level decisions. It is quite typical to find that the finance function is being performed by the treasurer and three or four assistants. It is inherent in the nature of financial problems which pervade every corner of the operating organization that the issues raised can only be usefully discussed and decided by those who are empowered to make over-all policy. Consequently, decisions such as the debt-equity choice will be made by the executive board, which will include the financial vice president or treasurer, and it is unlikely that any significant ideas on the subject will originate outside this group. These are typically men of senior years and this is perhaps more commonly true of the senior financial executive than it is of the senior executives in other areas such as production or sales. Without attempting to draw any sweeping and obviously unfounded generalizations from this, it is not surprising to find that the financial decisions made by such a group in a particular company are of a conservative nature.

The extent to which the senior financial executive influences the corporate attitude toward debt varies greatly from one company to another, as one would expect. In some cases the financial vice president or treasurer appears to have a dominant role; in other cases it is the president or some other key board member who makes the decisions; and in still others there is evidence of a genuine group decision. In some instances the chief financial executive appeared to be virtually on the outside looking in on this decision, merely implementing policies handed down to him. On occasion this produced a conflict in point of view which was sufficiently sharp that the financial executive felt it necessary to disassociate his own views from company policy. This point is significant in that it obviously bears on the extent to which formal financial analysis of relevant data by experts could have a bearing on the ultimate choice. In some companies the lack of such analysis was apparently a result of this fact and not of indifference or inability on the part of responsible financial personnel.

In this respect it is also interesting to note the changes in policy which followed changes in the individuals holding the office of treasurer or a key position on the board. In several companies there was a distinct relaxation of opposition to debt, particularly in the post-World War II period, as those men for whom the depression of the early thirties was the most vivid impression of their career were replaced by younger men whose period of executive responsibility followed that period. Even though businessmen who had experienced the Great Depression were invariably willing to concede that a repetition was unlikely, there was still some unwillingness to make debt decisions on the assumption of a remote probability.

One way of approaching management's concepts of uncertainty is through its utilization of financial forecasting. As previously mentioned, forecasting of fund flows by the companies in the study was in most cases taken seriously and was an important responsibility of the treasurer's office. The usual pattern included a monthly, quarterly, yearly, and, in some cases, a five-year projection. These were of course revised periodically and the amount of detail varied considerably, the extent being dependent as much or more on the need to be precise as it was on the ability to be so. In some cases the forecast was built up from detailed cash data and in others it was merely a rough interpretation from pro forma income statement and balance sheet data.

Confidence in the accuracy of these forecasts varied considerably from one company and one industry to another. The most significant and universal characteristic, however, was the notable lack of confidence in the accuracy of forecasts which extended beyond six months or at best a year. Several companies did not make any formal attempt to project funds expectations beyond a year on the grounds that the margin of error would be so great as to render the results useless. This attitude went so far as to result in deliberate discouragement of any efforts in this direction on the part of the treasury staff — and this in one of the largest corporations in one of the more stable industries. Other companies had such projections but they were not taken seriously by top management. The best that can be said of the relatively few that took the five-year forecast seriously was that it was useful as a rough check on the funds implications of major long-term policy — as a means of anticipating major excesses or deficiencies and the possible need for external financing.

The evidence on forecasting practice suggests that for these companies the financial horizon for practical purposes was at best one year out and beyond that was a largely uncharted land of uncertainty. This is not to suggest that these businesses did not project their thinking beyond a year. The nature of their operations forced them to do so from time to time. They knew the fixed elements and they could identify the nature of the variables. However, they appeared to have little confidence in anticipating the precise pattern of variation or even the limits of variation. This is obviously significant when related to the fact that long-term debt contracts invariably extended for at least five years and often twenty or thirty.

Under these circumstances of almost complete ignorance as to the shape of events during the greater part of the period over which the long-term debt contract will remain outstanding, it seems highly unlikely that the decision on long-term debt policy could be based on formal and logical reasoning. The question as to how the businessmen in these companies "got a handle" on uncertainty can be answered only in rather general terms since clearly there was no explicit analytical process. As might be expected the typical approach was an attempt to relate a given risk situation to others which came within the experience or knowledge of the individual concerned. These different situations were then ranked in order of increasing (or decreasing) riskiness according to whatever evidence suggested clear and substantial differences. The mental process was typically informal and to a considerable extent subjective.

Perhaps the most significant comparison was with the past experience of the same company. For example, in the rubber industry it was generally agreed that there had been a significant decline in risk in this industry due to the shift toward greater reliance on synthetic rubber and fibers and to the growing diversification in the industry. The implications of this change were clearly recognized in terms of the *direction* of the change, but no one had any quantitative yardstick of its magnitude. Nevertheless the change made management in the industry more disposed to consider the use of debt or, if they had been using it, to use it more extensively. Of course, it did not provide any clues as to how far to go.

For particular individuals in business the relative magnitude of the risk was established by comparisons with their own previous business experience outside the company. In one instance the top financial executive of a machine tool company had come directly to this job from a similar position in a much more stable industry. Differences in the magnitude and predictability of variations in funds flow were striking and led him to a negative attitude toward debt. Of course such attitudes may be modified by the new experience. In this case the executive's attitude happened to be further strengthened by the occurrence of one of the industry's periodic sharp and prolonged recessions shortly after the man joined the company.

Another basis for concepts of relative magnitude of risk was found to be through comparisons with other companies in the same industry. Such comparisons were in terms of obvious and significant differences which suggested significantly greater or less risk. To illustrate, one company in the machine tool industry operated a subsidiary which contributed a substantial amount each year to the revenue of the parent company. This subsidiary was of such a nature that this revenue had a high degree of stability over the years, unlike that derived from the basic industry. Both the management of this parent company and its chief creditor were clearly aware that this company was as a result not a "typical" machine tool company and it led both to a more receptive attitude toward the use of debt as a long-term source of funds. In purely rational terms it was questionable practice to translate a (justifiable) conviction that the risk was less in this company than in other machine tool companies into the conclusion that debt was justified, and, particularly, that any given amount was justified.

Finally the relative magnitude of risk in a company was established by comparisons of the industry in which it was located with other industries. Again the conclusion was merely that this industry was more or less risky than some other, particularly another industry that was similar in some respects and not in others. In some cases these were industries where corporate structures had brought the two together. For example, the people in the ethical drug industry frequently drew contrasts with industrial chemicals and vice versa.

Obviously this "ranking" approach to the measurement of risk did not in itself provide any satisfactory answers as to whether the company in question could (safely) assume debt and if so, how much. It is also apparent that it relied on major differences or changes which were apparent without resorting to refined analysis.

What it did do was to establish a base point from which the direction of thinking about debt could move. *The underlying assumption,* which was implicit in any attempt to use a comparative approach as the basis of debt policy and which appeared to be accepted without question, *was that the debt policy used as a point of departure and as a standard of comparison was an appropriate one for that situation.* For example, if it had been the practice of companies in the rubber industry prior to the economic change cited earlier to borrow some given proportion of their permanent capital, then the natural inference drawn from the change would be to continue to borrow in the future and in greater proportions than in the past. Likewise if it was the practice of firms in the ethical drug industry to borrow on occasion for long-term needs, then industrial chemical firms, believing themselves to be in a somewhat less risky industry, might also be disposed to borrow and to do so in somewhat greater amounts and more continuously. *The hazards inherent in an approach to policy formulation where everyone looked at his neighbor for guidance are readily apparent.* These will be discussed in detail later when the discussion turns to a consideration of the formulation of specific debt criteria.

CHAPTER 5

Corporate Debt Policy

and the Control of Risk

RESTRAINTS ON THE AMOUNT OF DEBT

Against the background of many arguments both for and against the use of debt as a long-term source of funds and employing a concept of risk measurement which was confined to a ranking of risk situations in terms of apparent risk differentials, corporate management somehow evolved a debt policy and reached specific decisions on the debt-equity question. The actual process of formulation is not clear. In spite of its enormously complex character the resolution of the problem appeared to involve surprisingly little explicit objective analysis in most cases. Evidence suggests that the typical decision was made by narrowing the appraisal to one or a few considerations which were regarded as paramount and, depending on how these were ranked and whether they were pro or con, the choice or rejection of debt was reached. This process of (arbitrary) simplification of the problem to the point where judgment, unassisted by formal analysis, could handle the "weighting" process is apparent when we examine the various forms in which corporate debt policy manifested itself in the companies included in this study.

Before turning to a consideration of corporate practice with respect to the control of the risk element as it can be observed in specific debt policies, it should be noted that not all companies have a debt policy — in the sense of a clearly articulated decision rule which influences or determines a sequence of decisions involving

93

the alternative of debt. As has been seen in Chapter 2, some companies so managed their financial affairs that there was rarely if ever a need to go outside the company for new funds; hence there was no need to consider the alternative of long-term debt, hence no debt policy. Whether the happy combination of investment policy, earning capacity, and dividend policy which produced this result was a matter of accident or design is clear in some cases and not in others. In those cases where the coincidence of these policies was deliberate, it is still not clear whether this coincidence was in fact a form of debt policy (no debt) because of the difficulty of weighing the influence of attitudes toward other external sources of funds.

There are other cases where the need and the debt did exist, at least from time to time, but where a consistent policy appeared lacking. More than one executive admitted that his company's capital structure had evolved in a haphazard manner and lacked logical consistency. This does not per se raise doubts as to the validity of individual debt decisions or even as to the soundness of the resulting capital structure, but the lack of consistency does suggest that the fundamental implications of debt and of the risks of debt had not been clearly and explicitly analyzed.

Most companies, however, did have relatively simple and clear decision rules regarding the use of long-term debt in which the method of disposal of the risk question was apparent. It is also accurate to say that these decision rules tended to be relatively inflexible over extended periods of time. In the sample of companies under consideration, the following debt policies have been identified and will be considered in detail.

DECISION RULE NO. 1 — NO LONG-TERM DEBT UNDER ANY
    CIRCUMSTANCES

A relatively uncommon rule within the sample of companies but nevertheless one that had some prominent exponents is that which excludes long-term debt entirely from consideration as a source of funds. It is a rule which has some important practical advantages. It cannot be excelled for simplicity and clarity. There is no room for doubt or confusion in its implementation. It is undeniably conservative and provides the maximum contribution to executive peace of mind. It also conveniently avoids the problem of evaluation of risk. This is not to suggest, however, that a "no debt" policy necessarily means inability or unwillingness to face up to this problem. It could in fact be the logical conclusion following a careful appraisal of expected gain and possible loss and the probabilities of their occurrence. It cannot be proved that this was not in fact the case in those instances where this policy was found. Nevertheless the external evidence suggested otherwise. In two instances in particular the probability of the event of cash insolvency appeared so small and the influence of *some* debt on this probability also so small that a policy of no debt under any circumstances could be justified only on an assumption of an extreme of ultraconservatism on the part of those who bore the risk. Further, it may be added that if a detailed appraisal did in fact take place, there was no evidence that it was done formally and explicitly which, in view of the complexity of the problem, suggests that it was not done at all.

Thus one possible interpretation of a "no debt" policy is that management felt unable to get any kind of a reliable appraisal of the risk associated with long-term debt and fortunately was in a financial position where it could avoid the question completely by relying solely on nondebt sources of funds. The outside financial observer must, of course, be always mindful of the possibility that considerations other than those which had a direct profit implication may have governed. For example, it is quite possible that a company may be so large or so profitable that a substantial use of debt leverage would induce unwanted competitive or governmental action.

DECISION RULE NO. 2 — BORROW THE MAXIMUM AVAILABLE

A policy of borrowing as much debt capital as is available from all sources is obviously the opposite extreme from the policy just discussed. It has, however, certain characteristics in common with the total abstinence policy, notably that it is a simple, unambiguous rule as to its application and that it avoids the necessity of appraising the risks associated with debt. To the extent that management is concerned about the event of insolvency, this policy places responsibility for the avoidance of this event on the supply side of the capital market. The suppliers of debt capital will presumably stop lending when they consider the existing-plus-proposed debt to be "excessive."

Like the no debt rule, the unlimited debt approach found few supporters among the sample of companies under examination. However, the underlying concept which turned at least a share of the responsibility for risk appraisal over to the creditors was found to be relatively common in the thinking of corporate financial officers. In several instances the corporate treasurer would say in substance: "Why should I concern myself with the (theoretical) question of debt capacity? My creditor will tell me how much I can borrow." This kind of statement had more than one implication. One was that the idea of debt capacity beyond the amount particular bankers or other creditors are willing to lend has no practical significance. Another implication is that institutional lenders are by experience better equipped to appraise risk and therefore that the corporate treasurer who borrows only once every five or ten years should not challenge his judgment. A further implication is that the borrower and the lender view risk in the same way. All these assumptions can be and will be challenged at a later stage in this study.

In practice only one company in the group had a debt policy which could be described as being restrained only by the consideration of availability. The company's capital structure showed the characteristic features of a relatively high and continuous proportion of long-term debt — a variety of debt instruments negotiated with different debt sources, periodic renegotiation of existing agreements, and other evidences of active exploration of the boundaries of the debt capital reservoir. Even in this case, however, there was evidence that the policy was not as undiscriminating in practice as it might at first sight appear. There were certain self-imposed restraints. One was that the search for debt capital was confined to the larger well-established and reputable financial institutions. The contracts which had been negotiated were for the most part conventional contracts with no more than the usual number and variety of protective covenants. Although the company had allowed its bond rating to decline to the "B" category, it showed concern about this and a resistance to further decline.

Thus when this and other companies side-stepped their own appraisal of debt capacity by leaving the decision to the creditor, it was not without some qualification. Two variations of this approach to debt policy will now be added to the list. The remaining debt policies which will be discussed, including these two, contain some concept of a self-imposed limit which leads to a debt position in between no debt and the maximum available. Very few companies were prepared to say that they would never borrow, but the large majority had at the same time a healthy respect for the hazards of borrowing and felt the necessity for a decision rule which in their judgment kept the hazards within bounds.

DECISION RULE NO. 3 — BORROW THE MAXIMUM AVAILABLE "AT THE PRIME RATE"

This concept of a debt limit is obviously a significant modification of the policy of leaving the decision to the creditor. The company that sets a ceiling on the rate of interest it will pay for debt capital is thereby excluding debt financing where a higher risk was compensated by a higher return. The extreme of this policy is the one stated above where if the money is not available at the then prevailing prime rate, a rate available only to companies with the highest credit standing, it will not be utilized. Clearly, such a policy provides a built-in margin of safety in the differential between what conservative financial institutions would consider as the maximum acceptable risk and the minimum risk reflected in the prime rate category. It leaves to the creditor the task of deciding the point at which more debt would exclude the financing on these grounds.

It is readily seen why such a debt rule might appeal to the corporate financial administrator. Like the two previous approaches to debt policy, it places a minimum of strain on the analytical skill and judgment of the borrower. In addition it is an approach which to some appears to be consistent with profit maximization. Within a certain frame of reference with respect to corporate investment, profit maximization is equated to cost minimization. As discussed in earlier chapters, those companies that have accepted investment limits other than the availability and cost of capital do not think so much in terms of the net incremental return from potential investment opportunities but rather in terms of minimizing the cost of capital on the existing investment. To some this means borrowing as little as possible and paying as low an interest rate as possible on what you are forced by circumstances to borrow.

Another practical consideration which ties in to the maximum interest rate form of debt restraint is the fact that the interest rate paid on long-term debt has become an important status symbol which some managements prize quite independently of any profit maximization goal. The ability to do one's financing at the prime rate is unquestionable evidence of rank within an industry and the industrial community at large and a proof of success which is not easily discarded merely to increase an already creditable return on investment. The importance of this consideration cannot, of course, be measured, but it is clearly important in some decision making and has no direct relation to concepts of risk-bearing capacity such as a debt limit implies.

DECISION RULE NO. 4 — BORROW THE MAXIMUM CONSISTENT
    WITH AN "A" RATING

Another approach to the control of the risk inherent in debt financing is one that sets a minimum acceptable value for the company's bond rating. According to this decision rule, no deliberate action would be taken that jeopardized this rating and no debt issues would be floated if, in the opinion of the company's financial counsel and the rating agencies, future ratings might fall below the level of "A" or whatever minimum was set. This decision rule is similar to the preceding one in that it provides for a margin of safety by setting a specific limit which is clearly above the minimum acceptable to the suppliers of debt capital. It is also similar in that the arbitrary adoption of a criterion which has been established by an outside party — the creditor or the bond rating agency — automatically transfers to that outside party the responsibility of determining what that standard means in terms of the specific circumstances of this company. Again the company's financial officers conveniently avoid their own appraisal of risk.

There is no doubt, of course, that the rating placed on public debt issues by reputable rating agencies is of considerable practical importance. It bears directly on the interest rate and on the acceptability of the issue in the minds of the buyers of such issues. Like the interest rate criterion of debt capacity, the minimum rating criterion is affected by considerations beyond the basic objective of controlling risk. To the extent that management was preoccupied with minimizing costs as opposed to maximizing profits, the bond rating was of obvious importance. Also, like the interest rate, the bond rating is a universal symbol of achievement which has considerable value in itself to those who consider themselves responsible for it. There is a real question as to whether it would be sacrificed merely to raise the rate of return on investment.

Among the companies interviewed there was widespread agreement that the straight "A" rating was the lowest rating a company could afford to have and still retain ready acceptance for the portfolios of the major investing institutions. It was felt that to expand debt to a level which caused the rating to drop below this would endanger the availability of debt capital in the future. Virtually all the companies attached great importance to preserving flexibility in future financing.

This concept of the capital market appears to be at variance with the usual assumptions of financial theory. It obviously implies that the sources of debt capital have clearly defined and absolute standards of risk-bearing capacity so that risk situations which are considered unacceptable by this (relatively conservative) standard would not find funds available at any price — at least from the established financial institutions. Financial theory, on the other hand, normally assumes that the availability of funds is a function of price — as in any market — and the higher risk situations merely require a higher interest premium to bring forth the necessary funds.

The facts of the actual capital market with which these businesses have to deal are probably somewhere in between these two extremes. Businesses do sell bonds publicly or make private placements where the rating would be below, sometimes substantially below, the equivalent of the "A" category. On the other hand, to the extent that borrowers prefer to associate only with those financial institutions (notably the better known commercial banks and insurance companies) which are generally accepted as "proper" and "respectable," it is undoubtedly true that the ease of obtaining funds is sharply reduced if the quality rating is much below the equivalent of "A." There is no doubt that the typical financial officer of a large and reputable business would not care to be on the defensive in negotiating a debt or other capital contract or to be humiliated by one or more refusals before locating a willing source of funds.

Further, a debt limit that preserves an "A" rating provides assurance of some cushion of borrowing power in the event of an emergency.

In summary, the approaches to debt policy that have been considered so far have either avoided the problem of appraising the risk associated with debt or passed the responsibility over to those who are supplying the debt capital. We now turn to those approaches to debt policy that have explicitly or implicitly recognized the responsibility of the borrower in making his own appraisal of risk and in using this to form his own independently formulated restraints on the voluntary assumption of the additional risk associated with debt. Typically these restraints take an objective and relatively uncomplicated form which are as a result often described as "rules of thumb," though they are not necessarily employed in the undiscriminating manner that this term implies. By far the most common of these standards is that in which a specific limit is placed on the principal amount of long-term debt as a percentage of the total permanent capital of the business. There are, however, other standards that have distinctly different form and implications, and a description of all observed variations follows.

DECISION RULE NO. 5 — LIMIT THE PRINCIPAL AMOUNT OF (LONG-TERM) DEBT TO "X" PERCENT OF TOTAL CAPITALIZATION

It is an almost universal custom in business to think about debt magnitudes in terms of balance sheet values. This of course means that the principal amount of the debt is compared to a valuation of owners' equity based on the original cost of the various tangible assets. The risk of debt is assumed to vary in a linear (inverse) relationship to the excess of such equity value over the total principal claims of the long-term creditors.

It is therefore natural that restraints on the assumption of the risk of debt are commonly expressed as an absolute limit beyond which the balance sheet debt-equity ratios must not be allowed to go. This is usually expressed as percentage value — debt as a percentage of total long-term debt plus equity (capitalization) — but it may also be expressed, particularly in debt contracts, as a ratio of Net Tangible Assets to total long-term debt. As a practical guide such a standard has the advantage of being precise and free from the possibility of differences of interpretation or judgment. It has the further advantage of adjusting the absolute limit on dollars of debt outstanding with any variations in the amount of owners' equity such as the gradual build-up resulting from retention of earnings.

As previously noted, any such self-imposed standard which places a specific limit on debt short of that which the creditor would impose implies that the borrower has made his own independent appraisal of the incremental risk associated with debt. It also implies that the decision is based on a knowledge of the willingness to bear risk on the part of those who are to assume it. Thus when the limit is set, it provides a clear boundary line beyond which the magnitude of the risk is considered too great in relation to the circumstances and objectives of the risk bearers. At a later point the question as to whether the establishment of such criteria was in practice preceded by explicit examination of the risk element will be considered in detail. At this stage it is appropriate to note that there was wide divergence in practice in this regard.

In those companies in which it was employed, the Percent of Capitalization debt limit had two distinct applications. In certain companies it was taken literally as the point up to which debt financing could and did go, assuming that the capital was needed and debt was in other respects the best financial medium. In other companies the debt limit, say 30%, was only a theoretical limit to which debt *could* go and be carried "with safety" but which in practice was never reached. This resulted from the fact that it was generally considered financially prudent always to have a reserve of debt capacity as protection against embarrassment from the unexpected. The determination of an "adequate" margin between the theoretical and practical limits was necessarily vague because of an obvious inability to measure the unexpected. At times circumstances pushed the debt of such companies up toward the theoretical limit, but when they did management became uncomfortable and took steps to widen the margin as soon as possible.

This point illustrates a more general characteristic of debt policy which is that decision rules were commonly rough approximations, based on relatively little specific analysis (or none at all), the primary function of which was to act like a radar system as a "distant early warning" device calling for a review of attitude to further debt financing. Within this limit management was generally receptive to debt, at least as regards the question of risk, whereas when the limit was approached or passed the management attitude shifted to one of active resistance to further debt, including attention to ways and means of reducing the existing risk as rapidly as possible. As to the precise location of this warning line, it was sometimes a matter of indifference so long as it was clearly far enough in advance of real danger to provide ample time for preparing the defenses.

Viewed in this light, the debt standard presents an interesting question as to whether it is sound business policy to have an absolute limit on debt at any point in time. In theory, at least, the voluntary assumption of risk is contingent on a concurrent evaluation of the potential reward, the potential penalty, and the relative probabilities of their occurrence. To be more explicit a simple example may be used. Suppose a bond issue is being considered for the financing of a new plant which will expand production and sales capacity. The potential reward or gain is the higher return on the investment of existing shareholders resulting from the use of debt rather than an equivalent common stock issue. The potential penalty is that in so doing the company may face cash insolvency in the future, being unable to meet the increased fixed cash outflows. This is normally considered a severe penalty should it occur, and the probability of its occurrence may be great or small depending on the individual circumstances. The question as to whether it is worth while to assume the risk of such a penalty would appear to depend in part on the nature and magnitude of the reward and cannot be decided without a knowledge of this consideration.

Consequently it seems inconsistent to have a fixed absolute limit on debt at any point in time and especially over time when the magnitude of the reward is subject to change. It seems quite reasonable to suggest that some businessmen would be disposed to assume more risk if the rewards from risk taking were increased.

One possible interpretation of practice is that this is in fact what happens, *but only within the range of debt capacity specified by the debt standard.* What the debt standard implies is that beyond some point the company is unwilling to assume any more risk *regardless of the reward.* The implications of this will be considered in a later critical discussion of these standards.

DECISION RULE NO. 6 — A MINIMUM EARNINGS COVERAGE STANDARD

The Earnings Coverage standard states a limit in terms of the amount of interest and sinking fund payments rather than in terms of the principal amount of the debt as in the Percent of Capitalization standard. In its common form it sets a minimum level for the excess of earnings available for debt servicing over the amount of the servicing charges. It is usually shown as a ratio, the Earnings Coverage requirement being twice or some other multiple of the annual interest charge or interest plus principal repayment. Since the whole purpose of the standard is to protect against adversity in the future, the earnings in question represent an estimate of the general or average level of future earnings. The margin of coverage is presumed to allow for temporary contractions in earnings below the expected average level, thus hopefully avoiding the possibility of cash insolvency through inability to meet the servicing charges.

It can be seen that this standard is a more complicated one than the Percent of Capitalization standard. The latter has the advantage of simple objectivity, provided one is willing to accept a framework dictated by accounting conventions. The Earnings Coverage standard requires a large element of judgment in its formulation. Typically this is resolved by using the earnings experience of the immediate past as the guide. Problems remain, however, as to whether one year or an average of several should be used, whether trends should be taken into account, and so on. Some who use this standard argue for the exclusion of noncash charges in calculating available earnings and some for their inclusion.

No doubt the greater complexity of this standard has had something to do with the fact that it was not widely used among the corporate financial officers included in this study. It was more commonly found among lending institutions, particularly insurance companies. It can be argued, of course, that the Percent of Capitalization standard is a rough but sufficiently reliable approximation of an adequate margin of earnings available for debt servicing. The higher the proportion of equity financing in the capital structure, the wider should be the margin of Earnings Coverage. The question is, assuming that the earnings comparison is the more meaningful one, whether the approximation is in fact sufficiently reliable.

Like Percent of Capitalization, the Earnings Coverage standard does not have a built-in dependence on the judgment of the creditor. It implies an independent appraisal of risk by the borrower and a judgment as to his willingness to assume this risk. The permissible debt is automatically adjustable for any variations in expected earnings. Within limits it provides for permissible variations in the principal amount of the debt depending on the specific terms of the debt contract. Taken at any point in time it represents an absolute limit, and as such the same questions regarding the theoretical validity of a single debt limit which were raised regarding Percent of Capitalization also apply here.

A final point of similarity is that both these standards view debt financing as an open-ended and continuous process — a point of contrast with other standards to be considered next. Both standards clearly imply that any time the company finds itself in the position where the actual ratio is above the minimum acceptable level, usable debt capacity exists and new long-term debt commitments extending over an undefined period in the future would be quite appropriate. This in turn suggests that the borrower's risk bearing capacity is founded on basic characteristics of the business and its environment which are relatively stable over extended periods of time.

In contrast there were certain companies that had what some described as a "one shot" approach to debt financing. The management of these companies held the point of view that it was inappropriate to use long-term debt as a continuous component of the capital structure but that under certain circumstances a limited use of debt might be advisable. Thus each debt decision would require a fresh appraisal of the risk element in the light of the circumstances at the time. The continuous debt concept of the standards previously described views risk in terms of the over-all situation and essentially independently of the circumstances of any particular financing proposal. In contrast the "one shot" approach appraises risk in terms of the circumstances surrounding the particular use to which such debt funds will be put. It implies that in such a company the general risk situation is unfavorable to long-term debt but that specific investment proposals may be considered independently of the general risk situation. This approach to long-term debt was observed to take two forms, as follows.

DECISION RULE NO. 7 — THE SINGLE-PROJECT APPROACH TO DEBT

The most notable examples of this approach to long-term debt policy were found in the machine tool industry, though they were by no means confined to this industry. Generally speaking, companies in this industry considered the periodic swings in sales and revenues too severe to justify the use of debt as a continuing source of funds. On the other hand, all appeared to accept the possibility that investment opportunities could arise for which debt financing would be appropriate.

The example most frequently cited was that of an acquisition of a going concern as a new subsidiary. The feature which distinguished this investment opportunity from internal investment opportunities was the fact that the acquired company's future earnings performance could be measured in terms of its past record and an "assured" payback could be anticipated. It should be noted that, while it was not stated, it may have been assumed that the acquisition would be at a bargain price so that a relatively rapid recovery of the investment would be realized. This was contrasted to internal investment opportunities such as new product development where the payback appeared relatively much less measurable and assured.

Thus the argument was that even in a comparatively risky business where debt was generally inappropriate, specific investment opportunities might present themselves from time to time where the level of risk was much lower than that characteristic of the business as a whole. Here debt might be used to finance the project. In practice there were no examples of such debt-financed acquisitions in the recent past of the companies included in the sample. This, however, did not necessarily suggest that they lacked the courage of their convictions. There were strong tax reasons why those who were selling out would prefer stock in payment rather than cash so that debt financing would be ruled out by the vendor and not by the acquiring company. Several acquiring companies stated that they would have preferred to pay cash but were unable to do so and had to offer an exchange of stock instead.

DECISION RULE NO. 8 — THE RAPID PAYBACK APPROACH TO DEBT

A second basis for acceptance of a limited amount of debt, and a variation of the "one shot" approach, was related to the time period involved. At certain points in time it is quite possible that a company has a high degree of confidence in the cash flows of the immediate future but little or no confidence in the cash flows of the more distant future. Further, this reasoning may be quite justified. To refer again to the machine tool industry, there may be good justification for a business in the early stages of recovery when backlogs are accumulating to have considerable confidence in the cash position for the next two or three years. On the other hand, knowing the industry, there is good reason to expect a sharp recession sometime in the more distant future. The latter consideration inhibits the acceptance of a continuous debt concept such as is implicit in most standards of debt capacity. Given strong assurance of a relatively high cash throw off for, say, two years, however, companies may be willing to assume a modest amount of debt in the expectation that they will be able to pay it back rapidly. What this is really saying, of course, is that the funds so attained are quickly replaced by equity funds and thus this is not really long-term debt. On the other hand, the loan may be arranged as a term loan and may extend over several years before it is completely extinguished. The goal of the borrower may be simply to pay down a major part of the loan during the period of "assured" income.

In practice the goal of retiring as much of the debt as possible in good years was widely held and was not confined to the highly cyclical industries. It was evident even in companies purporting to have a continuous debt policy. It reflected a certain lack of confidence in the "continuous" standard in use and a consequent desire to hedge against its long-term hazards by reducing debt when the company had the chance. In line with this, borrowers were usually anxious to have "prepayment without penalty" clauses in the debt contract and often made use of them. In certain instances this clause was considered to be as important to the borrower as the interest rate and the period of the loan. This approach to debt financing ties back directly to the general financial goals discussed in Chapter 2. In that chapter it was pointed out that several companies had the long-term objective of financing growth from retained earnings. In such cases debt was merely a means of handling unavoidable peaking of needs in excess of current internal generation, and it is obvious that such companies would endeavor to retire the debt as quickly as possible from retained earnings.

THE CONTROL OF RISK OTHER THAN BY LIMITING THE AMOUNT OF THE DEBT

In imposing restraints on the risks associated with debt financing, borrowers and lenders are primarily concerned with limitations on the principal outstanding at any given time and this is apparent in the standards of debt financing described so far. This emphasis derives in part from the traditional interest of creditors in the recoverability of asset values in the event of bankruptcy and liquidation, either with respect to assets in general or specific assets pledged or mortgaged as security for a particular loan. More realistically, however, the concern with the principal amount derives from the assumption that the financial burden of debt on the current or future earning capacity of a going concern is roughly proportional to the amount of the debt outstanding. Thus a restraint on the principal outstanding is a direct restraint on the amount of debt servicing.

In practice, the risk-conscious borrower will first negotiate the amount of the loan and then, having done that, will proceed to explore ways and means of minimizing risk within the variable terms of the debt contract. The vigor of this exploration and the price he is willing to pay for a reduction in risk (in terms of concessions to the creditor in other respects — e.g., the interest rate) depends on his evaluation of the general range of risk imposed by the size of the loan. It also depends, of course, on the receptivity of the lender to bargaining with respect to risk.

Because of the fact that present-day industrial loans of whatever form invariably require substantial periodic repayment of principal during the life of the loan, the magnitude of the annual debt service charge is directly dependent on the duration of the loan. Recognizing this, some borrowers will take considerable care in choosing the lender and the debt instrument and negotiate so as to extend the life of the loan as far as possible, thus minimizing the annual charge for repayment of principal. Thus, for example, a loan of

$1,000,000 at an assumed interest rate of 4% would have a maximum annual servicing charge of $140,000 if negotiated for 10 years and fully retired by maturity, $90,000 if negotiated for 20 years, and $73,000 if negotiated for 30 years. This is not to suggest that a borrower would necessarily have such a wide choice of maturity dates, but usually some variation is possible and this can be significant in the annual burden.

A related consideration is the question as to whether there will be a "balloon" payment on the maturity date or alternatively a full pay-down by maturity. The amount of such final payment, if any, may be negotiable — again within limits set by the lender, the debt instrument used, and the bargaining position of the borrower. To the extent that the balloon payment is substantially larger than the periodic repayments of principal prior to maturity, there is an interesting question as to how this affects the risk to the borrower. If it is assumed that the balloon can be renegotiated when the time comes, if necessary, then it obviously reduces the risk since the annual charges are thereby reduced. If, however, this cannot be assumed with complete assurance there is the problem of assessing the hazard of the single large (but distant) final payment as opposed to the smaller regular payment.

In direct contrast to the minimization of risk by stretching out the period over which principal is to be repaid, some borrowers believe that they are minimizing the risk by seeking as *short* a repayment period as possible. This approach stems from greater confidence in the cash inflow in the near than in the distant future and a desire to assure that priority is given to debt retirement over competing uses for available funds in the near future. Such an approach implies that self-discipline alone, unsupported by a legal contract, might be incapable of achieving the same result. Reasoning realistically, the financial officer and/or chief executive officer knows that a corporation is subjected to a variety of pressures for the utilization of funds, both from management and from shareholders, and if debt repayment is paramount the most effective way of assuring it is to commit the corporation to a legal obligation to repay.

A related consideration is the option to prepay a loan without a prohibitive penalty. It is natural that lenders, having made what they consider to be a satisfactory loan at a good interest rate, will want to keep the funds so invested for an extended period of time. Borrowers, on the other hand, usually seek a prepayment option partly as a means of minimizing the related interest payment when the opportunity for repayment presents itself, partly as insurance against excessive interest rates if and when the market changes, and partly as a means of reducing the risks associated with the fixed charges of debt.

The extent to which the prepayment clause is subject to negotiation depends most fundamentally on the state of the money market — the availability of funds and anticipated interest rate trends — as well as on the bargaining position of the borrower and his interest in the clause. Some borrowers asserted that they would not borrow at all without the "prepayment without penalty" clause. Others were less adamant. Clearly, however, the opportunity to replace debt with equity capital in periods of high cash inflow prior to the maturity of the debt could have a significant bearing on the risk.

Although not specifically included in the concept of risk used in this study, many debt contracts include covenants other than those relating to payments of interest and principal which if breached can be a threat to the whole debtor-creditor relationship and ultimately to the continued existence of the business. One of the most significant examples of such a covenant is that concerning the maintenance of working capital above some level specified by the contract. In some cases such a restraint is so far beyond normal experience that it can be conveniently forgotten by management. In other cases it is close enough that management must keep a watchful eye on the level of working capital and even take action to assure conformity with the debt contract. At such times the covenant is at best an annoyance and at worst a real hazard to management.

The best protection against the risks of such covenants is not to have them and some borrowers have the bargaining power to do just that. Other borrowers, however, and these are likely to include those where the covenant might become binding, may not be able to avoid it. One financial officer under such circumstances stated that when these covenants were forced on him, he endeavored to have them conditional rather than absolute. This is to say that instead of a covenant which required that Net Current Assets must not fall below "x" million dollars under any circumstances, the covenant would read that if Net Current Assets fell below "x" million dollars, dividends would be suspended until the position was restored. Thus the covenant would not be a condition of default but would merely enforce remedial action.

A consideration underlying all the terms of the debt contract and bearing directly on the practical significance of the event of default is the possibility of negotiating a modification or suspension of the terms. Interest on the part of the borrower in such a possibility arises not only with respect to the event of adversity but also the event of the unexpected during prosperous times. Debt contracts can exert undesirable restraints on managerial decisions in good times as well as being a potential source of embarrassment in bad times so that management interest in the negotiability of terms is only in part risk-oriented.

For the general purpose of maximum flexibility, however, managements do give consideration to this matter when selecting the lending institution and the debt instrument. One of the commonly accepted arguments for private placement lies in the intimate borrower-lender association and the fact that only one or a small number of lenders are involved so that renegotiation of terms is a manageable proposition — as contrasted with the public bond issue. Likewise borrowers pick up information about the experience of other companies with respect to particular lending institutions and, rightly or wrongly, characterize them as being either flexible or rigid in their original negotiations and subsequent handling of the agreement. In part this is one of several ways of attempting to minimize the hazard associated with any given amount of debt capital.

Before concluding this section on the minimization of risk for any given amount of debt capital, it should be noted that we have deliberately omitted consideration of modifications of the basic debt form as a means of reducing risk. Clearly the use of such securities as income bonds or convertible debentures has a major implication in respect to the risk to the borrowing corporation. The primary concern of this study, however, is with the basic debt instrument which involves periodic payments of cash to the creditor fixed at the time of initial negotiation as to amount and timing and legally binding throughout the life of the contract. Because of its overwhelming importance in practice, this basic debt form will absorb the entire attention of this study, and a consideration of the various modifications will be omitted.

Reviewing the general observations on risk minimization among the sample of companies in this study, some over-all comments may be made. In practice there appeared to be wide variations in the concern of management with the opportunities for risk minimization in debt financing. Similarly there was wide variation in the vigor with which managements bargained in this respect. Some appeared to bargain vigorously only with respect to the interest rate. Others had a precise and inflexible attitude as to which terms and covenants were or were not acceptable. In general there was very little evidence of interest in swapping interest rate concessions for major modifications of the risk element — on the part of either the borrower or the lender. Such negotiation as there was on this point appeared to be within a very narrow range. In general, and as one might expect, the active exploration of opportunities for risk minimization for any given amount of debt was found primarily among those companies which were actively exploiting the debt capital market.

THE ORIGIN OF STANDARDS OF DEBT CAPACITY

In the discussion of debt policy in preceding chapters it has been recognized that the decision to borrow or not to borrow rests both on an appraisal of the magnitude of risk and on willingness to bear risk. Since the latter aspect is subjective and personal on the part of those who make the decision, it resists objective analysis either by the outside observer or by the individuals concerned. Consequently our analysis of the reasoning behind specific debt policies must be confined to whatever evidence there is on the underlying appraisal of risk magnitudes. In particular this phase of the study centered on determining whether the standard was conceived inside or outside the borrowing corporation and in either case what was the rationale which underlay its acceptance as the best policy under the circumstances.

. Perhaps the most significant observation in this respect is that within the research sample there was *very little evidence of a serious attempt on the part of the borrowing corporation to make an advance appraisal of the validity of a debt capacity criterion in terms of its own unique circumstances.*   The most common practical test of a debt policy was the test of past experience — and a satisfactory policy was one which had not been a cause of financial embarrassment *as yet.*   The validity of this approach will be questioned later. Actually the only really reliable policy under this approach would be a no-debt policy.

To begin with, there were those companies that recognized the desirability of an advance appraisal of risk but that for one reason or another left this responsibility to the prospective creditor.   In the face of this admittedly complex problem some considered themselves incapable of making an intelligent attempt and deferred to the extensive experience of the lender who after all made his living doing just this.   (Some corporate treasurers faced a long-term debt decision at most two or three times in their career as the senior financial officer.)   Others took what they considered a realistic line of reasoning that reputable commercial banks and insurance companies were highly conservative lenders and after all it was of little practical significance if a borrower believed he could stand more debt when the creditor refused to lend it.   Thus they were unlikely to lend too much and so a company could safely take what it could get.

In a number of cases, however, the borrower had a specific standard of debt capacity that he applied in thinking through the investment and debt-equity decisions and that had no apparent connection with the opinions or practices of creditors.   Such a rule, for example, was that which rejected a debt issue if as a result total long-term debt as a proportion of total capitalization was raised to a point in excess of 30%.   Where did such a rule originate? The answer was not always clear.   One answer was that such rules were evolved from experience.   This implies an empirical approach in which particular debt proportions selected more or less at random are tested under actual recession conditions and thereby "proved" reasonable or excessive.   It also obviously implies that at some stage in its experience the company was operating without any meaningful guide lines as to the appropriate amount of debt.

The Capital Structure of Other Companies

While it is undoubtedly true that much of the decision making in this area is essentially a process of more or less cautious experimentation (less euphemistically known as "trial and error"), it is not accurate to suggest that the rule or standard of the moment is merely "picked out of the air." In practice businesses had two primary sources for such standards — both external. One source was the observable practice of other businesses in the same or in other industries. The other source was, again, the recommendation of lending institutions either directly received or indirectly received through the opinions of financial intermediaries. There was of course no reason why a company should not consult any and all such sources before reaching a decision.

In considering the possibility of a substantial increase in the amount of long-term debt outstanding, it was common practice for a company to take note of the capital structure of other companies, particularly those considered to be in similar circumstances. In this way the individual company became aware of general practice — the "typical" debt proportions as well as the extremes, high and low. In the absence of other criteria, the only meaningful interpretation of such data would be to stay within the limits of current practice and conservative management would likely want to be consistent with what the majority were doing, thus avoiding the extremes, particularly the upper one.

Such comparisons are not necessarily confined to the same industry. The author recalls reading an extensive study and report carried out for internal purposes by the financial division of a large nonmanufacturing corporation (not included in this study). The analysis was detailed and involved a variety of considerations but the basic thesis boiled down to this: "We observe that the public utility industry typically borrows around 50% of its total capitalization and that manufacturing industries generally borrow up to 30% of total capitalization. We believe that our business is somewhat more risky than a public utility and somewhat less risky than a manufacturing business. Therefore we conclude that our debt limit should be 40%."

At a later point we will come back to an appraisal of the validity of this approach. At this point we merely raise the question: What happens if the majority of businesses are coming to their debt capacity decisions in the same way?

In defense of this approach some financial people argued that regardless of how these proportions were arrived at originally, the stock market took cognizance of the "typical" debt proportions and was disposed to look with some alarm at a company whose debt was significantly out of line (on the high side). This deviation could lead to a lower price-earnings ratio in an attempt to compensate for the assumed higher risk and thus to a higher cost of equity capital — regardless of whether any real threat to solvency existed. This line of reasoning assumes that the stock market, like the corporation itself, has no better way of appraising the reasonableness of debt burdens in the individual case.

The Standards of the Lender

A source of ideas on debt capacity for the individual business which is of equal if not greater importance is the institutions on the supply side of the debt capital market. The evidence of this study supports the idea that borrowing corporations lean heavily on the debt capacity standards of lending institutions. The use of this source was most apparent in those debt criteria in which this dependence was total and explicit. But it is also true of a number of those corporations that had their own debt capacity criteria. In some cases the debt criteria of the creditors were actively sought after, in other cases passively accepted as an unavoidable fact. In some cases the information was received from a single creditor with whom the borrower had a close association; in other cases the information was generalized — drawn from "common knowledge" or the opinions of financial intermediaries.

For example, it was quite apparent that investment bankers played a significant role in shaping debt policy for those companies which made use of their services. Company "A" was planning an expansion of plant facilities and was considering debt as a means of obtaining the necessary funds. The Board of Directors, or certain influential members thereof, were unwilling to increase debt beyond 20% of capitalization which would happen if the entire investment was debt financed. The president of the company was disinclined to accept this limit as final and so wrote to a partner of an investment banking house with whom previous financial arrangements had been made. He reported the views of the Board and asked his opinion. The memorandum made by the partner at the time was as follows: "My answer was that 30% or even 35% is not out of line for the _____ industry at present." Subsequently debt was floated in an amount in excess of the 20% limit.

Company "B" was favorably disposed toward the use of debt and believed in continuous trading on equity as a means of raising the return on the common investment. The treasurer was not clear, however, as to the safe upper limit of permanent debt. On the occasion of a need to raise $10,000,000 of additional funds he consulted with a partner of an investment banking firm with whom he was acquainted. Together they reviewed the financial condition of the company and in particular two things: (1) the effect of $10,000,000 of new long-term debt on the balance sheet and (2) the effect of the added carrying charges on the ratio of Earnings Coverage. Long-term debt as a percentage of total capitalization worked out at 26% and was considered by the investment banker to be a "good conservative ratio." In later argument before the Board the treasurer pointed out that this percentage of debt had been reached and passed before in the history of the company with no ill effects. On the question of Earnings Coverage it was determined that over the past several years earnings available for debt servicing had been running at four to six times total debt servicing, including that on the proposed debt. This was considered to be an "obviously safe" margin. On the strength of this evidence both the investment banker and the treasurer appeared satisfied that the new debt would not be excessively risky for the company to undertake.

Company "C" was approaching the market for the first time with a public bond issue. It had no clear idea as to what the limits of its debt capacity were but had decided that the proposed issue lay within these limits. In working out the terms of the indenture with the investment banker, a limit on further borrowing had to be written in. Since a primary objective of the company was to have at least an "A" rating, it was necessary for the investment banker to discuss the proposed indenture with a bond rating agency and obtain an opinion as to the likely rating, given certain terms. The issuing company was quite happy to accept a limit on debt of 35% of its capitalization. The investment banker, however, said that this was "crazy" — unnecessarily restrictive — and recommended "trying" for 50%. It was finally agreed between the investment

banker and the rating agency that a 40% limit would be in keeping
with an "A" rating for this company.

Such examples illustrate the part which investment bankers and
bond rating agencies can play in the development of the specific
debt criteria used by industrial companies.   Such intermediaries
are presumed to be in continuous and intimate contact with the
individuals and institutions who supply the debt capital and are
relied on by some borrowers to tell them what is likely to prove
acceptable to creditors in general.   This then becomes the operating
guide for the borrowers' own financial policies.

Other companies relied on their direct contact with individual
lending institutions, particularly those with which they had satisfactory financial arrangements in the past.   Of course, not all
lenders were willing to take a position on debt capacity beyond any
amount currently outstanding or under negotiation.   To do so was
considered by some to imply a commitment as to willingness to lend
in the future, and they preferred to make each decision as it came
and only when it came.   As a result the borrower may decide that
the only practical operating policy is to do likewise — to let the
test of appropriate debt capacity be whether the bank will meet the
loan request as it arises.   This may or may not imply an absence
of "shopping around" among banks.   Taken literally, this approach
to the use of long-term debt obviously means that the borrower had
no independent standard of risk bearing capacity.

In contrast, some lenders were willing to take a position on over-
all debt limits and to make this known to the borrower.   Willingness was undoubtedly influenced by such considerations as the size,
financial strength, and bargaining position of the borrower, the
closeness of the lender-borrower relationship, and the condition of
the money market.   The opinion of the lender on this matter might
be made known in informal conversations but was more commonly
forced into the open by the necessity for a covenant with respect
to future borrowing as a part of a loan agreement.   Apart from
the relatively few companies that were able to negotiate a loan contract without any limit on the amount of future debt, the borrowers
generally operated under a specific restraint of this sort.   Given a
free choice the average lender appeared to prefer a complete pro-
hibition of additional debt beyond the amount negotiated under the
contract, regardless of its size.   A covenant of this sort would have

the important advantages of minimizing the risk, giving the lender the opportunity to review the situation before any new debt was assumed and bringing the borrower back to the original source of such funds for any new debt money considered to be reasonable.

Lenders were not always in a strong enough bargaining position to be able to insist on such a provision, however. Consequently, covenants often permitted borrowing beyond the amount negotiated according to some simple formula. The most common formula was one that expressed a limit as some relationship between Net Tangible Assets and Total Long-Term Debt. This type of formula obviously permitted an increase in debt as equity increased, in contrast to contracts in which the absolute dollar amount of debt was limited. For example, the debt contract might require that the company maintain Net Tangible Assets (Tangible Assets less Current Liabilities) equal to or greater than 275% of total long-term debt. This is the equivalent of a maximum debt to capitalization percentage of 36%. Insurance company debt contracts commonly added a second standard in terms of a minimum earnings coverage standard, with the two standards operating so that the more conservative applied at any given time.

It will be apparent that such covenants did not necessarily reflect in any precise way the appraisal of the borrower's maximum debt bearing capacity by the lender. It was in the lender's interests to keep the covenant as tight as possible, yielding (within limits) in those cases where the general bargaining position of the borrower was strong *and* where the borrower considered this to be a critical covenant. Some lenders had the reputation of being generally unyielding in their debt limit covenants and others of being open to a fair range of negotiation, assuming a give-and-take atmosphere in other respects. It is interesting to note here that very few borrowers suggested that this was in fact a critical covenant in their approach to the debt contract negotiation. In particular there appeared to be little interest in the possibility of giving a little on the interest rate in exchange for a more liberal covenant. In general, the borrowers seemed prepared to accept with little or no debate the standard restrictions which at their most liberal point held debt down to a level in the vicinity of 30% of capitalization.

Thus through the negotiation of debt contracts the borrower came to know something of the risk standards of the lender and often, for want of an independent criterion, was apparently prepared to accept the creditor's judgment and to adopt it as his own. As a practical matter what this issue reduces to is the question of whether the borrower can evolve his own standard of debt capacity independently of the lender and whether, given differing evaluations, the amount of debt capital available to a given company at a given point in time is open to negotiation.

The Independent Standard

Few corporate officials would be flattered by the assertion that such a critical element of debt policy as the limits of debt capacity was not an independent decision but rather was based largely on an uncritical acceptance of other people's opinions or actions. Nevertheless, the observations so far on the source of operating standards of debt capacity suggest that this is substantially true in a number of instances. This impression must be qualified by a recognition that the managements concerned had not completely abdicated from responsibility for the level of risk associated with debt. They still retained and exercised the choice between debt and no debt, between continuous and intermittent borrowing, between the absolute minimum and a substantially larger amount where the goal became leverage rather than meeting emergency needs. The fact remains, however, that many managements depended on the opinions and decisions of others as to the precise boundary line.

Within the sample of companies considered, only a small minority showed evidence of a serious attempt at making their own independent appraisal of appropriate debt limits. For the majority, the extent of independent appraisal was through applying the test of experience. If the decision rule on debt financing had been in operation for a number of years and if, in particular, it had survived a recession or two without serious financial embarrassment, then it was judged to be a good rule and continued in effect. If experience proved the rule too liberal, then it was modified — assuming of course that it was not so liberal as to result in bankruptcy. Naturally all businesses were alert to the lessons of experience but for the minority referred to above this was not sufficient. What they desired was some advance assurance of the validity of the standard other than the recommendation of creditors or the observation that roughly comparable companies were doing roughly the same thing.

PART TWO

THE ANALYSIS OF
CORPORATE DEBT CAPACITY:
AN APPRAISAL OF PRACTICE AND
A PROPOSAL FOR IMPROVEMENT

The character and extent of this independent appraisal varied. As one might expect it centered on an analysis of past experience within the company concerned and the implications of this for the future. In its simplest form it was an attempt to predict the range of earnings available for debt servicing as was done in the example of Company "B" referred to earlier in this chapter. In this case a comparison was made between the average net earnings before debt charges based on recent experience and expected debt servicing. There was no explicit analysis of the adequacy of the margin of such expected earnings over debt charges — merely the value judgment that it was comfortably in excess of the minimum required.

The most sophisticated analysis of debt capacity was undertaken by a company that was in a rapid growth situation and where a substantial amount of debt was necessary if the pace of growth was to continue. Here the management undertook what it referred to as a cash forecast under varying assumptions. What management did in fact was to approximate cash flows from income and balance sheet data. The objective was to observe what happened to cash flows under assumed recession conditions and to relate this to varying levels of cash outflow required to service varying levels of debt needed for expansion. The starting point was to calculate net profit at three levels, the upper being a projection of current earnings experience and the lower an assumed breakeven point. To these net profit figures were added depreciation charges and other income.

These sums of cash inflow were then matched against the comparable level of expenditures for plant and equipment, working capital requirements (if any), and dividends. It was assumed that a certain minimum of capital expenditures would continue even in recession — certainly for any capital projects which were already under construction or otherwise under contract at the time the recession set in. Dividends were arbitrarily assumed cut back at lower levels of earnings, falling to zero at the break-even level. As the calculations worked out, working capital proved to be a source of funds rather than a use at lower levels of earnings. The net effect of the analysis was to show what additional cash outflows for debt servicing could be assumed without jeopardizing the cash position of the company.

The final conclusion of this particular study was that "provided the recession didn't last too long and also provided that it did not throw the company into a net loss situation" a 30% debt rule (Percent of Capitalization) would not only be safe but would provide a margin so that if the company had a research "break-through" it could actually stand some more debt beyond that for financing unexpected and urgently needed capital expenditures. The company also pointed out that this "was not out of line" with the debt limit imposed on the company by long-term debt contracts (net tangible assets at least 275% of total long-term debt).

In summary, the evidence as to the sources from which these companies drew their standards of debt capacity indicates primary reliance on the judgment of others and very little independent evaluation. The independence came in the decision as to what external information to accept as the appropriate guide, but management appeared to have very little in the way of an objective basis upon which to make a rational choice. There was of course the test of experience, of trial and error, but this assumes that the adverse effects of an inappropriate choice are not so severe as to preclude subsequent modification. Challenged on this point, management tended to argue in one of two directions: (a) that the future was so uncertain that any attempt to appraise the risks of debt would be meaningless (assuming of course management knew how to approach the problem) or (b) that in the last analysis it was the creditor who set the limits on debt and independent evaluation was largely an academic exercise. These arguments will be considered at length as a part of the appraisal of debt policy which follows.

CHAPTER 6

An Appraisal of Corporate Practice in the

Use of Long-Term Debt

INTRODUCTION

Part One of this study has presented the significant observations derived from a study of business practice with respect to debt and related financial decisions and policies. Its purpose has been largely descriptive — to lay before the reader a detailed outline of current management thinking and practice within a hopefully representative sample of manufacturing companies in as accurate and unbiased a form as was possible for the external observer. In spite of this objective, however, it seemed appropriate to raise questions from time to time where the author was disposed to challenge the adequacy or soundness of individual corporate practices. Introduced at this stage, the intention was to stimulate a constructively critical attitude on the part of the reader in reviewing this sample of present-day business thinking.

Now that the description has been completed, it will be the purpose of this chapter to pull these critical questions together, to extend the analysis, and to develop some general conclusions as to the logical consistency and practical usefulness of the ideas currently accepted by business practitioners. Anticipating these conclusions, at least in one important respect, it may be stated here that the author believes that many corporate borrowers are too dependent on others for their standards of corporate debt capacity and that greater efforts should be made to develop criteria based on a detailed knowledge of the circumstances of the individual business.

123

As a consequence, the remaining chapters of Part Two of this study are devoted to a proposed method for developing an independent appraisal of the risk implications of long-term debt.

This chapter has two principal objectives. The first of these objectives is to assess the appropriateness of the basic sources of corporate debt capacity criteria, and the second is to examine the validity of the particular standards of debt capacity derived from these sources. A few related topics will also be discussed.

THE APPROPRIATENESS OF CONVENTIONAL SOURCES FROM WHICH DEBT CAPACITY CRITERIA ARE DERIVED

In reviewing the debt capacity concepts which have gained acceptance by a sample of business practitioners, it seems a useful point of departure to begin by examining the underlying sources from which individual debt criteria have been evolved. These sources have been described previously and will now be considered critically in terms of their appropriateness for the purposes of the borrowing corporation.

The Purely Subjective Debt Criterion

In the description of the problem of risk associated with debt given in the Introduction to this study, it was pointed out that we are dealing with two separate considerations when considering corporate practice — the magnitude of the risk and the willingness to bear risk. It has also been pointed out that the second consideration is a subjective, personal decision on the part of those who are to bear the risk and must be taken as given. This study focuses on the first — the consideration of risk magnitudes in debt financing. Nevertheless, in reviewing the policies in effect among the companies under consideration there are some which appear to be determined largely if not entirely by the second consideration. The best examples of this are companies that have a debt policy that may be described as being at an extreme position — one that permits no debt whatsoever or alternatively one that pushes debt to its maximum limit of availability. This is particularly true of the former, the "no debt" policy. These companies appear to say, in effect: "We are so opposed to the idea of adding unnecessarily to the risk of this business that regardless of how small that addition to the risk may be, we do not want to assume it." Consequently they see no point in attempting to measure the magnitude of the risk associated with any given amount of debt. Thus the debt decision is as close to a purely subjective one as it is possible to imagine.

Speaking in practical terms, it is quite within the realm of possibility that a conservative management in a generally sound and profitable business would take such a position. Considered in the cold light of rational behavior, however, the position appears inconsistent with the fact that every business has inherent in it the necessity for a balancing of the risk of loss against the opportunity for gain. This is the essential characteristic of private enterprise. In the normal course of business, management is continuously engaged in making decisions that modify the magnitude and certainty of cash inflows and outflows. Why should some managements arbitrarily exclude modifications of the capital structure from consideration along with other opportunities to assume risk in the interest of making a profit?

There is, of course, no single answer. Undoubtedly part of the answer lies in the significant phrase "adding *unnecessarily*" in the above synthetic quote. A company that can achieve and maintain a satisfactory and competitively respectable rate of growth and profitability without debt may not feel strongly motivated to add a new dimension to risk, however small the chance of loss may be or however large the potential reward. In an earlier chapter attention was drawn to the wide variation that may exist with regard to the sense of urgency associated with various investment opportunities. There is the very important distinction drawn in practice between those risks that the company "has to bear" — as an inescapable part of performing its established function in industry — and those that it is "free" to accept or reject without prejudice to the central activity.

Secondly, it must be recognized that the penalty for an error of judgment in making the debt decision — the prospect of insolvency and possibly bankruptcy — is one from which most managements shrink in horror. There are some people who, if offered the opportunity to participate in a game of chance in which they might lose all they owned, would instantly refuse without waiting to hear the odds. It is in this frame of mind that some people in management positions approach the opportunity of "trading on the equity," and it is another significant explanation for the purely subjective approach to the debt decision. It may be added here that it is also true of some managements that do borrow funds that they borrow only because they believe that what they are doing involves no real risk of insolvency. We repeat here the statement of one treasurer which was to the effect that his company was of such a size and maturity that it was completely out of character to "go for broke."

Finally, a consideration of equal if not greater importance is the fact that few businesses consider themselves adequately equipped to measure — or even approximate — the likelihood of the occurrence of cash insolvency which would be associated with any given amount of long-term debt. At best they can distinguish only between substantial risk differentials in terms of which is the greater and which the lesser risk. This way of thinking about risk, which is useful for some purposes, does not provide a means of identifying the "safe" limit to debt capacity, and consequently there will be a tendency to make the decision with respect to the debt on purely subjective grounds — according to the general disposition for or against more risk.

Nevertheless the pattern for rational behavior remains, always assuming of course that the goal is to maximize the value of the owners' investment. This is: (1) to identify the penalties associated with "excessive" debt servicing charges, the principal one being the occurrence of cash insolvency, and (2) to provide a measure of the chance of their occurrence which is associated with any given amount of debt. Management is then in a position to observe objectively the nature of the risk that it is being asked to bear and to decide whether it is or is not willing to accept this risk in the light of the expected gain from the use of debt as an alternative to an equivalent amount of equity capital. Obviously a rational decision cannot be made solely on the basis of one's general disposition or willingness to assume risk.

The Evidence of General Industry Practice

It is a natural tendency when formulating major policies, particularly where serious adverse consequences may follow from errors of judgment, to be influenced by the practices of others in similar circumstances. This is most noticeable when companies are considering debt for the first time or are considering a substantial increase in the proportion of debt in the capital structure above that to which the company has been accustomed. Where reliance on the experience of others was observed, it did not involve any formal process of establishing comparability and was usually confined to a comparison with companies in the same industry (and, where the numbers were great, to those companies that were believed to be similar in the sense of being competitors in the same market). The comparisons were generally confined to a calculation of current percentages of total capitalization represented by long-term debt. The extremes were noted and also the mode — the most common value in practice.

The significance of such evidence for the purpose of formulating individual debt policy has already been questioned. There is doubt as to whether the particular group of companies so assembled is sufficiently comparable as to cash flow characteristics to warrant the expectation of similarity in the risk associated with any given proportion of debt. Not only must the risk be roughly comparable but so also must be the willingness to bear risk — an even more unlikely assumption. The acceptance of such evidence as a useful guide also implies that the managements of these other companies have made their decisions rationally on the basis of meaningful evidence. Beyond this assumption there is the implication that such policies have been time-tested in bad times and good and so proved "safe" and workable.

There is reason to question whether the normal test of experience is adequate. This will be discussed at length shortly. There is also reason to ask whether this practice may not merely produce a clustering around some historical norm of accepted business practice which may be substantially out of line with the observable present-day evidence on risk and attitudes to risk bearing.

As previously mentioned, there is a sense in which this evidence, regardless of the absence of rational validity, can be of important practical significance. This consideration is the extent to which current practice with respect to the use of long-term debt becomes one of the standards used by participants in the stock market in determining individual price-earnings relationships. *If* the stock market is inclined to penalize a company for having "excessive" debt by requiring a higher earnings yield to compensate for the assumed higher risk *and if* its standard of excessiveness is the capital structures of comparable businesses in the same industry, then it follows that what others do in this respect, right or wrong, is of real, practical significance to the businessman and his over-all cost of capital.

To phrase this observation somewhat differently, the reasoning suggests that management should take its cue on debt from the stockholder who expresses his attitude in the price at which he is willing to sell or buy the stock. Further it implies that up to a point the amount of debt does not affect the stockholders' concept of the risk associated with the investment, that point being an amount which is in line with the amount commonly used by such businesses. Beyond that point the risk is significantly increased, at least in the minds of the stockholders, and the market price declines by an amount necessary to produce a compensating increase in the yield on the stock.

It is, of course, common sense to expect that the stock market will take note of any financial characteristic which is clearly and obviously out of line with what it is accustomed to expect. In practice, however, it is extremely difficult if not impossible to establish the degree of comparability among businesses that would warrant the desired confidence either in the observed relationship between debt and stock price or in its application in market decisions. Without denying its significance in practice, the conclusion is inescapable that this line of thinking merely enlarges the group that is relying on *someone else* to make an independent and rational decision which they can then safely adopt as their own. It does not of itself provide a sound basis for a rational decision in any given risk situation.

The Risk Standard of the Lender

From the observations made in this study it is clear that the two most significant influences setting the risk standard of the individual corporate borrower were found to be the risk standard of the lender and individual and/or company experience with debt burden. It is therefore of special importance to examine carefully the reliability of these particular guides for the purpose in mind.

As mentioned in the Introduction, the field work of this study included interviews with all lending institutions currently associated with the industrial companies included in the sample. The primary purpose of these interviews was to learn as much as possible about the consideration of risk in the decisions to lend which matched the decisions to borrow and in the process to compare the approaches and standards of the two parties to the contract. In most cases the interview was with the lending officer who had been personally involved in the negotiation. In a public offering of bonds the individual concerned was the partner or executive of the investment banking house that had primary responsibility for the underwriting. This section will first describe the general characteristics of the lenders' approach to the question of debt capacity, covered in part in Chapter 5, and then proceed to appraise the usefulness of lenders' standards as a guide for the borrower.

In most of the cases included in this study the debt financing was privately negotiated as a term loan arrangement, with a commercial bank or insurance company acting alone or as the prime negotiator for a small group of financial institutions. Thus the corporate officers were able to deal at first hand with the men who would make the lending decision and gain direct impressions of the lender's point of view on all considerations including that of the risk associated with the proposed loan. It must be recognized, however, that in any debt negotiation the lender is making a decision on a specific investment and loan proposal at a given point in time and is not disposed to generalize beyond this proposal. The lending officer or loan committee must decide whether it is within their current risk standards to loan "X" million dollars to the ABC Company for a finite period of time beginning now. Since the risk factor is not the only consideration in this decision, a refusal does not necessarily mean that the lender considers the risk excessive. On the other hand, approval of the loan request implies that in the lender's judgment the risk is reasonable, in the sense that the lender does not expect the company to default on its contractual obligations during the period of the loan: hence the frequently used borrower practice of making debt decisions by continuing to submit a succession of loan requests until the lender says "no."

It must also be recognized here that the lenders in question were among the most conservative to be found in the capital market, with relatively high standards of safety. At the same time, however, their eagerness for new loan opportunities varied from time to time as the flow of funds into the capital market varied and as their particular portfolio requirements shifted. Thus it might be that an unusually large flow of funds available for investment could lead to a temporary though perhaps modest relaxation in the risk standard of the lender. The timing of the particular loan request therefore had some bearing on the risk decision.

Thus, at best, the approval of a loan request told the borrower that the amount of debt then outstanding was within the standard of acceptable risk in the judgment of one lending institution, within the framework of its particular circumstances at that point in time. This is a long way from defining a long-term debt policy for the borrower — nor would it be so represented by any intelligent lender. Regarding the apparent evaluation of debt capacity found in debt contract covenants, it was pointed out in Chapter 5 that it was in the interest of the lender to have as tight a debt limit covenant as possible. Such a covenant served to inhibit any additional drains on funds available for debt servicing and to give the lender the chance to review the present and future prospects before giving its consent, if and when a further need arose at some future date. It also avoided the danger of an inference that the lender considered the existing loan well below the company's real debt limits, thus weakening the current bargaining position of the lender unnecessarily and carrying the undesired implication that the lender could be counted on for more debt money in the future.

Although there was considerable variation in the form of this covenant, the usual rule, as previously indicated, was some ratio between Net Tangible Assets and total long-term debt. The number of instances were too few to draw any significant conclusions from the data, but these ratios tended to fall in the 30% to 35% of capitalization range. The actual form of the covenant depended a great deal on the bargaining position of the borrower, the interest of the borrower in keeping the debt route open, and the confidence of the lender in the responsibility and basic conservatism of management. In any case it could not be taken as a realistic yardstick of the lender's judgment of the borrower's over-all debt capacity.

As previously noted, discussions with both borrowers and lenders suggested a relatively low level of concern on the part of the borrower with such restraints on future borrowing capacity. This was not one of the covenants which generated vigorous negotiation in the majority of cases. The inference is that these borrowers did not give high priority to probing the outside limits of the lender's willingness to lend. This apparent indifference may have been based in part on a confidence in the ability to renegotiate the entire loan agreement by the time any new need for debt funds presented itself. The relative frequency of renegotiation prior to maturity on the part of continuous borrowers tended to support this expectation.

The approach taken in reaching specific loan decisions by the large majority of loan officers interviewed was such that it would be virtually impossible for the borrower to form an independent appraisal of the basis of the lender's judgment, were he so inclined. The decision making process was generally represented as a highly individualized process of transforming a complex of (often conflicting) evidence on many relevant considerations into a simple "yes" or "no." Successful decision making was considered to rest on some combination of native ability and experience — a nontransferable skill. There was a frequent tendency to play down the role of formalized explicit analysis, primarily on the grounds that for many considerations there was no common denominator. Likewise there was a tendency to play down the role of explicit standards for industry as a whole or even within industries. No self-respecting loan officer cared to be identified with decision making by rule of thumb. In support of this contention a loan officer might cite an instance where a loan of 50% or more of capitalization was granted. As a consequence of this approach the borrower had to take the wisdom of any particular loan decision largely on faith — faith in the competence of the man or men making the decision.

There was, however, some evidence on the approach of some lenders to the appraisal of risk. This was to be found in the nature of the data assembled by the lender and used in his quantitative analysis. In its most advanced form this analysis rested on the most recent income statement and balance sheet data plus a cash forecast prepared by the borrower for a period extending one to five years into the future. The conventional financial statements gave evidence on the soundness of the financial structure and on the magnitude, trend, and stability of earnings. The cash forecast gave evidence on the expectations of management as to future earnings, including the impact of new capital expenditures, additional capital requirements, if any, and expected sources of funds. Such a forecast was considered useful for reasons other than the specific information contained. It forced management to do more precise and explicit thinking about the future. It produced evidence on the character of management's forward thinking — the degree of care, conservatism, and so on. It emphasized the necessity for adequate anticipation of cash needs including the servicing of the proposed debt.

As to the specific data provided in the cash forecast, they were potentially useful in appraising the capacity of the business to meet mandatory cash payments during the forecast period and beyond. Since the forecast was dealing with expectations as to cash flow it was getting to the heart of the information needed to appraise the risk of cash insolvency. However, the lender recognized important practical limitations as to its usefulness. Since expansion of the invested capital is commonly contemplated in a period of prosperity and general optimism, the forecast commonly failed to take a realistic look at the full range of adverse circumstances which could affect the actual result. The lender was also aware that this was a document submitted as a part of a negotiation and that it would be unrealistic to expect the borrowing corporation not to give its future prospects the benefit of any doubt. Consciously or unconsciously, it was biased information. Finally there were the obvious limitations on the ability to forecast the financial future beyond six months or a year.

In view of these limitations the lender was not generally disposed to trust his conclusions with respect to risk to a literal interpretation of the cash forecast or to carry on a detailed and sophisticated analysis based on unsophisticated and biased data. At the same time the lender recognized the necessity of a test of debt bearing capacity under possible adverse circumstances. The typical solution of the lender, recognizing the limitations of time available for predecision analysis and also the limitations of the data available to an outsider, was to work out a rough approximation. This analysis usually was reduced to an estimate of the impact on net earnings available for debt servicing resulting from one or more recession sales assumptions based on company and industry experience. This estimate was then related to the amount of debt servicing contemplated and a judgment was made as to its adequacy. Whether or not the loan officer was influenced in this judgment by some predetermined standard drawn from his own experience or that of others is for this study a matter of speculation. In any case this standard, if it existed, was not often explicit.

The approach to a determination of debt capacity to be recommended in this study has a rough parallel in the approach of the lender just described. The success or failure of risk appraisal lies in the ability to predict the probable limits of cash flow. It will be shown later, however, that the usual efforts of the lender in this direction are too rough and approximate to be really useful in setting the debt policy of the borrower.

At the same time it must be recognized that there are good, practical reasons why the lender may be content with such approximations, beyond the reason of expediency. The reader is reminded that the companies under consideration were all relatively large, mature, and historically profitable companies. The amounts of debt requested by these companies (and granted to them) were for the most part modest. Very few companies had debt in excess of 35% of capitalization outstanding at any time, and the average debt outstanding was substantially below that figure. Further, the debt standards of the lender as reflected in loan covenants usually contained not one but several built-in margins of safety. By focusing on net earnings in recession the lender ignored the potential release of funds resulting from contraction of working capital needs. Likewise that portion of the inflow of funds which was obscured by noncash expenses, notably depreciation charges, was often disregarded. It was often considered conservative to ignore the potential earnings resulting from the investment of the funds provided by the loan.

The sufficiency of a rough guide was also supported by the fact that the lender had the secondary defense of asset values when considering the prospect of insolvency. While the amount of the debt servicing probably would remain constant throughout the life of the loan (the critical consideration from the borrower's point of view), the lender could look forward to a steady improvement in the asset-debt ratio by the dual influence of repayments of principal and the accumulation of retained earnings. Since debt limits were commonly expressed in terms of initial debt proportions, doubts about the cash flows in the more distant future could be in part appeased by the prospect of a constantly increasing margin of asset values.

It should also be noted that while the borrower must of necessity be as concerned with the timing of a cash payment as he is with the amount, the lender may well be able to be more casual about timing if things work out more adversely than expected. When it comes down to it, an unavoidable postponement of payments under the terms of a debt contract does not necessarily mean ultimate loss of principal or interest. A realistic lender expects to have some loans that "go sour" and have to be "worked out" over time. On the other hand, a borrower would be ill-advised to plan a debt policy which presumed a patient lender — though doubtless some do.

It is quite within reason to expect that a particular financial institution, and lending institutions as a whole, will have evolved from experience a risk standard that precludes the event of insolvency among industrial borrowers except in an acceptable minority of cases. Such losses as result from defaulted loans can in the long run be considered as an acceptable cost of operation. If experience shows the standard to be too liberal and the "cost" of such defaults becomes "excessive," the standard can be raised. Some lenders clearly indicated that their risk standards were essentially of this evolutionary character. By such means the lender protected himself against a standard which was actuarially too low (excessively risky) for the industrial loan portfolio as a whole (given the possible range of interest charges for such loans). On the other hand, there was no limit on how high the standard could be when loan opportunities were outrunning the funds available for this category of investment opportunity.

It should be apparent that however appropriate such a standard may be for the lender it is faulty reasoning to assume that it is therefore an appropriate guide for the debt policy of an individual borrower to whom it is applied at a particular point in time. Without a careful examination of the special circumstances of the company and the industry at a given stage in their history, the individual borrower has no way of knowing whether he is "typical" or not — and the penalty for being wrong in this one case is infinitely greater for the borrower than for the lender.

There is a further point of difference in point of view between borrower and lender which has been mentioned before but needs to be re-emphasized in this context. This centers on the fact that the lender, in his concern about future cash flows, is primarily if not

wholly concerned with his contractual claims and such other contractual demands on cash which may rank ahead of his. The borrowing corporation, on the other hand, must also consider other
cash flows — such as dividend payments — which in terms of policy may be equally mandatory. The mandatory nature of such
payments derives from the judgment of management as to what is
in the best long-term interest of the corporation. Consequently if
it is considered in the long-term interest of the company to preserve
the continuity of certain payments, management will be inclined to
refrain from any deliberate act — such as an increase in the debt
proportions — which clearly jeopardizes such continuity. It is for
this reason that the suggestion was made earlier in this report that
the lender's criterion of debt capacity stands a chance of being too
liberal as well as too conservative from the borrower's point of
view.

The conclusion of this study with regard to the usefulness of the
lender's standard of debt capacity as a guide in the formulation of
the borrower's debt policy should now be apparent to the reader.
It is that for a variety of reasons the lender and the borrower can
and do quite justifiably come to differing appraisals of risk and of
debt capacity in any given situation. *Consequently it is considered
inappropriate for the borrower to use the lender's standard* (assuming it can be determined) *as his primary criterion of debt capacity.* In saying this it is recognized that, if the sample survey of
corporate practice is any indication of corporate practice in general, this conclusion is sharply at variance with a considerable segment of corporate practice. This is not to say, however, that the
viewpoint of the creditor does not have to be reckoned with or that
his judgment is not a significant piece of evidence to be recognized
in the formulation of corporate policy.

The Criterion of Past Experience

While the importance attached to the practices of competitors
and the standards of lenders in the formulation of individual corporate debt policy varied considerably, there is no doubt of the universal and often dominant influence of individual experience in
guiding the use of this source of funds. Obviously the new business
or the business approaching debt for the first time is more dependent on the experience and opinions of others. The companies in

this study, however, were neither new nor for the most part completely inexperienced in debt financing. In attempting to resolve a problem the essence of which was uncertainty, it was natural and proper that management should review all the evidence, including the outcome of whatever policies had been employed in the past.

The primary concern was, of course, with the burden of debt in the event of a serious and sustained recession. Actually the extent of firsthand recession experience which could be drawn on by any top level executive during his span of responsibility for such matters was distinctly limited. Some financial officers and other top executives now in office in certain industries have had virtually no firsthand experience with management during a recession. Others have been through from one to four or five significant dips in the sales trend. Firsthand experience is, however, supplemented by the available records of the business and the experience of predecessors under whose tutelage the individual in question may have evolved his own opinions.

It is interesting to note that among the companies studied there were several cases where there was a noticeable shift in the attitude toward debt in the post World War II period and that this was traceable at least in part to a change in the personnel of top management. The men who had had firsthand experience in management during the depression of the early thirties were being replaced by men whose experience had been gained in a period of recovery and of war and postwar "boom" conditions. The veterans of the Great Depression were invariably cautious men, keenly aware of the hazards of excessive rigidity in cash outflows. While they generally believed that such an extreme experience would not be repeated in the foreseeable future, reason appeared to be in advance of conviction and their actions belied their words.

This illustrates the important limitation of personal experience as a guide in decision making which was suggested in the preceding paragraph. Not only is the individual experience with the phenomenon of a recession strictly limited but the variation in this experience within the same industry and company can be very great from one decade to the next. When it is also recognized that for certain companies the experience with debt was limited and that proportions varied significantly over time, the chances of that combination of maximum debt proportions and maximum contraction in sales that would provide a rigorous test of debt-bearing capacity were in a number of cases rather remote.

The plain fact is that the test of experience *as it is usually applied* is not necessarily a reliable test of debt-bearing capacity. The critical consideration of cash flow is, at any period in time, subject to a variety of influences which are to a considerable extent interdependent but which by no means operate in fixed patterns. These influences include the decisions of consumers as to the magnitude and timing of purchase orders, the capacity of the business to fill these orders either from inventory or production to order, the conventions and consumer practices with respect to payment following shipment of goods, the nature of the productive process and the manner in which materials and services are drawn into the production stream including necessary or conventional leads and lags, the manner of payment for such materials and services, and so on. The net cash flow during any given period of time is the combined result of the individual behavior patterns of these several influences, any particular combination of which may never recur during any imaginable forecast period. This behavior during a recession period is in part dependent on certain characteristics of the preceding period of prosperity and in part dependent on the response of these elements of cash flow during the recession period itself.

Recognizing these facts, it is apparent that there is no easily recognizable relationship between net cash flow and the customary measures of recession severity such as sales or net earnings. It is also apparent that the actual cash flow experience in any given recession period in the past and the impact of any given amount of debt thereon are unlikely to be an accurate guide as to the future should a recession occur again. Thus the confidence inspired by a debt policy that was successful in the past — in terms of freedom from the threat of insolvency — may well be false confidence. This is not to say that the evidence of past experience cannot be useful in formulating debt policy. Indeed, the approach to the question of debt capacity suggested in the remaining chapters of this study rests heavily on past experience. A vital distinction must be made, however, between an uncritical acceptance of the net results of experience and a critical evaluation of the full range of possibilities which a careful and detailed study of experience can reveal. The next chapter will deal directly with the broader implications of experience in a selected group of companies.

THE CONCEPT OF CONTINUOUS VERSUS DISCONTINUOUS BORROWING

One of the major considerations in the development of a concept of debt capacity is the question of whether it is to be applied on a continuous or discontinuous basis. It is apparent that the expected advantage of debt leverage in which the earning capacity of equity capital is extended by borrowing at a low fixed rate and investing at a higher rate is a function, not only of the rate differential and of the proportions of debt in the capital structure, but also of the period of time over which the leverage is exercised. Recognizing this fact some companies take a positive approach to the use of debt and think of debt capacity in terms of an "ideal" capital structure toward which management should always be striving. Other companies, on the other hand, take an essentially negative approach to the use of debt by thinking of it as something which under the pressure of circumstances may be assumed up to some "reasonable" level but which should be minimized and if possible eliminated as quickly as needs and alternative resources permit. These differing approaches are apparent in the observed practices with respect to debt policy and debt capacity described earlier in this study. The question arises as to whether either or both of these approaches "make sense" and if so under what circumstances.

In practice, circumstances in the typical industrial company tend to work against a policy of continuous borrowing at or near the desired debt limit. The evidence of this study supports general observation that within the accepted framework of investment opportunities for any given company there is a significant fluctuation in the need for funds over a period of years. This fluctuation leads to periods of exceptional need and also to periods of temporary excess of funds. With debt normally considered as the most flexible of long-term sources it tends to absorb the major shock of these changes, both up and down. Under these circumstances the maintenance of continuous leverage would require much greater flexibility in the use of equity capital (from either or both external and internal sources) than is apparent in common business practice. It is only in those situations where substantial long-term growth is a characteristic of the business or the industry — growth substantially in excess of the capacity of internally generated funds — where the practice of continuous debt leverage is to be observed among industrial companies.

Another factor that obviously works against the concept of continuous leverage is the attitude of the lender and the form of the typical industrial debt contract. The general practice in industrial loans, whether publicly or privately placed, is to require a regular repayment of most or all of the principal amount over the life of the loan. From the lender's point of view this serves the dual purpose of reducing the risk and increasing the flexibility of his loan portfolio in the face of uncertain trends in the interest rate. The repayment schedule invariably involves a straight-line formula of equal annual repayments with the possible exception of the first one or two years to allow for the start-up time on the income generation of the new investment. Such repayments are related not to the need for funds and their possible release from active employment but rather to income generation and the capacity of the user to replace debt by internally generated equity capital. In other words, the typical long-term industrial loan contract is deliberately designed so as to inhibit continuous borrowing and to ensure a continuous growth in the "cushion" of equity capital.

Of course there are ways of getting around this problem. Under certain favorable circumstances a borrower may arrange a series of overlapping loan agreements. It is also common practice to renegotiate privately placed loan contracts with the result that while the repayment schedule remains in effect, the unpaid principal amount is periodically revised upwards and the schedule is prevented from running its full course. Naturally such actions presume a continuing flow of new investment opportunities at a level in excess of the rate at which funds are internally generated and retained. At best, however, they lead to a variable debt component where the variations are usually of considerable magnitude and the average amount of debt outstanding is substantially below what might be considered a "safe" maximum.

In addition to these practical considerations, which make for discontinuous rather than continuous borrowing, mention should be made of variations in the availability of debt capital. There is no doubt that the financing decisions of many businesses are significantly influenced by periodic dips in the flow of capital through their customary sources of loan funds. An abundance of debt capital is unlikely, of itself, to cause debt proportions to rise above the accepted upper limit, but a shortage which coincides with a time of need may well cause debt proportions to fall below this level for a significant period of time. On the other hand, among the companies included in this study there was very little evidence that, *at the levels of debt which they were prepared to consider,* variations in the supply of debt capital — up or down — had a significant bearing on usage. Obviously the fact that these were typically large, mature, and profitable companies had a lot to do with this.

Apart from the practical limitations on continuous borrowing at any given level, it is still appropriate to consider whether the goal of continuous debt leverage is sound from the risk standpoint. Assuming that the basic considerations involved in the debt decision (the expected rewards and penalties, the probabilities of their occurrence, and the attitude toward risk bearing) do not change significantly over any given period of time, then it is perfectly rational to bear the risk continuously during that period. If any of these considerations should change, then of course it would be necessary to reappraise the debt policy and adjust the debt burden up or down as seems appropriate. If anything significant should happen to the expected return on the invested funds, either in amount or in certainty, to the probability of occurrence of cash insolvency, or to the basic willingness of the shareholders and management to bear the risk of insolvency, then, depending on the net result of any such changes, the amount of the fixed cash outflow associated with debt might be increased or reduced as soon as conditions permitted. As will be emphasized later, a rational debt policy requires continuing alertness to such changes and a detailed reappraisal whenever they occur.

In the light of these circumstances a policy that accentuates variations in the amount of debt outstanding, variations which bear no apparent relation to the kinds of changes mentioned above, does not appear to be entirely rational at least so far as income maximization is concerned. If the primary purpose in borrowing is to gain the advantages of income leverage and if after due consideration of the relevant factors it is considered appropriate to borrow up to some level, then it continues to be appropriate so long as this situation obtains, and management is under an obligation to explore ways and means of preserving the maximum appropriate leverage. To permit or to deliberately plan for a substantial and sustained reduction in debt below this level implies one or more of three conditions: (1) that considerations other than income maximization are governing policy; (2) that circumstances have in fact changed — for the worse — and that management is adjusting to them; or (3) that the level of debt which previously obtained was in fact "excessive" and management is seeking an early opportunity to restore a reasonable and appropriate level of leverage.

Observation suggests that all three of these conditions plus the influence of factors beyond managements' control have played a part in producing the widespread evidence of discontinuity in the use of long-term debt. With reference to number (3) above, there was evidence in several cases that while management considered it necessary to raise funds from time to time through debt, management was unwilling to bear this risk over extended periods of time, and consequently chose the first opportunity to substitute enough equity to restore the desired balance. Beyond this, however, it was also true that many managements did not really know the magnitude of the risks associated with any given amount of debt and therefore could not rationally appraise what the appropriate level should be. While under certain circumstances conservative management might be prepared to borrow funds in amounts which were in keeping with creditors' standards or general industry practice, the lurking fear remained that the risk might be excessive for their company and the obvious course of action was to reduce it, as circumstances permitted, to a nominal level or to eliminate it entirely. In the face of an unknown hazard, real peace of mind was obtainable only by complete elimination.

Assuming, however, that management approaches the decision rationally and in the light of the best information available on the pertinent considerations, including the magnitude of the risk involved, and concludes that some debt servicing can be carried, then the income objective will be best served by maintaining the debt at this level until such times as the pertinent considerations change. When change comes, in such factors as willingness to bear risk and the magnitude of the risk, it is likely to be gradual — which suggests that the sharp and erratic changes in the amount of long-term debt in use by some companies are not the result of a strictly logical and income-oriented process of reasoning.

THE FRAGMENTED APPROACH TO RISK APPRAISAL

Observation indicated that in the majority of cases management approached the problem of risk associated with debt on a total company basis. The decision was made as to whether the company as a whole could or could not borrow and if so, how much. As mentioned earlier in the description of the various forms of debt policy, however, some managements were disposed to take what may be called a fragmented approach. By this statement is meant that they tended to distinguish between the levels of risk associated with different investments and in line with this reasoning to recognize the possibility of debt financing for one (the less risky) and exclude the debt alternative for another (the more risky). This approach is illustrated by an example cited earlier of the machine tool company which would not consider debt financing for the production of a new internally developed and largely untested product but would use debt to acquire the assets and management of a going and profitable subsidiary, even though it was in the same or a related industry, because the payback, relatively speaking, was "proven."

This fragmented approach to risk appraisal has definite appeal, especially for the company which in its general operations is relatively risky and where from time to time investment opportunities are presented that are clearly in a different risk category. It suggests a simple and precise solution to the dilemma of debt magnitudes — which is to use debt to finance investments of low risk and equity to finance investments of high risk. The desired debt-equity proportions then become the automatic by-product of the particular balance of risky and "safe" investments undertaken by the company at any given time. Further, the debt-equity proportions would automatically shift as the balance of investments shifted.

It is the opinion of the author, however, that this line of reasoning can lead to faulty decisions. Since the fundamental problem is the event of cash insolvency, the only realistic boundaries to this problem are those imposed by the limits of legal liability. The solvency of any given corporate entity obviously cannot be subdivided; and distinctions among the patterns of cash flow associated with various investment projects, useful as they are for certain decision-making purposes, become meaningless when a company is pressed for cash to meet a specific obligation. The only exception to this might be where an investment opportunity is retained as a separate corporate entity (as a wholly or partially owned subsidiary).

Any company taken at any point in time has certain characteristics in its pattern of cash flows which determine the response of cash flow under recession conditions. These characteristics may be modified from time to time by the addition of new investments, the extent of the modification depending both on the extent of the departure from the general risk level and the relative magnitude of the new investment. Depending on its nature, the new investment may introduce a modification of the variability and timing of cash inflows, various expenditure categories — such as raw materials and labor, inventory levels, and the use of trade credit. The net effect may be to dampen or to accentuate the swings in cash flows, depending on the character and sequence of events in a particular recession period.

Although the net effect of any given investment does not necessarily work in the same direction under all circumstances, for the sake of argument we can assume that it does. Let it be assumed that a new investment made by a company is substantial and that it is clearly less risky than the kind of investment which characterizes the business as a whole. The recognition of this would lead some managements to consider debt as a means of financing this investment following the line of reasoning that the comparative certainty and stability of income warrant it. The fact is, however, that the investment appears "certain" only in comparison with the company's normal activities, that it is not by any means risk-free (unless it be the purchase of Federal Government bonds and even here risk can exist), and that therefore at best the risk characteristics of the new investment *may* justify debt as a means of financing *some portion* of it. If this is so, then it is only because the new investment has so altered the *over-all characteristics* of cash flow that the *company as a whole* is now in a position to safely bear some incremental fixed cash outflows for debt servicing. In any case the amount of the new investment is a meaningless guide for the decision as to how much of an increase in fixed cash outflows is warranted. To repeat — within a single corporate entity the risk of cash insolvency must be considered on a company-wide basis.

THE VALIDITY OF THE SINGLE CORPORATE DEBT LIMIT

For companies disposed to borrow, it is the invariable custom to think of a single company-wide standard for the upper limit of safe debt financing. Over a period of many years such a company is likely to operate on a rule such as that which precludes debt in excess of 25% of total capitalization. It will borrow up to but never deliberately in excess of this proportion (though adversity may reduce the equity to the point where the ratio is out of line). In previous discussion a question has been raised about the rationality of any *single* debt limit for a corporation, however that limit may be conceived, in view of the kinds of considerations which underlie the risk-bearing decision. Even assuming no change in the basic willingness to bear risk on the part of the corporate ownership (or in management's understanding thereof), there are still likely to be changes in the magnitude of the risk confronting the business from time to time and in the rewards for risk bearing in terms of the expected rates of return on investments.

Consequently a rational weighing of the potential rewards and penalties resulting from debt financing of investment opportunities, and of their related probabilities of occurrence, may be expected to lead to a concept of debt capacity which varies with any significant modification of one or more of these considerations. As a minimum this approach to the problem suggests continuing alertness and periodic reappraisal of a company's standard of debt capacity. It also suggests that it may be quite appropriate for a company to change its debt limit, up or down, from time to time with no deliberate trend in one direction or another.

If this is so, then it seems surprising that so many companies show such a high degree of rigidity in their debt capacity standards over extended periods of time, giving the appearance at least of an "absolute" concept of capacity rather than a relative one as suggested above. What is even more surprising is a common acceptance of the idea that it is possible to generalize about the debt capacity of a whole industry and, indeed, of such a vast conglomeration of businesses encompassed by the broad category of "manufacturing industries." One of the most surprising results of the field study was the frequency with which lenders and borrowers cited a 30% (or 33⅓%) of capitalization debt limit as the appropriate guide for some members of the diverse group of companies and industries represented.

There were, of course, situations where there was considerable stability in the underlying factors involved in the debt financing decision. Assuming no change in the general make-up of the shareholder group or in its circumstances and objectives, no change in management personnel and viewpoint and no basic shifts in the character of the industry in which the company is engaged, then it is reasonable to expect that a company will have a relatively fixed standard of debt capacity. Within the customary range of investment opportunities in an industry there will, of course, be variations in expected return on investment and in the uncertainty or risk associated therewith. The company debt standard reflects an averaging of the risks within this customary range of opportunities, however, and it would be unrealistic and, in fact, unsound to expect a company to make frequent adjustments in its appraisal of risk and in its debt capacity standard to allow for every temporary shift in the balance which a random sequence of investment opportunities would produce.

In contrast there were other situations where it was clear that there were major and relatively permanent shifts taking place in the company's "investment portfolio" or where the corporate entity had no single industry affiliation and ranged over a wide variety of investment opportunities. Thus without assuming any change in the willingness to bear risk there was good reason to expect that the concept of debt capacity should have been re-examined and probably changed significantly. The fact that this re-examination did not always occur is undoubtedly due in considerable measure to debt standards which were largely or entirely unrelated to the circumstances of the individual firm and to the related fact that most managements interviewed did not have a workable formalized approach to the appraisal of risk within the company which would enable them to clearly identify the ranking of investment opportunities in terms of risk or to establish a trend. It is not surprising that when debt standards are drawn from the sources described at the beginning of this chapter — where they are largely subjective or drawn from the folklore of finance, from observed industry practice, or from the pronouncements of creditors — these standards tend to remain fixed over an indefinite period of time. Provided the standards are sufficiently conservative, experience only tends to confirm their validity in the minds of the users.

One of the dangers of the fixed single standard is that it gives an unwarranted impression of absoluteness. At times such standards appear to be employed as if debt up to some predetermined level involves no risk but debt beyond that level produces a sharp and unacceptable increase in risk. This can be very dangerous thinking. The fact is that any net addition to fixed cash outflows involves *some* risk and that increases of whatever magnitude necessarily heighten the risk. As this study stated at the outset, the debt limit decision is not a choice between some risk and no risk *but a choice as to the level of risk which management and the owners are willing to assume in the interests of basic corporate objectives.*

Among the companies observed in the field study there were instances of significant changes in the concept of debt capacity. While these were not numerous, there was enough evidence to suggest at least three important reasons for such changes in practice. The evidence was not sufficient to indicate a ranking of these in order of importance relative to each other or to other possible motivating circumstances. One reason for a change in the concept of debt capacity was illustrated in the change in the character of the rubber industry which has been referred to earlier in this study. It became generally accepted in the industry that the shift to synthetic rubber and fibers plus the growth of the replacement market in tires had all worked together to stabilize the industry and substantially reduce the risks of investment. Since the change was recognized as substantial and of long-term significance, it was generally agreed among the rubber companies included in the study that their capacity to bear long-term debt with safety had substantially increased. It should be noted, however, that this did not lead all the companies in question immediately to so modify their policies as to create the circumstances favorable to a substantial increase in borrowing.

A second and important reason for a change in the concept of debt capacity was a change in the personnel comprising the decision-making group. It is clear that the use of debt is a subject on which there can be sharp differences of opinion not only from one company to another but also within the same management group. The policy that prevails at any time depends very much on whose voice dominates management councils. This brings out once again the highly subjective nature of the risk appraisal in many cases. If the dominant personality is aggressive, venturesome, expansion-minded, then the company is likely to have a debt policy to match. If, on the other hand, he is (or they are) conservative and preoccupied with conserving and preserving the company's accumulated resources, then the debt policy will be of a totally different character. It is obvious that under such circumstances the replacement of a key man — the chairman of the board, president, or financial vice president — by a man of a distinctly different stamp may profoundly affect debt policy and the accepted standard of debt capacity. Mention has been made before of the noticeable change in attitude between men who had executive responsibility during the depression of the early thirties and those who had not.

A third reason for a change was the matter of financial need. In Chapter 4 the importance of the recognized need for funds in shaping the pattern of debt usage was emphasized. It was also brought out that most companies experienced a periodic peaking of need which could be substantially in excess of current internal generation of funds. It might be assumed that on such occasions a company would be ready to borrow up to its predetermined debt capacity and either find alternative equity sources if a further need existed or postpone the remaining expenditures. There were instances, however, where the need seemed so urgent and the equity alternatives so undesirable that management abandoned, at least temporarily, its earlier standard. This raises a question as to whether the earlier standard was a valid limit or merely a talking point which suited the circumstances of the moment. Evidence suggests that both situations existed and that it was possible for management to continue to believe in the predetermined debt limit as the proper long-term guide while at the same time yielding under pressure to assume an excessive risk for a short period of time. Where there was an unusual degree of confidence in the prospects for that particular period and a chance to reduce the debt back to "reasonable" levels, management might not consider this as an excessive risk situation. If the experience proved that the company could carry the new level of debt indefinitely without apparent hazard, then this might become a new long-term debt capacity standard.

Considering these three circumstances under which there were changes in corporate practice with respect to debt capacity and relating them to the approach adopted in this study, it may be observed that they are not any of them necessarily in conflict with that approach. It should be expected that if there is a significant change in the nature and degree of risk, in the willingness to bear risk (as reflected in the persons making the decision), or in the rewards from risk bearing (as reflected in the urgency of the need), there should be a reappraisal of the debt capacity standard and probably a change in that standard. On the other hand, it was also apparent in many cases that management had not gone as far as it could in appraising the magnitude of the risk of cash insolvency or the impact of any given amount of debt on that risk. Similarly there was no reliable evidence that a change in willingness to bear risk as reflected in the personality of the decision maker necessarily reflected a similar change in the willingness on the part of those (the shareholders) who were actually bearing the financial risk. Finally, it was not at all certain that in yielding to the pressure of the current need for funds management was consciously weighing the potential rewards and penalties as opposed to merely following the dictates of expediency, unaware of the true magnitude of the associated risks.

THE QUANTITATIVE FORM OF DEBT CAPACITY STANDARDS

A description of the specific standards of debt policy found to be in use among the companies included in the study was given in Chapter 5 (pages 94–106). These included the formulae for determining the appropriate limits of borrowing where such existed. In this section it was pointed out that some such formulae clearly passed the responsibility for risk appraisal to the creditor and we have already discussed the weaknesses of this course of action. We have also discussed the limitations of a "one shot" or discontinuous approach to debt which was evident in certain standards. We now turn to a consideration of the validity of the specific quantitative criteria used by companies which had assumed the responsibility for individual appraisal of risk and which approached borrowing, in theory at least, as a continuous concept.

In this regard there were two commonly accepted ways of quantifying a debt capacity standard — Decision Rules 5 and 6 as described on pages 100 to 105. These two approaches, Percent of

Capitalization and Earnings Coverage, will now be discussed in turn.

The Balance Sheet Standard — Percent of Capitalization

It appears to be almost universal practice in business among lenders and borrowers to think of debt magnitudes in terms of the principal as a fraction of total asset values, asset values being measured according to conventional accounting concepts. The balance sheet is the document from which the data are drawn for a measure of debt at any point in time. The advantages of a standard expressed in these terms were reviewed in Chapter 5. The standard is simple, apparently precise, and expressed in terms which are commonly understood. These characteristics are particularly desirable for the purposes of workable contractual covenants in connection with which there is the additional important feature that (asset) values are subject to periodic confirmation by an independent authority — the auditor — through the annual financial report. Further, the standard automatically adjusts for any change in the owners' investment which presumably stands behind the safety of the loan.

These are, however, considerations of contractual convenience and do not have any necessary bearing on the primary question of the risk of insolvency. For the standard to be meaningful there must be a measurable relationship between the standard and the element of risk so that changes in the criterion reliably reflect changes in the degree of risk. For practical purposes this relationship must be comparatively simple and direct. The commonly accepted rule with respect to capitalization ratios is, of course, that the higher the proportion of debt, the greater the risk of insolvency. Following the same line of reasoning, if the percentage remained constant over a period this could be interpreted as a constant risk factor.

In an earlier era much significance was attached by creditors to the values assumed to be inherent in individual assets, and safety was judged in part by the cushion of asset values in excess of those directly financed by the debt. In addition to the fact that experience, particularly with specialized industrial assets, has shown this to be an unreliable test of safety, it is apparent that the cushion of asset values is a liquidation concept. Our concern — the concern of the borrower — is with a decision rule which will prevent the event of insolvency and liquidation from occurring.

To repeat — a satisfactory debt criterion must reliably reflect the impact of changes in debt on the risk of cash insolvency. The conclusion of this study is that balance sheet ratios are in this respect unnecessarily crude and unreliable and as a result can be a dangerous way of expressing a risk-bearing standard, at least so far as industrial borrowers are concerned. The balance sheet proportion of debt can change significantly with no change in the risk and vice versa. Further, comparisons of such ratios among companies can lead to misleading conclusions. Illustrations of these statements follow.

One of the main reasons for the inadequacy of the balance sheet standard lies in the fact that industrial loans invariably require the serial repayment of the principal amount over the life of the loan. For the typical term loan the amount of the principal repayment is at least as large as and may be considerably larger than the interest payment and is not deductible for tax purposes. It is obviously therefore of great importance in the picture of cash flows. The significance of this method of repayment will be apparent — *as the debt proportion declines over the life of the term loan and the balance sheet picture steadily "improves," the amount of the annual cash drain associated with the debt remains fixed right up to the last payment.* The declining debt proportions may decrease the risk to the lender (in the sense of the secondary line of defense of asset values), but the change does not in any way directly diminish the risk of cash insolvency to the borrower until the debt is fully repaid. In fact, in a limited sense, the risk may be considered to increase since the last year often requires a balloon repayment of principal substantially larger than the previous annual amounts.

A related consideration is the wide variation in the term of such industrial loans. In the experience of this study they varied from 5 to 100 years with a common range between 10 and 25 years. It can be seen that with the principal repayment representing such an important part of the burden of debt on cash flows, the term of the loan is of great importance to the risk. Given any principal amount of debt the hazard to cash solvency could vary significantly depending on the term and the decision on balloon payments. The simple debt-equity proportions do not reflect such variations.

It should also be recognized that while amounts of debt are clearly fixed by contract and change only according to the specific terms of the contract, the asset values as shown on the balance sheet are not nearly so reliable. It is unnecessary here to discuss the reasons why accounting values are subject from time to time to significant changes quite unrelated to cash flows and hence unrelated to the problem of cash solvency. To illustrate, changes in inventory values and depreciation rates directly affect the debt-equity ratio but need not have any direct bearing on the amount or timing of cash flowing into the business.

On the other hand, there can be changes in the composition of the company's assets which, although they do not change the debt-equity ratio, may have great importance for the solvency of the company. A build-up of the proportion of highly liquid assets in a period of prosperity can be of enormous significance for the chances of survival in an ensuing recession and likewise for a decline in this proportion. It may be added that increasing attention has been given recently to certain off-the-balance-sheet items (e.g., lease contracts) which again bear directly on the problem of cash solvency.

This is not a complete list of the inadequacies of this standard but should be sufficient to show that it is much too crude to be reliable. To be fair to many of those who continue to use this standard, it should be said that they are not all as naive as they may appear. The more sophisticated look on the debt-equity ratio as a rough but adequate measure of the relationship between the amount of debt servicing and the net earnings available for this purpose. It is assumed that the smaller the proportion of debt financing of earning assets the greater will be the earnings coverage. The discussion of this section has pointed out the many qualifications that would have to be introduced in order that this might be roughly valid. The discussion of the next section will bring out the reasons why the author believes that there are also weaknesses in the earnings coverage approach and why a new approach is needed.

The Income Statement Standard — Earnings Coverage

The introduction of the Earnings Coverage criterion for debt capacity represented a substantial advance beyond the debt-equity ratio. This ratio focuses directly on the dollars required for the annual servicing of corporate debt and relates them to the net earnings that the income statement shows are available to meet such payments. While it is sometimes applied to interest charges alone, it is more properly related to interest plus sinking fund payments and would appear as follows:

$$\frac{Available\ Net\ Earnings\ (Before\ Taxes)}{Interest + \left[S.F.\ Payments \times \left(\frac{1}{1 - Tax\ Rate} \right) \right]}$$

The denominator in this ratio represents the total amount of before-tax income necessary to equal the interest and sinking fund payments, and the numerator would be expected to be some multiple of this — say 2:1 or 3:1, depending on the assumed degree of risk. The Net Earnings are those which remain after all other expenses of the period, except federal corporate income taxes, have been provided for. They represent some sort of "normal earnings" concept, and the margin by which they exceed the debt servicing is presumably enough so that in the event of a recession the earnings available for debt servicing will not fall below the amount needed.

The use of an earnings coverage standard for debt capacity, by shifting attention away from assets to what they actually earn and away from the principal amount of debt to the related fixed annual cash outflow, moves a long way in the direction of relating the standard to the factors directly involved in cash solvency. Obviously several of the potential misconceptions inherent in the balance sheet standard are avoided. In view of this it is a little surprising that the standard was not found in common use except by insurance companies and some investment bankers.

In spite of its advantages, however, two major problems detract from the usefulness of the earnings coverage standard. One relates to the question as to whether Net Earnings is an adequate representation of the *cash* available for debt servicing, since in the last analysis solvency can only be preserved if the ability to make cash payments on time is assured. The other relates to the question of the precise meaning of the "coverage" and how the minimum adequate coverage (maximum debt service burden) is to be determined. Taking up these questions in order, it may be noted that some analysts would make the earnings coverage ratio more of a cash flow comparison by adding back noncash expenses to the item of Net Income (principally depreciation charges). With this important exception, however, the ratio relates the annual cash burden of debt to annual income as defined by the conventions of accrual accounting. Under certain circumstances net income, particularly when adjusted for noncash expenses, can be a reasonable approximation of net cash inflow. Under other circumstances it may be a very misleading indicator of cash flow and this is particularly likely to be the case in industrial companies during the recession periods with which the risk analysis is inevitably preoccupied.

At this point only a few of the more obvious discrepancies will be pointed out. The complete description of a full cash flow analysis given in the following chapter will bring out the potential inadequacies of the earnings coverage standard more forcefully. One obvious point of difference is that between Sales and Cash Receipts. So long as the level of sales is more or less static or gradually adjusted from year to year, the difference between these two can probably be ignored. If, however, there is a sudden sharp change in the Sales level, the differences may be significant. If there is a substantial lag in the timing of Collections behind Sales and there is no major lengthening of the Collection Period coincident with the Sales decline, there will be a release of cash as Accounts Receivable decline which is not apparent on the income statement. Likewise there may also be an important difference between Cost of Goods Sold and expenditures for goods produced, the latter being the cash consideration. The drawing down of inventory as a substitute for current production can make a great deal of difference in the recession cash flow picture. There may of course be offsetting changes in the short-term credit extended to the company but there is no reason to believe that these will necessarily counterbalance each other.

Similarly there are other important items of cash flow which do not show up on the income statement. One of these, capital expenditures, is sometimes allowed for by omitting the noncash expense adjustment in the ratio on the grounds that these two will roughly cancel out. This method also appears to be unnecessarily crude and possibly dangerous. Another item, dividend payments, is commonly dismissed on the grounds that these are not mandatory and therefore do not enter into the consideration of the risk of insolvency. This study has emphasized, however, that the debt decision is being approached from the point of view of management — not the creditor — and that some demands on cash although not mandatory in a legal sense may be so for decision-making purposes.

To turn to the second problem which stands in the way of a usable and reliable earnings coverage criterion for debt capacity, it can be seen that such a criterion does not come with a built-in guide as to the desirable margin of safety. Investment literature contains flat assertions regarding the minimum permissible ratio for investment purposes and lenders have their rules of thumb. Similarly it is possible to draw conclusions from data in the balance sheets and income statements of comparable companies. The limitations of such sources have already been described. Commonly the earnings coverage ratios are stated with reference to broad industry groupings and are not normally refined beyond the "all manufacturing" category. The ratios are commonly expressed in multiples of one (2:1, 3:1) and distinctions are never carried beyond a .5 differential (2½:1 vs. 3:1). It should be noted that when such differences are translated into amounts of debt the distinctions are quite crude and a choice between 2:1 and 3:1 or even 2½:1 and 3:1 will make a significant difference in the permissible debt burden.

The determining considerations in this choice lie *behind* the Available Net Income figure in the behavior of income and expenditures which lead to variations from year to year. So long as these variations have the potential of reducing Net Income to zero or below, the debt servicing would be vulnerable no matter what the margin of Earnings Coverage, be it 10 or even 20 to 1. Thus for any particular company a realistic choice of the appropriate margin of safety over debt burden would require a careful examination of patterns of behavior within the circumstances of the individual firm. In this respect there are major differences from one industry to another within the manufacturing group which are obscured by an "all manufacturing" standard.

This line of reasoning — that a meaningful Earnings Coverage standard can be developed only by a careful examination of the patterns of variation of income and expense in a given situation (or comparable group) — leads to the conclusion that *the most useful approach to an appraisal of risk and a meaningful debt standard lies in such an analysis — but not in terms of accounting values, rather in terms of cash flows.* The next chapter is devoted to the description of a method for such an analysis.

Before proceeding to this recommended approach as an alternative to the conventional standards of debt capacity, one further comment should be added. In general the common practices with respect to debt standards have been described in this chapter as unnecessarily crude and at times meaningless and misleading. This is a harsh comment on the financial practices of many well-managed and obviously successful businesses. Further, there is no reason to believe that the companies included in the study were atypical in this respect. There appear to be four main reasons why this situation exists in industry today:

(1) The debt concepts of public utility finance developed in an earlier era have been uncritically adopted in an area of business activity and in a debt framework where they do not apply.

(2) The corporate financial officer has all too frequently sought his standards in those of the creditor and investor where crude criteria may not only be adequate but necessary due to time and data limitations.

(3) Many corporate financial people have not been stimulated to think through the full implications of risk associated with fixed obligations.

(4) Many who are aware of the job to be done and have the data to do it believe that the cost of such an analysis would outweigh the possible gains in refinement.

It is the contention of this study that this last reason is invalid. The cash flow analysis proposed in the next chapter is considered essential not only to a sensible debt decision but also to many other related financial decisions. In spite of the fact that it does require a considerable expenditure of executive time and some money, the educational benefits of conducting such an analysis and the information it provides have a potential which far outweighs whatever cost may be involved.

CHAPTER 7

A Cash Flow Analysis for the
Appraisal of Risk and the Determination of
Long-Term Debt Capacity

INTRODUCTION

Two purposes of this study of debt capacity have now been accomplished. One has been to describe how a sample of industrial corporations think and how they behave with respect to the use of long-term debt. The other has been to examine the rational framework of existing decision rules regarding the use of debt and form some judgments on their validity for the purposes in mind. This second phase of the study of debt capacity criteria has suggested a number of inherent and operative limitations to conventional criteria. These are considered so serious that a third phase is required, namely, the exploration of alternative approaches to the debt capacity decision. One such approach is developed in this and the succeeding chapter. The objective of this third phase is not only to suggest a different and hopefully a better way for a company to look at its debt capacity but also to provide a basis for further appraisal of the validity of decision rules currently in use. Illustration of the latter objective will be the subject of the final chapter.

A basic criticism which the preceding chapters have levied against conventional debt capacity rules is that they are derived from sources external to the business concerned, are cast in a form which is more appropriate to the lender than to the borrower, and do not provide a means for relating the rule to individual company circumstances. Thus the primary point of departure for this study is to develop an approach to debt capacity that grows out of a knowledge of the risks in the individual firm and that can therefore be sharply contrasted with generalized rules of thumb. The evidence of debt capacity thus produced is internally rather than externally generated. It should be clearly understood that the aim is not to replace existing debt capacity rules. A borrower or potential borrower must of necessity take account of how others view his capacity to assume debt, however irrational that view may be. The aim is rather to reduce management's dependence on outside opinion and enable it to develop appropriate modifications of debt policy consistent with individual circumstances.

At the end of the preceding chapter, the general direction of an internal appraisal of risk and of debt capacity was indicated. It lies in a study of the behavior of cash flows within the firm and in particular with the circumstances under which shortages of cash might develop and threaten the ability to fulfill fixed cash commitments. This chapter is concerned almost exclusively with methodology, and it will describe in some detail a cash flow approach to the debt question. For those who are more interested in the results of the analysis than in the method of getting there, Chapters 8 and 9 where these results are described and discussed will doubtless be more interesting. However, the usefulness (and limitations) of the results will not be fully appreciated unless there is at least a general understanding of how the results were obtained.

THE OBJECTIVES OF A CASH FLOW ANALYSIS

The conventional debt capacity rule such as that long-term debt should not exceed 30% of total capitalization clearly implies that debt in excess of this limit is "too risky." Just what this phrase means is not always clear as earlier chapters of this study have indicated. The obvious inference may be drawn, however, that if further additions are made to fixed debt servicing charges the time may come when the company does not have enough cash to go around. In the extreme case this may mean that there is not enough cash to meet legal commitments and hence the company would be insolvent. In a less extreme form it may mean that under such circumstances the drain of debt servicing would prevent management from covering expenditures it desires to preserve — for any one of a variety of reasons. This situation will be called in this study "cash inadequacy" as opposed to cash insolvency.

We have already alluded to the obvious fact of private enterprise life that inflows are uncertain and therefore that *some* chance of these adverse events occurring exists regardless of whether there is debt in the capital structure. Thus a 30% or any other debt rule represents someone's arbitrary judgment that above this point the chances of occurrence of these adverse events have become so high as to be intolerable to those who would experience the adverse effects. The reader is once again reminded of the need to separate the appraisal of risk magnitudes from the subjective decision as to whether the rewards from risk bearing warrant the assumption of risks of any given magnitude. The cash flow analysis is concerned only with the former. The possibilities of a formal treatment of the willingness to bear risk along the lines of utility theory will not be attempted. If, however, it is possible by means of a cash flow analysis to come up with objective evidence on the magnitude of the risks involved with any given level of debt, then by comparison with existing debt capacity rules it is possible to draw inferences as to management's willingness to bear risk. This will be attempted in Chapter 9.

Turning to the immediate objective, therefore, the goal of Chapters 7 and 8 is to develop an approach which provides as much information as possible on the chance of any given company "running out of cash." As the discussion develops, it will be seen that an analysis of the risk of cash inadequacy, of which cash insolvency is the extreme case, can become highly complex, involving a variety of sophisticated mathematical and statistical techniques. It is not the purpose of this study to lay out the framework of a comprehensive and rigorous analysis of risk. Neither the necessary data nor the techniques have been developed for a working model which could be applied to the illustrative cases. Rather the purpose has been to carry such an analysis as far as it seems practical to go using cash flow data which is readily derived from conventional financial records and analytical concepts which can be readily integrated with the conventional framework of financial decision making. The intention has been to suggest something of immediate usefulness in business practice. At the same time, however, this approach although relatively crude by any rigorous standards is intended to be logically sound. The requirement of practical usefulness imposes significant limitations on refinement of analysis but not on logical consistency.

Throughout this chapter the analysis will focus on the extreme case of cash inadequacy — the event of cash insolvency. This is the hazard which has been traditionally associated with excessive borrowing and which debt limits have been designed to prevent. In the initial examination of the behavior of cash inflows and outflows, we shall be concerned with the margin between inflows and unavoidable, nonpostponable outflows — that is, outflows which are vital to corporate continuity. This would include not only expenditures that are mandatory in a contractual sense, such as bond interest, but also the minimum expenditures required to sustain current sales and maintain the available cash inflow from sales. Other expenditures which have longer term implications, such as dividend payments, certain capital expenditures, and the like will be considered discretionary and will be brought into consideration in Chapter 8 where the lesser risks of cash inadequacy will be considered along with cash insolvency.

With respect to the risk of cash insolvency, we would like information on the following basic questions:

(1) Given a company's current financial condition and capital structure, its record of past experience and current expectations, is there a possibility that it may face the event of cash insolvency during the period a debt contract would remain in force?

(2) If this event does appear possible within the limits set by an objective analysis of cash flow behavior, what is the magnitude of the chance of its occurrence — what are the "odds" of its happening?

(3) How are these odds affected by the addition of any given amount of debt?

We now proceed to see how far we can go in answering these questions which are critical to a rational decision on debt capacity.

CASH FLOWS AND THE EVENT OF CASH INSOLVENCY

Management's expectations as to future cash flows will inevitably be strongly influenced by its experience with cash flows in the past.

Thus the raw data of any cash flow analysis will largely consist of the historical record as it exists in financial documents and in the minds of those who were involved. This study has already raised strong objections to the simple "test of experience," however, which draws impressions from the specific events of the past and concludes that these events constitute an adequate test of the future. History need not repeat itself — at least so far as any precise set of relationships is concerned. Consequently, a way for using the evidence of past experience must be found which avoids the fallacy of blindly extrapolating the past into the future.

In recent years, there have been important developments in the application of cash budgeting to financial decisions. In some companies such forecasting of cash flows has been developed to a high degree and with considerable success. It is quite apparent that in such instances the evidence of the past and the impressions of the present are carefully and intelligently blended to produce meaningful expectations for the future which may be considered relevant to the problem posed in this study. Unfortunately, however, cash forecasts are as yet seriously limited as to the period over which projections can be made with confidence. The findings of this study support common observation that confidence drops off sharply beyond the period of a year. Thus while such forecasts may tell a great deal about the chances of insolvency in the immediate future (six months to a year), the tool of analysis has not yet been developed in a form which is useful for the period covered by the typical long-term debt contract. Forecasting of the exact nature and timing of the pattern of events in a business is still a relatively crude art and not one upon which most managements are likely to base fundamental risk decisions.

Considering the dark void of the future which lies beyond the brief range of light cast by the current market expectations and the related cash forecast, management may be inclined to assume that "anything can happen." While this cannot be denied, it is a mistake to assume that available evidence on cash flows is totally irrelevant so far as the longer term future is concerned. Clearly some assumption must be made about the course of events in the more distant future, and it is the responsibility of management to make this as sensible as possible.

For the purpose of this analysis, it will be assumed that the primary concern of debt policy with respect to risk is a concern with what would happen under conditions of an industry or general business recession.   This is an obvious over-simplification since there are other circumstances which could precipitate cash insolvency — for example, bad management or a prolonged strike. This study has been approached from the point of view of mature, basically profitable, and apparently well-managed companies, however, and in such companies it is the event of a possible recession or depression which appears to be the center of concern with respect to the risk of debt.   Thus the analysis will be concerned with the expected behavior of cash inflows and outflows during recession periods.   In line with the preceding statements about the limited range of business forecasts, we must assume that management cannot tell when such recessions will occur and thus must be prepared for a decline in cash inflows at any time during the life of the debt contract.   At the same time, however, past experience does provide some evidence as to what may be expected when such recessions do occur and from this some estimates may be made as to the probable impact on net cash flows.

THE DETERMINANTS OF CASH FLOW

In the preceding chapter it was pointed out that the Earnings Coverage form of debt capacity standard is generally intended as a crude approximation of risk measurement in cash flow terms — the higher the risk the higher the required cushion of "normal" net earnings available for debt servicing in excess of debt servicing charges.   In this sense the flow of net earnings is assumed to be the rough equivalent of a flow of cash of comparable size.   By subtracting the amount of the debt servicing from a net earnings figure which is some multiple thereof, the remainder presumably represents the anticipated shrinkage in annual cash inflow which would result under recession conditions.   In theory such a standard if properly defined would provide absolute protection against the risk of cash insolvency from debt since the assumption is that the earnings (cash) available for debt servicing would not get below a 1:1 relationship even under recession conditions.

It was pointed out in Chapter 6 that while such a standard may be adequate for creditors' loan portfolios it is inadequate from the borrowers' point of view.   Net earnings as described by the conventional income statement (even adjusted for noncash charges) does not provide a reliable measure of net cash flows, particularly in periods of substantial changes in the scale of operations, and the potential shrinkage in cash flows during a recession can only be assessed by taking the behavior of *all* major determinants of cash flow into consideration. We now turn to the task of describing total cash flow and of identifying its primary determinants as the first step of the analysis. As a means of simplifying this description, some simple symbols will be used and so far as possible these symbols will relate to the first letters of the words or phrases they stand for.

The ultimate concern of this analysis is with the probability that net cash balances during some future recession period (CB_r) will be involuntarily reduced to zero. This will happen if net cash flows during the recession (NCF_r) become negative and the deficit flow is large enough and lasts long enough to exhaust the cash balances on hand at the onset of the recession (CB_0). The relationship here may be expressed in general terms as follows:

$$CB_r = CB_0 \pm NCF_r$$

For the moment we will consider the entire recession as one period and the critical segment of time is the period up to the low point of the recession or alternatively, if NCF becomes negative at some stage, the period up to the point where it turns positive again.

The figure for net cash flow for any period is obviously the result of Total Inflows minus Total Outflows. In proceeding to describe the customary make-up of inflows and outflows in an industrial firm, we have a choice between a description in purely cash terms of receipts and payments and a description in terms of a conversion of accounting data back into cash equivalents.

Contrast, for example, the specific cash expenditures required to produce a given number of units during a year — the direct labor payroll, raw material, purchases, etc. — versus an approximation derived by working back from Costs of Goods Sold by taking account of changes in Inventory levels. Since this is an analysis intended primarily for internal purposes and since it is reasonable to assume that the internal analyst has ready access to a large amount of primary cash flow data, it seems unnecessarily roundabout to derive cash data from conventional accrual accounting records and statements. For a variety of reasons, however, this study will describe the component elements of cash flow in both cash and accounting terms. One of these reasons is that the approach can be used by the external analyst (including the author) whose starting point will be conventional account records. Another and perhaps equally important reason is that many internal analysts and decision makers find it convenient to think in terms of accrual accounting approximations of cash flow.

Expressed in purely cash terms, the recession net cash flow can be shown in an oversimplified form as follows:

$$NCF_r = (C_s + OR) - (P_a + RM + \cdots + E_n)$$

where:

C_s	represents	Collections from Sales
OR	"	Other Receipts in Cash Form
P_a	"	Expenditures for Payroll
RM	"	Expenditures for Raw Materials
E_n	"	the last of a series of such nondiscretionary cash expenditures.

(At this point the reader is again reminded that this chapter will focus only on those items of cash flow which are mandatory in the sense of being continuously and unavoidably associated with current sales and income generation.)

As previously asserted, NCF_r is not the same as Net Income for the period and this can best be emphasized by converting an income statement into a cash flow statement. Very briefly, Net Income (NI) can be expressed as follows:

$$NI \ (B.T.) = S - (CGS + SGA)$$
$$NI \ (A.T.) = .48 \ NI \ (B.T.)$$

where:

S	represents	Sales
CGS	"	Cost of Goods Sold
SGA	"	Selling, General, and Administrative Expense

and *B.T.* and *A.T.* represent Before (federal income) Tax and After Tax. Using balance sheet as well as income statement data, *NCF* may be expressed in the following general form:

$$NCF = \{(AR_0 + S - AR_1) + OI\} - \{[CGP + SGA + T] + [(AP_0 - AP_1) + (AE_0 - AE_1)]\}$$

where new symbols introduced are:

AR_0 which represents Accounts Receivable at the beginning of the Period

AR_1 " " Accounts Receivable at the end of the Period

OI " " Other Income

CGP " " Cost of Goods Actually Produced

T " " Federal Income Tax

AP_0, AP_1 " " Accounts Payable

AE_0, AE_1 " " Accrued Expenses

It should be noted that in order to convert credit sales into gross cash inflow it must be considered as an addition to Accounts Receivable and the cash inflow is then the liquidation of Accounts Receivable during the period. On the outflow side Cost of Goods Produced represents a variation from Cost of Goods Sold not only because noncash expenses are ignored but also because account is taken of the extent to which current orders have been filled out of inventory or conversely current production has added to inventory. Finally, the various legitimate expenses of the period are converted into expenditures by taking account of any changes in payment lags reflected in Accounts Payable and Accrued Expenses.

The two statements of Net Cash Flow on page 163 may be placed side by side as follows:

	NCF	$=$	Inflow	$-$	Outflow
Cash Flow Symbols			$C_s + OR$		$P_a + RM + \cdots + E_n$
Accounting Symbols			$(AR_0 + S - AR_1) + OI$		$[CGP + SGA + T] +$
					$[(AP_0 - AP_1) +$
					$(AE_0 - AE_1)]$

One intended effect of this symbolic representation is to emphasize that a consideration of the prospects for cash solvency involves far more than merely a comparison of debt servicing charges with net income levels. Solvency cannot be segmented and an appraisal of risks must of necessity involve all major dimensions of cash flow. Of greater immediate importance, however, is the point that the first step in a process of risk appraisal is to identify the major elements of cash flows, variations in which collectively determine the variation in Net Cash Flow. These elements or determinants of cash inflow and outflow, such as Sales volume or Inventory levels, will be loosely referred to in this study as the *determinants* of cash flow. The identification of all major determinants is an obvious prerequisite to observation of the effect of changes in their behavior on NCF and hence on CB.

Looking back over this and the previous section, the reader will observe that the cash position of the company at the low point of a recession (CB_r) is going to be influenced not only by the initial cash position (CB_0) and the behavior of the determinants of cash flow during the recession period but also by certain aspects of the company's financial condition immediately preceding the recession (designated as Period Zero). Thus AR_0 represents potential cash inflow in addition to the Sales of the recession period, I_0 (Inventory, beginning of period) represents an anticipation of expenditures necessary to meet the Sales of the recession period, and AP_0 represents expenditures over and above those related to the specific items produced and sold in this period. A complete analysis of recession cash flows must take these factors into account.

The Underlying Causes of Change in Net Cash Flow

In considering the circumstances under which NCF might become negative to the point where CB_0 would be reduced to zero, the first step is obviously to consider the recession behavior of the several determinants of inflow and outflow noted in the preceding section. The determinant of dominant significance is, of course, Sales (S), and we can begin with a consideration of the recession behavior of Sales drawing on past experience and present knowledge to create sensible expectations for the future. Similarly, separate consideration can be given to collection experience on Accounts Receivable under recession conditions and expectations here can be combined with expectations for Sales levels to produce the anticipated recession behavior of C_s. The various determinants of outflow can then be examined one by one with the objective of relating individual recession behavior to Net Cash Flow.

In examining these various determinants of cash inflow and outflow, it becomes apparent that we are dealing more with the effects of change than with causes. There is danger in taking the word "determinant" too literally. The danger is twofold. First, there is the possibility that in examining the historical record of recession experience the full potential of change may be obscured. For example, changes in dollar sales are normally the net result of changes in physical volume, price, and the mix of products sold. Changes in each of these may at one time be offsetting but it is also possible that they may be reinforcing, and unless the possible variations in each of these elements of dollar sales are identified the possible variations in dollar sales may be understated. The second danger of failing to probe for underlying causes of change is that inter-relationships and interdependence among the various determinants of inflow and outflow may not be identified. Thus, for example, the factors making for a decline in sales volume may also produce a lengthening of the collection period. Such information would be vital to the prediction of adverse limits of net cash flow behavior in a recession period.

It is therefore essential to look behind the historical record of variation in the elements of cash flow if the full potential of recession cash flow behavior is to be described. Here a critical examination of the historical data coupled with the knowledge and experience of competent management can be of great value in identifying the significant dimensions. There is undoubtedly room for considerable research on this subject of cash flow behavior on an aggregate, industry, and company level, and the analysis proposed in this study would be greatly aided by such research. At the practical level, however, it is obvious that we must work with what we now have. It is also apparent that there are limits on the extent to which refinement in the analysis is useful. The operating guide to debt policy which is the end result will inevitably be a rough approximation and will be so used by management. In practice judgment based on experience must be exercised in deciding what is relevant and significant.

The meaning of these comments on the underlying causes of change in cash flow will be more apparent if reference is made to the procedure followed in the analyses of recession cash flow which are to be found in Chapters 8 and 9. As an external analyst, the author began with a detailed examination of recession experience of cash inflows and outflows, working with the company's published financial statements and other records. This required a conversion of accounting data into cash flow approximations along the lines described on page 163. In carrying out this conversion the analysis was aided by the fact that the companies selected had unusually detailed records. If the examination had stopped here, however, as it would for many external analysts, the conclusions would be limited by many elements of uncertainty in interpretation.

Fortunately, the author was also able to view the problem from an internal point of view as well, having access to additional information made available by management and, more importantly, to the experience and judgment of management. Fortunately, also, the critical variable, Sales, has in most companies been subjected to a great deal of careful analysis as a part of conventional sales forecast and cash budgeting procedures. Thus management already has considerable knowledge of the factors which produce change in the dollar volume of Sales and can give a valuable interpretation of the historical record without which the record could be highly misleading. Similarly, the behavior of other determinants of cash flow were explored in discussions with members of management responsible for each aspect with the purpose of probing the true limits of recession behavior and of identifying interrelationships among factors not apparent from the observed record. Thus added information on collection experience, inventory levels, and so on was gained. Under the circumstances of the study, there were limits as to how far this exploration behind the published data needed to be carried or should be carried without straining the hospitality of the companies concerned. Obviously, the internal analyst doing this for his own purposes could carry the analysis as far as it seemed useful to go.

As a part of the identification of causal relationships, the author found it useful to classify the various items of cash outflow along the following lines:

(1) Cash expenditures directly related to the volume of Sales (Physical levels or Dollar Value).

(2) Cash expenditures directly related to the Number of Units Produced.

(3) Cash expenditures which have no precise relationship to the number of units produced or sold but which are influenced by significant changes in the general level of Production or Sales (e.g., Advertising and Sales Promotion).

(4) Cash expenditures directly related to the level of Net Income.

(5) Cash expenditures which vary in response to factors other than the current level of Sales, Production, or Net Income (e.g., Heat and Light).

(6) Cash expenditures which are fixed in amount and/or timing of payment over a period of two or more years.

It is apparent from this list that in the examination of outflows attention will focus particularly on variations in the levels of sales and production, and in this regard the linkage between the two requires very careful attention. With respect to expenditures for raw materials, for example, close attention must be given to the operating relationship among orders received, finished goods inventory levels, and work scheduled into production. One of the problems in this regard is the role played by management discretion. In this study the initial simplifying assumption is made that management will behave in the future within the limits described by actions in the past. At a later stage, when the results based on this assumption are in hand, this can be relaxed if desired.

Thus from whatever sources are available, the analyst develops an understanding of the underlying causes of change in the several elements of cash flow and how they interrelate. The next step in the analytical sequence is to describe in objective terms the anticipated recession behavior of each of the major determinants of cash inflow and outflow. Given this information and a description of the interrelationship or interdependence of these determinants, it will then be possible to set down an objective description of the recession behavior of Net Cash Flow itself.

THE RECESSION BEHAVIOR OF INDIVIDUAL DETERMINANTS
OF CASH FLOW

In order to describe the full range of possible variation in Net Cash Flow during recession periods, we must first describe item by item the full range of possible variation in each of the factors which determine *NCF:* sales volume, collection experience, inventory levels, payroll, heat, light, and power expenditures, and so on. To be somewhat more precise, the focus here will be on the range of *independent* variation, bearing in mind the necessity of also describing the nature of interdependence between or among the variables.

Lacking powers of prophecy for the time period in question, expectations for the future inevitably fall back on past experience interpreted in the light of present information. Consequently, it is appropriate to examine past experience in the most rational manner possible in order to come up with reasoned and reasonable expectations. The question as to *what* past experience is relevant must of course be a matter of judgment. Our aim here, however, is to include the full range of events which have a chance of recurring in the future, including all possible combinations of these events. It follows that the decision as to what experience data to include and what to exclude is simply a question of relevance for the future period and not a judgment on how probable is the chance of recurrence (at this point). It is particularly important that the experience base of the analysis not be confined by considerations of what management would like to see happen or of the risks management is prepared to take.

For the companies involved in the illustrative data of these chapters, the experience base was generally that which had been observed over the past twenty years. It is apparent that this base excluded the Great Depression of the early thirties and some readers may question the adequacy of any cash flow test which excluded this experience. It was, however, the considered judgment of the managements concerned that this experience would not be repeated in the future and, therefore, decisions should not be affected by it. Whether this action was or was not appropriate does not, of course, affect the method of analysis.

This point brings us to a fundamental argument upon which this study is based which is that while it is theoretically true that "anything could happen" in the future, experience strongly argues against such an assumption as a valid framework for decision making. Take as an example Collections from Sales. Assume a single product company selling entirely on credit and assume that we are concerned only with the factors of Dollar Volume of Sales and the Collection Period on these credit Sales. There is no law or force in the business universe which guarantees that the Sales volume of the company in question will not go to zero in some future recession and/or the Collection Period stretch to some indefinite period of days or months.

On the other hand, assuming this to be a mature company with

proven management and acceptable profit performance, experience
will deny this expectation. There are in every industry a variety of
underlying characteristics which tend to shape the nature of the
response of a business entity to a general business recession and
to set limits or restraints on this response. Among these characteristics are those which relate to the nature of the demand for the
product, the buying habits of customers, their income characteristics, the competitive situation, the nature of the product (durability,
unit value, et cetera), the nature of the productive process, the
character of the assets used in production, the credit conventions of
the industry on buying and selling, the character of management,
the conventional decision rules on such things as inventory levels
and production scheduling — and so on. *In general, these characteristics are known to management, sufficiently measurable* for the
purposes of financial policy, *and relatively stable over time* so that
if they change, the change is gradual and the direction of the trend
observable.

Intimate acquaintance with a business and an industry over a
period of time, such as is represented in the companies included in
this study, indicates the nature and behavior of these characteristics
in the past and provides a basis for predicting their probable behavior in the future.

Thus while it is not considered possible to predict with confidence when a particular recession will occur or its severity and
duration, it is considered possible that a well informed management
can *with considerable confidence set finite limits on the expected
impact* of any future recession period on the business *with respect
to sales and other elements of net cash flows.* In illustration of
this prediction, suppose that in our imaginary company, recession
contractions in dollar sales volume have never, over the relevant
past history of the company, been less than −4% of the Sales of
the preceding peak period or more than −32% (measured at the
lowest point of the recession). Underlying these bald statistics
will be a wealth of intimate management experience related to the
recessions as they occurred which leads to convictions as to whether
the figures fairly represent the extreme limits of experience during
this period. Figures that would "make sense" in this respect in the
baking industry would not make sense in the machine tool industry
and vice versa. Management's conclusion in this respect would be

against a background of knowledge of the industry and of the company's position in the industry.

Thus management may conclude that while it has no basis for knowing when the next recession is going to occur or what its magnitude or duration will be, it is prepared to make decisions on the assumption that the contraction in sales will be no less than -4% and no more than -32%. (For the moment we ignore the question of the timing of this contraction.) Throughout this study these limits will be referred to as the *Maximum Favorable Limit* and the *Maximum Adverse Limit*. The terms favorable and adverse refer of course to their anticipated impact on cash flows and cash balances. Similar values will be derived for all determinants of cash flow. Because we are preoccupied with the event of insolvency, it will be the Maximum Adverse Limit that will be of greatest interest.

A COMPREHENSIVE METHOD OF RISK ANALYSIS

Having derived these "absolute" limits of variation — absolute in the sense that they describe the full range of expected behavior — it is natural to ask whether we can say anything useful about the pattern of behavior of the determinant of cash flow *within* these limits. The answer to this question is critical to the nature and complexity of the process of analysis which follows. A useful way of responding to it is to state first what we would like to know about the recession behavior of the variable and what could be done with this information if it was available. This will be done in a few pages here and in a supporting Appendix and will constitute a sort of rough blueprint of how risk appraisal could be approached if certain kinds of data were available. This will be followed by the main body of the analysis which is designed to carry the risk analysis as far as it is useful and meaningful to go, given the kind of data normally available in an established business firm.

Returning to the example of sales variations, it is apparent that the actual contraction of sales in any particular recession — the next one perhaps — could be -4% or -32% or anything in between. A consideration of contractions of 10%, 20%, or 25%, or any other value within these limits, will be meaningful only if there is some basis for drawing distinctions among these various possibilities according to the likelihood or probability of their occurrence. There are two ways in which this may be done. Assuming that a company has had considerable recession experience, there will be records of the frequency with which changes in Sales (or the other variables) of different magnitudes have occurred in the past. From these data a "frequency distribution" can be drawn up which shows the number of times Sales contractions of 5%, 10%, 15%, and so on have occurred. Such data could then be used as a basis for future expectations, on the general assumption that those contractions which had occurred most frequently in the past would also occur most frequently in the future (assuming no current evidence to the contrary). A purely hypothetical example of what the results might look like is seen in Exhibit 5.

EXHIBIT 5. PROBABILITY TABLE OF RECESSION
SALES CONTRACTIONS

Range Number	*Range of Percentage Contraction of Sales*	*Sales Contraction Representing Mid Point of Range*	*Estimated Probability of Occurrence*
1	1%–10%	− 5%	One in Ten (.1)
2	11 –20	−15	Five in Ten (.5)
3	21 –30	−25	Three in Ten (.3)
4	31 –40	−35	One in Ten (.1)
All Possibilities Included in Ranges (1–4)		=	a "Certainty" (1.0)

How this information might be used will be discussed shortly. It should be noted, however, that in practice relevant recession experience is limited and the statistically minded analyst is frustrated by the absence of a sufficient number of occurrences for a meaningful frequency distribution. Even in a recession-prone industry like machine tools, the full record of recession experience is likely to appear as follows:

Recession Number	*Percentage Over-All Sales Contraction*
1	− 4%
2	−13
3	−18
4	−22
5	−23
6	−32

In the absence of adequate objective data, the statistician could turn to a second approach. This would take the form of detailed interviews with the experienced manager in order to elicit his subjective expectations of the chances of occurrence of various degrees of contraction such as those shown in Exhibit 5. The figures in the last column showing the "odds" or probability of occurrence in the future would thus be provided by the judgment of those skilled observers who had passed through the experiences such as those listed above.[1]

Granted the possibility by one means or another of drawing these probability distinctions for Sales contractions within the Maximum Favorable and Maximum Adverse Limits of variation, the same possibility obtains for describing the recession behavior of each of the major determinants of cash inflow and outflow. A simple, hypothetical example of how this information might be put together and what the end product would look like is shown in Appendix B, pages 274 to 284. The reader is warned that in practice this would not be a simple procedure. Beyond the considerable problem of deriving the ranges of variation of each of the determinants and the distribution of probabilities within the ranges, there is the major task of working out the Net Cash Flows associated with all possible combinations of Sales contraction with the other variables. There is the nice statistical problem of establishing the right relationship among the determinants of cash flow in terms of independent and interdependent variation. It is possible that in addition to the need for competent statistical assistance the use of a computer for processing all possible combinations would be required.

The end product of the analysis, as shown in Appendix B, Table B–2, would be a range of all possible recession Net Cash Flows and for each value of *NCF* the associated probability of occurrence. These could be arranged in order of decreasing adversity with the Maximum Adverse recession Net Cash Flow at the top and the Maximum Favorable recession Net Cash Flow at the bottom. Given an assumption with respect to the opening cash

---

[1] For a rigorous description of this approach, see Robert Schlaifer, *Probability and Statistics for Business Decisions,* McGraw-Hill Book Company, Inc., New York, 1959. Note in this connection, Chapter 1: The Meaning of Probability.

balance (CB_0), these figures could be converted into a series of minimum recession net cash balances. For each of these combinations of events, the *cumulative* probability of recession experience being *at least* as adverse as the figure shown could be provided by summing the probabilities of all CB_r's down to that point.

Referring to the hypothetical example given in Appendix B, Table B–2 shows that the recession cash balance could vary from a deficit of $1,065,000 to a surplus of $4,450,000. At some point in between these values the table will show the cumulative probability of CB_r being zero or negative and this, then, is the probability of cash insolvency. Suppose this is .05, or one chance in twenty. We would then have the basic information upon which the debt capacity decision could be based. By the process of analysis referred to above, the expectations of management would have been translated into the single objective measure that, as of now, there is one chance in twenty of the company's "going broke" in a recession. It is a very simple process to adjust these figures for any given increment of debt servicing charges, and to observe the change in this probability value. The obvious effect would be to add to the number of combinations of events under which the cash balance would be zero or negative and thus increase the cumulative probability of cash insolvency by a measurable amount. It would then be for management to decide whether this change in the "odds" of insolvency was acceptable to it in terms of the expected rewards from the added debt financing.

This brief sketch of the general outline of a full-blown analysis of the risk of cash insolvency in the individual firm is not intended to be a satisfactory model either for theory or for practice. Its main purpose is to picture for the reader what a detailed analysis of the whole spectrum of risk would look like and to suggest the nature of the data and the analytical processes required for a comprehensive description of risk magnitudes. As such it serves to suggest both the opportunities for the analysis of individual business risks and the limitations of approximate or partial analyses, one of which will be described shortly. Since the primary concern of this study is with operational analysis, the critical question is whether such an approach could be employed in practice. At the present time, there are three serious obstacles to practical application. These are: (1) the complexity of the analytical process,

(2) the difficulty of deriving the probability data, and, most importantly, (3) the difficulty of motivating management to undertake such an analysis.

The problem of methodology is an obstacle not because the appropriate methods have not been formalized but rather because their use requires mathematical and statistical skills not commonly found in business and because even where these skills are available — in the larger corporations — the process is likely to be relatively costly in time and money compared with existing decision rules. The problem of generating data, particularly on probability distributions of the behavior of the various determinants of cash flow, is more serious because, as we have seen, it requires a disposition on the part of management to draw distinctions regarding the likelihood of future events and an ability to participate in a formal analytical process which at best would appear unfamiliar and at worst highly academic.

It is apparent that both of these obstacles to the adoption of a comprehensive approach to risk analysis by business will appear large or small depending on the dimensions of the third obstacle cited above, namely, the motivation of management to get more precise information on the dimensions of the financial risks of the business. It is the author's opinion that many businesses today desire such information but that few would be ready to make such a radical departure from the practice of the past. The large majority would be unwilling to base such a critical decision as that concerning corporate solvency on an analytical process involving a degree of refinement which appeared inconsistent with the apparent uncertainties of the real world and on a methodology which was foreign to conventional business practice.

Thus since the availability of the critical data on probabilities requires the active support and participation of management, the current prospects for the application of a comprehensive risk analysis appear remote except in those relatively few companies which are the pioneers of improvement in practical decision making. In view of the goal of this study, which is to make a contribution to general business practice, the author has turned to an exploration of ways of utilizing this concept of risk analysis in terms of data presently available to and accepted by management and in a form which could readily be related to existing decision rules. The result has been what may be described as an approximate or partial risk analysis in terms of the adverse limits of recession cash flow behavior. It has already been stated that management can and does have strongly held expectations as to the *limits* of variation in the basic determinants of cash flow. The analysis takes advantage of these expectations and while it avoids the necessity for assigning probability values within these limits it does, as will be seen in the pages which follow, introduce the crude beginnings of a probability distinction. We now turn to the details of the method involved.

AN ANALYSIS OF THE ADVERSE LIMITS OF NET CASH FLOWS

Having described the general outlines of a full-scale analysis of the risk of cash solvency, and having given information on the entire range of possible events and the related probabilities in quantitative terms, we now return to an intermediate stage of this analysis in order to develop an analytical tool for management which does not depend on the assignment of specific probability values within the expected range of experience. This tool will as a result be less "realistic" in the sense that the problem is more crudely formulated but more realistic in the sense that it can be more readily related to present-day criteria and the analytical framework to which management is now accustomed.

The stage to which we refer is the point where the limits of expected variation for each of the determinants of cash flow had been developed (page 171). It has been previously explained that the data drawn from past experience, when considered in the light of present knowledge as to long-term trends in demand for the product, technological change, customer buying habits, the competitive situation, and so on, may quite sensibly lead to a strong presumption that future variations will be restrained within certain bounds which can be given specific values. Thus, for example, the experience on Sales contractions summarized in the table on page 172 when interpreted in this way may lead to a firm expectation that in future recessions the sales contraction will not exceed 32% of the sales of the preceding peak point, referred to previously as the Maximum Adverse Limit. This expectation on the part of management with respect to this and other determinants of cash flow is useful information which can be used in assessing the risk of insolvency and therefore in assessing the impact of varying amounts of debt servicing. We now proceed to develop how this may be done.

So far we have said nothing about the *timing* of the sales contraction, merely giving a measure of the over-all change in level of sales from peak to trough. Recessions may last several years and if the company is going to run out of cash, we are interested in when this is going to occur. There is also the point that different determinants may respond differently over the period of the recession and it is therefore dangerous to deal only with net change. To bring in the timing problem adds to the complexity of the analysis but does not change the basic concept. The symbolic description of Net Cash Flow shown on page 163 can be described period by period as follows:

$$NCF_1 = \{(AR_0 + S_1 - AR_1) + OI_1\} - \{[CGP_1 + SGA_1 + T_1] + [(AP_0 - AP_1) + (AE_0 - AE_1)]\}$$

$$NCF_2 = \{(AR_1 + S_2 - AR_2) + OI_2\} - \{[CGP_2 + SGA_2 + T_2] + [(AP_1 - AP_2) + (AE_1 - AE_2)]\}$$

— and so on for n periods. (The subscripts indicate successive periods.) Thus the Net Cash Flow for the relevant recession period (NCF_r) would then be shown as:

$$NCF_r = (NCF_1 + NCF_2 + \cdots + NCF_n).$$

The added problem here is that of distributing the anticipated over-all change in each determinant over the several periods involved on a logical and consistent basis.

In the example of the sales contraction cited above, it will obviously make a great deal of difference as to whether the 32% contraction is concentrated early in the recession, comes mainly at the end, or is spread evenly over the entire recession. For the sake of illustration, we may assume expectations to be that the maximum adverse recession period will be four years and that the maximum adverse timing would be one-half of the 32% contraction concentrated in the first year, the balance evenly distributed over the remaining years. Then, considering the possibility of a recession in the immediate future and assuming a current (prosperity) sales level of $68 million ($S_0$), the Maximum Adverse Sales pattern would be:

$$S_1 \qquad \$57,200,000$$
$$S_2 \qquad 53,600,000$$
$$S_3 \qquad 50,000,000$$
$$S_4 \qquad 46,400,000$$

In the previous simplified symbolic statement of Net Cash Flow, the element of Cash Inflow, C_s (Collections from Sales) was determined by S (Sales) and the Collection Period on Sales, assuming all sales were made on credit terms. Having determined the maximum adverse behavior of Sales, the next step in the analysis would be to determine the recession behavior of the Collection Period and in particular *its* Maximum Adverse Limit of variation. Given this value, it is then possible to put this together with the data on Sales to produce the Maximum Adverse Limit of C_s.

As has been noted previously, in any precise formulation of *NCF* there are problems of establishing the range of independent variation in a situation where interdependence may exist. For example, the magnitude of the sales decline and the variation in the collection period may be related so that the greater the decline the longer the collection period becomes. If substantial evidence of such interdependence exists, it will be a necessary part of the analysis to define this relationship in objective terms so that unrealistic combinations of values will be avoided. If the interdependence should be at the extreme of having one determinant completely dependent on variations in the other, then once the nature of the relationship was established the two could be treated as one variable. In practice, however, it is more likely that there will be a degree of independent variation as well as interdependence. Whether it will be sufficient to approximate the dependent relationship in a crude form — as suggested by a simple linear relation between sales and the collection period — or whether a more complex formula is necessary will depend on the need for precision in the end results. For the purposes of this study, it has been assumed that crude approximations are sufficient. Given this information, we can then turn our attention to the expected range of independent variation to determine what combinations of Maximum Adverse values are possible.

In this as in all parts of the analysis, the values used are not the result of generalized concepts but are derived from individual company experience. In some companies, collection experience may be closely tied to sales volume and in others it may be quite independent. As an example, the following observations may be made about the Collection Period of the company whose recession sales levels were described on the preceding page:

(1) The Collection Period invariably lengthens when a recession period occurs, and the weight of evidence suggests that the longer and deeper the recession the longer the Collection Period becomes.

(2) The Collection Period has never been shorter than 30 days or longer than 80 days.

(3) Given a Collection Period in Period Zero in excess of 30 days, the expected recession range will be between that value (say, 45 days) and the upper limit of 80 days.

(4) In spite of the proportional relationship between Sales and the Collection Period, there is a range of independent variation which is approximately ±10 days. Thus the Collection Period associated with the maximum Sales contraction (the $46,400,000 level previously described) would be 70 days plus or minus 10 (60 − 80 days).

This example indicates in simple form the general nature of what is meant by interdependent and independent variation between the various determinants of cash flow. From this point on this description of the analysis will refer only to the ranges of *independent* variation and will assume that any interdependence has been established and is implicit in these ranges. Thus the end product of the analysis — a description of Maximum Adverse recession Net Cash Flows — will be the result of combining the Maximum Adverse values of the several determinants of cash inflow and outflow which are possible within the limits of interdependence.

The preceeding paragraphs may have served to alert the reader to the fact that the recession cash flow will depend in part on the point in time from which the recession is assumed to occur. Since the long-term debt contract extends over a long period of time and since we do not know when the recession may begin, the precise circumstances of Period Zero are in doubt. One alternative is to assume that it may happen in the near future so that the values for S_0, AR_0 and so on are given by the current financial circumstances of the company. This may not always be so, however, and as the eventuality could happen five or ten years from now the change could be significant. For example, the working capital position of the company could become substantially more or less liquid with major implications for solvency in a recession. Thus it becomes necessary to add one more dimension to the problem. This is a statement of the limits of variation in relevant financial characteristics during peak prosperity periods. Once again, the interest focuses on the adverse limits — those financial characteristics with respect to such matters as inventory levels, credit to customers, and payables which would be least favorable to subsequent cash flows.

One of the most important of these characteristics has been recognized explicitly in the original statement of the problem on page 162 — CB_0, or the cash balance of the company immediately preceding the recession. Past experience would give evidence as to possible minimum levels, taking into account the surrounding circumstances and established company cash policy. This will be discussed in more detail later.

Having illustrated what is meant by the process of identifying the adverse limits of recession behavior of each of the major elements of cash flow and relating these to produce the anticipated adverse limits of cash flow itself, no further attempt will be made to illustrate the process in detail. The same data are produced for the elements of Outflow as for Inflow. It should be mentioned, however, that the outflow side is likely to be more difficult, in part because there are more variables and in part because of the potential effects of management discretion. There is also the problem, for the external analyst, that outflow data may be so condensed that interpretation may be very difficult. Here the internal analyst, for whom this analytical process is primarily intended, has an enormous advantage. He can be as detailed as he wishes, he can look behind dollar figures to observe physical changes (e.g., inventory), and he can observe behavior patterns and decision rules (e.g., production scheduling) directly rather than try to infer these from historical data.

In the matter of management's behavior, as in other aspects of the analysis, past experience will be the primary guide as to what is to be expected in the future. It is particularly important here to insulate the analysis from the effects of unwarranted optimism.

The data of the analysis should *not* reflect how an ideal management with perfect information would behave, or even how the present management says it will behave in the future but rather how it has behaved in the past under realistic conditions. Barring clear evidence of changed circumstances, an assumption of improved performance over the past is unwarranted in a risk analysis. Once the results of the analysis are known, management may then consider the possible effects of changes in its own behavior on the prospects of insolvency and make a rational choice between the gains in terms of lower risk and the inevitable "costs" of such changes. For example, tighter controls over production scheduling and inventory levels may significantly affect recession cash flows but they have a variety of potential costs in their impact on production and sales. These moves cannot be realistically evaluated in advance of some information on their approximate effects on the risk of insolvency.

Where this analysis is being done internally, there may be some doubt as to the objectivity of assumptions with respect to management behavior. However, this possible lack of objectivity need not be as serious as it might seem at first sight. In practice, the analysis is likely to be undertaken by the treasurer's office and the management action of greatest significance to cash flows lies outside this office — action by the board, the president, and in the sales and production areas. Because of this separation of analysis from action it seems reasonable to assume that the analysis can be sufficiently objective and realistic, though collaboration with a competent external analyst would be a valuable check on bias.

The net result of this entire procedure is to produce figures for the Maximum Adverse limit of Net Cash Flow year by year for the entire recession period from the preceding peak to the low point or trough (or, alternatively, to the point where annual Net Cash Flow becomes positive again). The analysis has translated the detailed expectations of management into their cash flow implications and *tells management what the historical record alone cannot tell, namely, whether a net cash outflow is within the realm of possibility and if so, its magnitude and timing.*

Deriving Data on the Chance of Cash Insolvency

The above analysis when applied to all determinants will have produced the data on recession Net Cash Flows by years ($NCF_1 + NCF_2 + \ldots + NCF_n$) as they would be expected to occur if the expected limits of adversity were approached or reached. The reader is once again reminded that the cash flows with which we have been concerned are those associated on a mandatory and continuous basis with the generation of income. The final step necessary to determine whether continued operations under these adverse circumstances would pose a threat to solvency is to bring in values for CB_0 — the cash balances of the company immediately prior to the recession experience. When this value is combined with NCF_1, NCF_2, etc., on a cumulative basis, the result will be CB_r — the cash balance during the recession as it changes over the entire period. We wish to know whether CB_r ever becomes negative and if so, when, by how much, and under what sets of assumptions.

Since the liquid reserves of a company are commonly one of its primary defenses against the unpredictable adverse event, this is obviously a very critical element of the cash flow analysis. It is intimately bound up with debt policy and is commonly considered along with unused debt capacity as one of the "cushions" against risk. Thus it is really impossible to consider appropriate levels of cash balances independently of an over-all risk appraisal.)| For the purposes of this analysis, however, it will be assumed that cash balances have not as yet been integrated in this sense.

There is, of course, wide variation in corporate practice in managing cash balances. In some companies cash balances are maintained at high levels as a substitute for careful planning and accurate forecasting. In other companies cash balances are held at low levels on the grounds that cash is an unproductive asset and full employment of resources in "earning assets" is the way to maximize profits. It is probably true of most companies that they steer a middle course between "excessively low" balances which create the risk of temporary inability to make payments on time and "excessively high" balances which create other kinds of risk — the risk of complaints that management is inactive, the risk of demands for higher dividends or even of corporate raiders.

The cash balances of a company at any point in time are not likely to be entirely planned balances. In some degree they are the incidental by-product of the current financial circumstances and of other financial policies — the level of earnings, dividend payout, capital expenditures, and so on. There is in most companies an unplanned range of variation of significant breadth between the acceptable lower limit, at which point management takes deliberate steps to increase the liquidity of its existing assets or bring in new liquid assets, and some more indefinite upper limit, at which point management will be disposed to step up capital expenditures or, perhaps, increase the dividend. Our concern here is with the lower limit, the "absolute" minimum below which liquid asset balances must not be allowed to go in facilitating current operations, its relationship to the level of sales and operations, and whatever excess or deficiency may exist between this level and the actual cash balance at the time the recession sets in.

As in previous analyses it is possible to approach this problem in terms of crude approximations. As a general rule, cash balances tend to be roughly proportional to the level of sales. One of the common rules of thumb in business is to have a minimum balance expressed as the equivalent of "x" days' sales or expenditures. The external analyst can make an attempt at estimating the minimum acceptable percentage relationship between year-end cash balances and annual sales. (In a few cases the data may even be available on a quarterly basis and thus be more useful and reliable.) Once again, however, the internal analyst has a major advantage. Detailed historical data supplemented by intimate knowledge of the company and industry can be used to build up an accurate picture of characteristic intramonth and seasonal variations in cash flows and their relation to the scale of operations.

Here the question will arise as to what extent, if at all, minimum cash balances should go beyond predictable, measurable needs. There is the problem of the unexpected need which by definition cannot be predicted as to magnitude or timing. Of course, the experience of 20 or more years should give some indication of what these "unexpected" needs are likely to be and should provide a rough indication of frequency and magnitude. At this stage of the analysis, however, it seems appropriate to consider only the readily measurable needs for cash. When the analysis has been completed and a tentative debt decision is reached, it will be desirable to review this assumption and consider whether a higher "absolute minimum" should be planned. It is only at that point that the question of cash balances can be fully resolved since, as previously stated, unused debt capacity is an integral part of planning for the unexpected.

Having arrived at a measure of the minimum desired cash balance, which may be expressed as a percentage of Sales, this value may be compared with the Current level of cash to determine any excess or deficiency. The existence of a significant amount of marketable securities over a period of years is in itself a strong indication that such an excess exists. It must be recognized that here also the significance of the Current cash position will diminish over time and it is necessary to consider Maximum Adverse values for Cash prior to the recession period. Consistent with previous practice in this analysis, no basic change in company policy will be assumed at this stage so that if it has been a consistent policy for the company to hold generous cash balances, the Maximum Adverse value may still be substantially above the absolute minimum previously derived. Consequently, it is possible that some and perhaps all the assumptions with respect to the initial cash balance will provide for some release of cash during the recession for purposes of offsetting any recession cash deficits.

With this information available, it is a simple step to translate NCF_1, NCF_2, et cetera into CB_1, CB_2, . . . , or the cash balances at the end of each period or year of maximum adverse recession behavior in cash flows. The prospect of cash insolvency will be demonstrated if any of these values becomes negative and, indeed, when the approximate nature of the data is taken into account it can be considered a possibility if CB approaches close to zero at any point. It will also be apparent that the chances of insolvency will normally be considered to vary directly with the size and timing of any deficits that show up at the extreme of adversity.

Before leaving this topic it should be noted that the assumptions with respect to cash must be tied into and be consistent with the other working capital assumptions used earlier in the analysis — regarding the levels of Accounts Receivable, Inventories, and Payables. It is obviously a part of the general consideration of the financial condition of the company prior to the recession but has required special attention because it is a major policy area.

Evaluating Adverse Limits — Maximum Adverse versus Most Probable Limits

Having derived values for the Maximum Adverse cash position of the company during future recession periods, the obvious question arises as to its significance. In response to this question, it may be said that the meaning and usefulness of the data depend in part on the basic attitudes of management in the particular case — whether it is a risk-minimizing or a risk-exploiting management — and in part on the character of existing debt policy and debt capacity decision rules. The uses will be illustrated in the two final chapters. Regardless of the possibilities, however, the usefulness is limited by the fact that we are talking about an event which has a remote probability of occurrence. By combining the worst possible event in every one of a number of factors governing cash flow, we have produced a figure representing "the worst of all possible worlds" — the Maximum Adverse net cash flow. The probability of occurrence of the net result is affected not only by the probabilities of its several determinants but also by the number of the determinants. There may be a relatively high probability for each event individually but a low probability for any particular combination of events.

This may be illustrated very simply by saying that if four coins are being flipped simultaneously the chance that any one of these coins will turn up "heads" is greater than the event of all turning up heads at the same time. The average person would say for any one coin that the chances were 50–50, but it would obviously be a mistake to assume that the chance of them all coming up heads when tossed simultaneously is also 50–50. The chances of the latter, instead of being 1 in 2, are 1 in 16.

Thus, assuming that the behavior of each of the primary determinants of cash flow is independent of the others and that there is no common tendency to reach maximum adversity in the same recession period, the probability of experiencing the net cash flow associated with the combined adverse limits of the various determinants is considerably more remote than the probability of occurrence of any single adverse limit.   The extent of the difference is a function of the number of independent determinants involved.

To the extent that the determinants are interdependent, however, as for example through a common dependency on the level of sales, this interdependence reduces the extremes of remote probability which the above paragraphs suggest.   In such an event it would be the probability associated with the sales level which would become the dominant consideration.   Thus the significance of this question depends on the individual circumstances of the company and the industry with respect to the recession behavior of the determinants of cash flow.   In any event there will be ranges of independent variation and this fact does tend to produce a relatively remote probability of occurrence for the *specific values* of recession cash flows associated with the maximum adverse assumptions.   Thus it seems desirable to look for another reference point on the possible range of future experience involving events of higher probability of occurrence with which to compare the Maximum Adverse Limit.   This is the subject of this section.

At this point it may be helpful to express the ideas graphically. Assume for a moment that the data on recession behavior of one of the determinants of cash flow, say dollar sales, is extensive so that we could construct a table of the frequency with which Sales contractions of varying magnitudes have occurred and that this is to be used as a guide to the future.   These frequencies could then be graphed as in Chart 5.   In the absence of evidence to the contrary, we may assume that these frequencies are more or less normally distributed about the mode or contraction of greatest frequency of occurrence.   According to the terminology of this study, the point at which the curve starts nearest to the origin would be the Maximum Favorable Limit and the point where it terminates would be the Maximum Adverse Limit.

From the graph it is apparent that the number of times the Sales contraction has reached its Maximum Adverse Limit is close to zero and the probability of actually hitting that limit is very low — this is really by definition.   Having ruled out the possibility of assigning probabilities in the range between the limits of experience, the question comes as to whether it is possible to derive a crude measure of what changes would take place in recession cash flows and cash balances if the analysis was confined to events with a substantial probability of occurrence. Of course, the word "substantial" cannot really be used in any general sense since it relates to an individual's utility scale — his willingness to bear risk. What is substantial to one would not be substantial to another.

CHART 5. GRAPH OF FREQUENCY OF SALES CONTRACTIONS IN RECESSION PERIODS

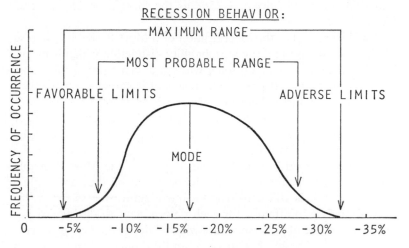

RECESSION BEHAVIOR:

MAXIMUM RANGE

MOST PROBABLE RANGE

FAVORABLE LIMITS   ADVERSE LIMITS

FREQUENCY OF OCCURRENCE

MODE

0   -5%   -10% -15% -20%   -25% -30%   -35%

CONTRACTION IN SALES LEVEL
(MAXIMUM SALES CONTRACTION AS A PERCENT OF
SALES OF PRECEDING PEAK PERIOD)

There is a way of introducing an element of objectivity in this search for a second reference point, however, and that is to determine what will be called the *Most Probable Range* of behavior as opposed to the *Maximum Range*. The Maximum Range includes all possible events regardless of the likelihood of recurrence. The Most Probable Range would cut off the "tails" of the frequency curve and exclude events considered to have only a remote chance of occurrence. Of course, looking at continuous data such as that illustrated in Chart 5, there is really no *one* point where the Probable Range begins. On the other hand, it is obvious that there is a critical section of the curve at each end where frequency drops off sharply and the curve approximates a parallel position with the horizontal axis close to zero frequency.

Speaking in more practical terms it is quite reasonable to assume that the actual experience with recessions such as that shown in the figures on page 172 will lead management to firm impressions as to what the Most Probable Adverse Limits of recession behavior are — as opposed to the "outside chance." For the figures referred to, it is possible that management might look on a Sales contraction of −32% as an outside chance and a contraction of something in the vicinity of −25% as the Most Probable Adverse Limit.

It will be seen that the identification of a Most Probable Adverse Limit is an attempt to draw a probability distinction which is meaningful to the business practitioner without assigning a specific value to that probability. It provides a means of isolating events considered to have a remote chance of occurrence from events which have a significant chance of occurrence. It must be recognized that for some determinants this may be a distinction which cannot be drawn — in other words, the experience curve may not have the bell shape assumed in Chart 5 and, therefore, the Most Probable and Maximum Limits may have to be taken as the same value. Nevertheless, it is still considered a meaningful process for the financial analyst to attempt for each determinant to distinguish between that range of adverse values which evidence indicates to have only a remote chance of occurrence and the range of values which describes the normal or typical recession experience. In this way, any tendency to treat the adverse limit of cash flows lightly will be averted.

Applying this concept to each of the determinants of net cash flow, the analyst can produce a figure for the Most Probable Adverse Net Cash Flow in the same manner as the figure for the Maximum Adverse Net Cash Flow was produced. The procedure will be identical.

ASSEMBLING THE DATA ON RECESSION CASH BALANCES

The final step of this analysis of adverse limits of recession cash flows is to assemble the data in the most useful form for decision-making purposes. There is no one right way of doing this but the author has adopted a form which he has found most useful and this will be used in the two remaining chapters. According to this form, three basic dimensions of the cash flow are highlighted:

(1) The Recession Behavior of Sales Volume

(2) The Recession Behavior of the Other Determinants of Cash Flow

(3) The Financial Condition of the Company immediately preceding the Recession.

There are good reasons, as regards to both interpretation and use of the data, for separating the influence of variations in the conditions prior to a recession from variations in cash flow and management behavior once the recession is under way. For example, if management as a result of the analysis decides it wishes to do something about improving the chances of avoiding insolvency in a recession *in advance* of such recession, it will probably concentrate its efforts on modifying the conditions which will obtain in Period Zero — building up CB_0, improving the liquidity of I_0, et cetera. (It might also, of course, try to do something to the product mix to influence the behavior of S during the recession but this is a more gradual, long-range proposition.) If such action is contemplated, management should be able to isolate these variables and have a measure of the probable impact on recession cash flows of such changes.

There is also value in separating the effects of variations in dollar Sales from the other factors which shape the behavior of net cash flows during the recession period. Sales is undoubtedly the most important variable in most cases. It is also the one least open to influence by management, at least in the short run. Consequently, it is valuable to observe the separate effect of Sales and of the other determinants which may be more susceptible of managerial influence.

For each of these three basic dimensions of the analysis, we have sets of figures which describe their effect on net cash flows and cash balances at the two adverse limits of behavior:

(a) Maximum

(b) Most Probable

For the Financial Condition preceding the Recession, there is a third set of figures which describes the condition of the company at the time of the analysis and will be referred to as:

(c) Current Condition

These data may be combined in several possible ways (twelve to be exact) to produce different pictures of recession cash balances. For example, the worst possible combination would be to have all three dimensions: Precedent Conditions, Sales contraction, and recession behavior of other determinants operate at their Maximum Adverse Limit — the combination of [(1)(a), (2)(a), (3)(a)]. For the near future, however, the Current values with respect to Precedent Conditions would be the most relevant and thus for the near future the Maximum Adverse would be [(1)(a), (2)(a), (3)(c)]. It is also interesting to observe the effect on cash flows of an assumption that adverse behavior will not exceed the Most Probable Limit [(1)(b), (2)(b), and (3)(b) or (3)(c)]. Recognizing the fact that some degree of control over the variables may exist but that this is not equally true in all basic dimensions, management may wish to look at recession cash balances when Sales is taken at Maximum Adverse and either or both of the other dimensions are taken at the Most Probable Limit [(1)(a), (2)(b), (3)(b)].

Not all of these sets of adverse assumptions will be relevant in every case. Nevertheless, they do present a range of possibilities which will help to describe the chances of cash insolvency in the individual firm.

SUMMARY

The conventional decision rules for the control of risk in long-term borrowing are cast in a form which implies a discrete division between amounts of debt which are "safe" to assume and amounts of debt which present a substantial and unacceptable threat to solvency. The nature of these decision rules is such that it is impossible to appraise their appropriateness for this purpose — even assuming that this approach to debt policy is a valid one. It has been the purpose of this chapter to consider a method of examining the risk of cash insolvency in the individual firm by analyzing in detail corporate experience with respect to those elements which have a significant bearing on variations in cash flows. The ultimate use of the data generated by the proposed method of analysis is to provide a rational interpretation of existing decision rules and, with the expectation that they may be found inadequate, to offer a sensible and practical alternative approach to the problem.

A portion of this chapter was devoted to developing what is considered by the author to be a valid conceptual framework for measuring the risk of cash insolvency. Because of the expectation that a direct, practical application of this framework is seriously restricted by the level of abstraction it requires — a level to which most of today's financial decision makers are quite unaccustomed, its primary function in this study of operative decision rules is the very important one of providing a way of thinking about debt in terms of the special circumstances of the individual firm. Given this framework the chapter then proceeded to consider a way of reshaping the data and judgments currently in use and in which businessmen have confidence in a form which approaches the more rigorous framework as far as it seems practical to go. The result was an analysis of the adverse limits of cash flow and of cash balances in recession periods which, as will be seen in the two remaining chapters, can be used as an approximate index of the risk of cash inadequacy in recession and a rough measure of the impact of debt servicing on this risk. Crude as this form may appear to the analytic purist, it is believed to be an improvement over existing rules of thumb.

Before turning to an illustration of this method and its implications for corporate debt policy, a word should be added on a point which may be troubling some readers. The analysis of recession cash flows has stopped short at the low point of the recession or, if the low point happens to be a period of net cash outflows, at the point on the succeeding upturn where annual net cash flows again become positive. Some may consider that this is incomplete since it omits the cash needs of the succeeding upswing. This may appear particularly important if the recession has involved a substantial depletion of opening cash balances.

The analytical approach does not prevent the inclusion of such considerations. This omission, however, stems from one of the initial assumptions which was that we were dealing with the recession experience of a company which was otherwise "mature, basically profitable, and apparently well managed." Under such an assumption it seems reasonable to assume that any depletion of equity resources during a recession was more than offset by the accretion of the preceding period of prosperity. Further, the analysis does not assume any new borrowing during the recession so that there will in the normal process be a significant reduction in outstanding long-term debt through the debt servicing which the test of solvency is designed to preserve.   Consequently it is assumed that in the succeeding prosperity the company will find adequate equity and debt capital available to it to take full advantage of its opportunities.   If this assumption is invalid, then the recession analysis will be realistic only if the needs of the following period are taken into account.

CHAPTER 8

The Application of a Recession Cash Flow Analysis to the Debt-Equity Choice and Its Integration with Other Long-Term Policies

INTRODUCTION

The approach to recession cash flow analysis described in the preceding chapter and its application to debt and other policy decisions can be discussed in a more meaningful manner if it is related to a specific business organization. The approach has been applied to five of the companies included in this study, one in each of the five industries. The results of these five analyses and their implications for existing debt policies will be described in Chapter 9. Before considering the implications for individual corporate policy, however, it will be useful to discuss in some detail the meaning of the results of the analysis in more general terms. This is the purpose of this chapter. The figures used for illustration are taken from one of the five companies considered in Chapter 9.

AN EXAMPLE OF RECESSION CASH FLOW ANALYSIS

The data on the impact of extreme recession conditions on corporate cash balances given in the following pages have no connection with the hypothetical examples used in Chapter 7 but are drawn from the actual experience of a company in the rubber industry. Because of the necessity for disguise, background information on the company must be kept to a minimum. It can be stated, however, that past experience and present expectations of management suggested that the Maximum Adverse Limit of Sales contraction should be approximately 20% of the Sales of the preceding peak period and the maximum duration be taken as two years. The Most Probable Limit so far as duration was concerned was taken as one year, with the magnitude of contraction somewhat less than that assumed for the first year of the Maximum Sales contraction.

The data upon which the analysis was based were a combination of internal and external information. The analysis began with an examination of historical evidence on cash flows derived from a reconstruction of unusually informative but conventional financial statements. This reconstruction was worked out along the lines suggested on pages 161 to 165 of Chapter 7. In its initial phase, therefore, the approach was essentially that of the external analyst. However, the company was chosen because it was found to have a management which was unusually cooperative in discussing fully and frankly the experience which lay behind the figures, without which the interpretation of the data would have been much more tentative. Thus, for example, evidence on variations in the Collection Period of Credit Sales was given much greater depth by an interpretive discussion with the company's credit manager. The same procedure was true for questions of sales levels, inventory positions, and other key elements.

Under the circumstances, of course, the analysis was considerably more rough and approximate than would be possible or desirable if carried out by internal analysts with specific decisions and policies dependent on the outcome. For the most part, judgmental approximations replaced precise statistical measures in establishing relationships among the variables. Here the purpose has been merely to illustrate a method and the specific results are not of critical significance. At the same time, however, the analysis has been made as precise as the data would justify so that the end result could be compared with existing company concepts and practices as a test of validity and consistency.

The figures shown in Exhibit 6 are the results of the first stage of the analysis in which recession net cash flows directly related to the generation of current income are determined. It will be noted in the heading that initial cash balances are assumed to be zero so

EXHIBIT 6. ESTIMATED NET CASH FLOWS ASSOCIATED
WITH THE ANTICIPATED ADVERSE LIMITS
OF RECESSION EXPERIENCE
COMPANY "A"
(Initial Cash Balance Assumed to be Zero)

Assuming Recession Experience with respect to:

Financial Conditions Preceding Recession	*Behavior of Determinants of Cash Flow During Recession*		*The Resulting Net Cash Flow is Estimated at:*	
	Sales Contraction	*Other Determinants*		
Reaches its Adverse Limit described as:			*In Year One*	*In Year Two*
Maximum	Maximum	Maximum	$ (4,970,000)	$ 1,280,000
		Most Probable	14,940,000	16,800,000
	Most Probable	Maximum	(2,460,000)	
		Most Probable	16,250,000	
Most Probable	Maximum	Maximum	1,430,000	11,280,000
		Most Probable	17,340,000	21,510,000
	Most Probable	Maximum	1,480,000	
		Most Probable	20,400,000	
Current Condition	Maximum	Maximum	4,830,000	18,200,000
		Most Probable	25,260,000	27,700,000
	Most Probable	Maximum	5,140,000	
		Most Probable	25,940,000	

that these figures are simply the net cash throw-off from opera-tions, year by year.

On page 189, Chapter 7, we indicated a method of grouping the assumptions underlying the cash flow analysis with a focus on (1) the underlying assumption as to the contraction in Sales, (2) the financial condition of the company preceding the recession, and (3) the behavior of the determinants of cash flow (other than Sales) during the recession. All possible combinations of these groupings are presented in Exhibit 6, twelve in all. The headings of the first three columns indicate the three factors enumerated above and under these the various combinations of their ad-verse limits. For example, the first horizontal line of figures show net cash flow assuming *all* groups of assumptions were taken at their Maximum Adverse Limit or value. This is the worst imaginable event within the realm of practical expectation of the management of this company.

Similarly, the last horizontal line of data is the net cash flow from operations which would result if the recession occurred in the immediate future, so that the Current financial condition was most relevant, and the Sales contraction and behavior of the other determinants of cash flow was according to the Most Probable Adverse Limit or value. The columns on the right of the exhibit show the related net cash flows year by year and are *not* cumulative. These cash flow figures taken as a group answer the basic question in the analysis of risk and debt capacity: Given management's expectations as to the limits of behavior in the underlying conditions governing cash flows, is it possible that the company could experience a negative cash flow from operations, and if so, under what assumptions and of what magnitude?

It will be seen from the exhibit that in this case there were only two sets of assumptions which produced a net cash outflow. These were: (1) when the Maximum Adverse behavior of every variable affecting the cash position coincided during the recession period — in which case the first year of the recession was expected to produce a net cash outflow of $4,970,000; (2) when every variable excepting the decline in Sales behaved in the Maximum Adverse manner and the Sales contraction was at its Most Probable Adverse Limit. Here the net cash outflow in the first year was estimated at $2,460,000. In every other combination of circumstances, there was some excess of inflow over outflow in each year of the recession. It is interesting to note that in this company it was expected that the second year of the recession would be an improvement over the first in spite of some further decline in Sales and in the most adverse set of circumstances the second year actually produced a small surplus of inflow over outflow.

In view of the fact that certain combinations of these assumptions produced substantial cash surpluses, the reader should be reminded that the most favorable of these assumptions are still at the negative end of the whole range of possibilities for the company. The most favorable assumption in any case is the Most Probable *Adverse* limit, except for the Initial Conditions where the Current condition could be substantially better than this. In this case the influence of this latter assumption was to raise the cash surplus from $20,400,000 to $25,940,000 under the most favorable set of assumptions with regard to the other variables.

It is helpful to regroup these data as seen in Exhibit 7 by ranking the various combinations of assumptions in order of the net effect on cash flow, showing the least favorable result first and the most favorable last. It can be seen that there is a range of $31,000,000, from −$5,000,000 to +$26,000,000 (approximately). These data suggest that although there is a chance of an operating cash deficit (and therefore possibly a chance of cash insolvency) this chance is confined to the "absolute" limit of adverse circumstances and by definition is an event to which management would attach a very low probability of occurrence. Those circumstances which manage-

EXHIBIT 7. RESULTS OF CASH FLOW ANALYSIS AS SHOWN
IN EXHIBIT 6, REGROUPED IN ORDER OF INCREASING
NET CASH FLOWS
COMPANY "A"

			Assuming Recession Experience with respect to:		
			Financial Conditions Preceding Recession	*Behavior of Determinants of Cash Flow During Recession*	
	Net Cash Flow from Operations in Year:			*Sales Contraction*	*Other Determinants*
No.	*One*	*Two*	Reaches its Adverse Limit described as:		
1	$(4,970,000)	$1,280,000	Maximum	Maximum	Maximum
2	(2,460,000)		Maximum	Most Probable	Maximum
3	1,430,000	11,280,000	Most Probable	Maximum	Maximum
4	1,480,000		Most Probable	Most Probable	Maximum
5	4,830,000	18,200,000	Current Condition	Maximum	Maximum
6	5,140,000		Current Condition	Most Probable	Maximum
7	14,940,000	16,800,000	Maximum	Maximum	Most Probable
8	16,250,000		Maximum	Most Probable	Most Probable
9	17,340,000	21,510,000	Most Probable	Maximum	Most Probable
10	20,400,000		Most Probable	Most Probable	Most Probable
11	25,260,000	27,700,000	Current Condition	Maximum	Most Probable
12	25,940,000		Current Condition	Most Probable	Most Probable

ment considers the most likely limit of adverse variation provide what appears to be a very comfortable margin of safety in cash flow.

This is, however, only a partial analysis. It provides the data on NCF_1 and NCF_2 only, and in order to consider the possibility of insolvency it is necessary to bring in CB_0 — initial cash balances which may be used to offset any net cash outflows. For the company in question, the following estimates were made of the cash which would be available over and above that required for the current level of operations. As can be seen, the amount varies depending on the assumption as to the initial financial condition and the magnitude of the sales contraction.

	Assumed Limit of Sales Contraction		
	Most Probable	Maximum	
Assumed Level of Initial Cash Balances	Year One	Year One	Year Two
Current	$2,500,000	$2,700,000	$200,000
Most Probable Adverse	1,600,000	1,700,000	100,000
Maximum Adverse	1,400,000	1,500,000	100,000

The reader will observe that the primary release of cash is from idle balances and only a modest amount is the result of the expected decline in level of sales and operations, as seen in the figures for Year Two of the Maximum Adverse Sales contraction.

We are now in a position to estimate the recession cash balances associated with the adverse cash flows assumptions of Exhibit 7. These are shown in Exhibit 8. The figures show the *cumulative* cash balance of the company at the end of each recession year related to each of the twelve sets of adverse behavior limits. It can be seen that the cash balances were not large enough to radically alter the impressions on the adverse limits of recession experience gained from Exhibit 7. The threat of insolvency as a result of mandatory operational cash flows appears to be confined to the extreme limits of adverse recession experience.

INTERPRETING THE DATA ON ADVERSE LIMITS OF RECESSION
CASH BALANCES

The next and obvious question is: How is the information of Exhibit 8 to be used as a tool of practical financial policy? In order to simplify the answer to this question, initial consideration will be confined to four sets of figures for recession cash balances:

(A) Recession Cash Balances associated with (1) Maximum and (2) Most Probable Adverse Limits for all variables, assuming a desire by management to *borrow continuously for an indefinite period.* (Nos. 1 and 10 in Exhibit 8.)

(B) Recession Cash Balances associated with (1) Maximum and (2) Most Probable Adverse Limits for all variables, assuming a desire by management to *confine borrowing to the near future only* (the "one shot" concept). (Nos. 5 and 12 in Exhibit 8.)

The recession cash balances related to these sets of conditions are:

Set of Conditions	Year One	Year Two
(A) (1)	$ (3,470,000)	$ (2,090,000)
(A) (2)	22,000,000	
(B) (1)	7,530,000	25,930,000
(B) (2)	28,440,000	

EXHIBIT 8.   CASH SOLVENCY AT THE LIMITS OF ADVERSITY
COMPANY "A"

Anticipated Recession Cash Balances Associated with the Adverse Recession Cash Flow Assumptions of Exhibit 7

	Cumulative Net Cash Balance at End of Recession Year:		Financial Conditions Preceding Recession	Behavior of Determinants of Cash Flow During Recession	
				Sales Contraction	Other Determinants
No.	One	Two	Reaches its Adverse Limit described as:		
1	$(3,470,000)	$(2,090,000)	Maximum	Maximum	Maximum
2	(1,060,000)		Maximum	Most Probable	Maximum
3	3,130,000	14,510,000	Most Probable	Maximum	Maximum
4	3,080,000		Most Probable	Most Probable	Maximum
5	7,530,000	25,930,000	Current Condition	Maximum	Maximum
6	7,640,000		Current Condition	Most Probable	Maximum
7	16,440,000	33,300,000	Maximum	Maximum	Most Probable
8	17,650,000		Maximum	Most Probable	Most Probable
9	19,040,000	40,610,000	Most Probable	Maximum	Most Probable
10	22,000,000		Most Probable	Most Probable	Most Probable
11	27,960,000	55,860,000	Current Condition	Maximum	Most Probable
12	28,440,000		Current Condition	Most Probable	Most Probable

Since it is apparent that cash insolvency is possible within the range of expectations of the management of this company as shown by the conditions of (A)(1) above, a debt policy which builds in *any amount* of continuous debt servicing over an extended future period (say beyond five years) will necessarily involve and increase the risk of cash insolvency. This knowledge may arouse concern on the part of some managements who have assumed that their current debt restrictions serve as an effective barrier to insolvency. In this case, even a "no debt" rule cannot assume complete peace of mind on this matter.

Many, perhaps most, managements would not be surprised by this information but would merely want to know whether the risk of insolvency for any given amount of debt was "substantial" or "excessive." The latter term implies a value judgment by those on whom the risk falls and must be related to their attitudes toward risk bearing. A rough measure of substantiality, however, is to be found in the recession cash balances related to Most *Probable* Limits of variation reflected in the (A)(2) cash balance shown above. Suppose, for example, that the management of this company was considering a plan to borrow permanent funds through a 20-year term loan amounting to 20% of the company's capital structure. Translated into an approximate amount of annual interest plus sinking fund payments, this would involve a cash drain of roughly $3,400,000 at its maximum point, assuming a 5% interest charge and repayment in equal annual installments.

When this figure is compared to the cash balance at the adverse limit of the *Probable* range of experience, (A)(2), it will be seen that the amount of borrowing under consideration does not pose a threat to solvency unless conditions are significantly more adverse than this. Since this Limit was conceived as a judgment which divided the "normal range" of experience from "abnormal" extremes of adverse behavior (which by definition have a low probability of occurrence), it is apparent that the chances of cash insolvency even with this amount of new long-term debt are remote.

If the company in question was contemplating the use of debt in the near future only and was planning to retire it as the need for funds passed and/or retained earnings accumulated, then the picture is even more favorable. The figures indicated as (B)(1) and (B)(2), which are based on the financial condition of the company prevailing in the near future, show that there is *no* chance of insolvency within the limits of management's expectations, even when the most adverse combination of events is assumed. It is also evident that the amount of debt contemplated above would not be large enough to produce a chance of insolvency.

Thus, in summary, the data show for varying amounts of debt (1) whether there is a chance of cash insolvency and if so (2) whether the risk of insolvency is of major or minor proportions. This information, while admittedly stated in imprecise and rather subjective terms, is of considerable value in interpreting the implications of specific debt alternatives and the meaning and validity of existing debt capacity decision rules. As indicated in previous chapters, these restraints on debt are commonly conceived as protecting the company from any (substantial) threat of insolvency. By implication debt in excess of the stated limit does pose a serious threat to solvency, and company action when debt approaches or exceeds the limit commonly supports this interpretation. Suppose, for example, the company in question had a rule not to borrow in excess of 20% of its total capitalization. The inference would be drawn that debt in excess of 20% was excessively risky, and should debt happen to exceed this limit for some reason drastic adjustments in financial policy should take place in order to restore a proper relationship as soon as possible.

We recognize of course that the assumed 20% rule is, in theory at least, the net result of an appraisal of the risk magnitude and management's subjective reactions to the bearing of such risk. The same rule could reflect either a low risk and a cautious management or a high risk and a venturesome management. Ordinarily it is impossible to separate these two components, and ordinarily management does not have adequate information to attempt to do so. Our recession cash flow analysis has, however, demonstrated that for this company a 20% debt burden would involve *no* prospect of cash insolvency in the immediate future and only a remote chance in the more distant future.

Since management presumably knows whether it is cautious or venturesome in bearing the risks of debt leverage, it can now separate the two elements which go to make up the decision rule and proceed to set one in relation to the other. While the data are not sufficiently refined to indicate precisely what the debt restraint *should be,* they will serve to identify rules which are substantially out of line with the facts as perceived by management. As previously stated, every debt capacity rule contains implicit assumptions about the magnitude of the risk involved. These can now be checked against the results of an analysis in which the event of insolvency has been examined explicitly and in detail. In the above example, management may find the chance of insolvency with 20% debt higher or, more probably, lower than it formerly believed was the case. If so, it now knows the direction in which modification should go. On the other hand, the cash flow analysis may only serve to confirm the previous impressions of risk, and assuming no change in the willingness to bear risk, the debt policy is not likely to change. In any case the recession cash flow data give a sense of perspective in which to view existing decision rules which the rules themselves cannot provide.

CASH INADEQUACY VERSUS CASH INSOLVENCY

The use of an example in which there appears to be a very remote chance of cash insolvency during economic recessions may have raised some questions in the reader's mind as to whether the threat of cash insolvency was in fact the primary consideration which led management to establish its particular debt capacity decision rule. Assuming that management was not completely "off base" in its appraisal of risk and was not unduly conservative, a debt restraint which lies within the conventional 30% of capitalization range appears somewhat irrational if insolvency was its sole concern. Not only is this risk remote but debt in this amount appears to have a very modest effect on its magnitude. Apart from the idea of a reserve of debt capacity held in anticipation of future investment opportunities, there remains the important consideration of debt as a potential threat to other expenditures which management wishes to preserve in periods of depressed business activity.

This may be described as the risk of cash inadequacy, as opposed to cash insolvency, and the inadequacy may be in respect of any one of a number of expenditures. It will be recalled that the cash flows considered so far included only those items of inflow and outflow which were directly, continuously, and unavoidably involved in the generation of income. These items would exclude dividend payments, capital expenditures, some kinds of research and development expenditures, employment stabilization expenditures, and other like items not directly involved in sustaining current sales and income levels. An analysis of the circumstances of insolvency must necessarily strip the company down to the immediate essentials of survival.

As a matter of policy, however, management may choose to give priority to such expenditures over the opportunity of debt leverage. If so, then management's concern over excessive debt may be only remotely connected with bankruptcy and may be primarily a fear that it will necessitate an interruption of research projects or capital expenditures vital to long-term competitive strength and profitability. Given a choice, management would not deliberately jeopardize these activities, and the potential income advantages of debt financing over alternative sources of funds may not be sufficient to overcome this concern for such expenditures. Such an approach may not be completely rational in the sense that management may not have carefully weighed the comparative gains and losses. Nevertheless, it is a very common way of thinking among practitioners.

There is another reason why we may wish to relax the assumptions of the "insolvency analysis" and bring in expenditures other than those which are unavoidably associated with the generation of income. It is an implicit assumption of the previous analysis that the recession was recognized by management from the outset and that it could immediately cut back quickly and drastically on "nonessential" expenditures. While this rapid response is possible, we must recognize that management does not always do so in practice. In spite of improved forecasting of recessions, there is still some uncertainty about the shape of things to come and some lag in responding to conserve cash. During this period there will likely be some cash drain for "nonessentials" which of course cannot be recovered.

Fortunately, this new dimension of the problem can be handled within the cash flow framework previously described. Instead of being concerned with the point at which initial cash balances plus cash inflows become inadequate to meet mandatory outflows, we are now concerned with the point where they fail to cover mandatory cash outflows *plus* some minimum level of expenditures dictated by policy considerations. To illustrate we return to the rubber company example. For this company, the principal expenditures in question were dividend payments and capital expenditures. At the time of the analysis, the company was paying $6,000,000 annually in dividends (disguised data). Past actions plus current statements of management indicated that the company would be disposed to cut the dividend under conditions of a substantial decline in sales of the magnitude assumed in this analysis. The management would, however, resist any decision (such as an increase in debt) which would imply a possible necessity for cutting the payments below a $3,500,000 level. In view of the fact that there was likely to be some delay in recognizing the onset of a serious recession and also a desire to stagger any cutback in the dividend so as to ease the blow to the stockholder and the market price of the stock, it could not be assumed that dividends would drop to the $3,500,000 level in the first year of the recession. Some reasonable assumption, therefore, had to be made as to the lag involved. The calculations were based on the assumption of a minimum dividend payment in the first year of the recession of $4,500,000 and in the second year of $3,500,000.

A more sophisticated assumption regarding dividend cuts in the recession could have been made but did not seem warranted in this case. If there were substantial differences in the contraction of Sales and Earnings between the Maximum Adverse and Most Probable Adverse, an attempt could be made to tie the size of the cut to the magnitude of the contraction. This assumption implies a policy to this effect, however, and there was no evidence of this.

With respect to capital expenditures the level at the time of the analysis was considered above average and was taken as being the Most Probable Adverse Limit as well as the Current value. The Maximum Adverse Limit was estimated as being about 60% higher. In view of the relatively short recession period and these comparatively high levels of capital expenditures, it was not considered practicable to assume the kind of cutbacks in recession expenditures for this purpose that one might have liked. The lowest level of outflow assumed in the second recession year was $2,500,000.

With these data in hand, it is a simple matter to convert Exhibit 8 into a table showing net cash balances which would remain after *all* expenditures considered mandatory by management under the various combinations of assumptions. The different assumptions as to

EXHIBIT 9. CASH ADEQUACY AT THE LIMITS OF ADVERSITY
COMPANY "A"

Revision of Exhibit 8 Showing Maximum Adverse Recession
Cash Position after Provision for All Expenditures
Considered by Management to be Mandatory

				Assuming Recession Experience with respect to:		
				Financial Conditions Preceding Recession	Behavior of Determinants of Cash Flow During Recession	
	Cumulative Net Cash Balance at End of Recession Year:				Sales Contraction	Other Determinants
No.	One	Two		Reaches its Adverse Limit described as:		
1	$(15,970,000)	$(22,090,000)		Maximum	Maximum	Maximum
2	(13,560,000)			Maximum	Most Probable	Maximum
3	(6,370,000)	(990,000)		Most Probable	Maximum	Maximum
4	(6,420,000)			Most Probable	Most Probable	Maximum
5	(1,970,000)	10,430,000		Current Condition	Maximum	Maximum
6	(1,860,000)			Current Condition	Most Probable	Maximum
7	3,940,000	13,300,000		Maximum	Maximum	Most Probable
8	5,150,000			Maximum	Most Probable	Most Probable
9	9,540,000	25,110,000		Most Probable	Maximum	Most Probable
10	12,500,000			Most Probable	Most Probable	Most Probable
11	18,460,000	40,360,000		Current Condition	Maximum	Most Probable
12	18,940,000			Current Condition	Most Probable	Most Probable

capital expenditures were matched up with the parallel assumptions
on the exhibit and the single assumption with respect to dividends
was a standard modification throughout. The final results are
shown in Exhibit 9. Once again, it is helpful to focus attention on
a few critical combinations of events, and the figures shown below
are the new cash balances for the same sets of assumptions referred to previously on page 199.

Set of Conditions		Year One	Year Two
(A)	(1)	$(15,970,000)	$(22,090,000)
(A)	(2)	12,500,000	
(B)	(1)	(1,970,000)	10,430,000
(B)	(2)	18,940,000	

By comparing these figures with those on page 199, it can be seen that whether we are considering the possibility of a recession in the immediate or more distant future, the chances of being "out of cash" for the purpose in mind, namely, the payment of minimum dividends and minimum capital expenditures, have significantly increased. Assuming the Maximum Adverse behavior of the determinants of cash flow, including Sales, there is a definite possibility of being unable to cover these payments. On the other hand, if we exclude the most extreme behavior and consider only the Most Probable range, then it is apparent that long-term debt in almost any amount that is likely to be available does not pose any threat to dividends or capital expenditures. Speaking generally, therefore, the threat to such payments is clearly a remote probability. As previously noted, however, the margin has narrowed and should any other expenditures, such as research and development or employment stabilization, be given precedence over debt leverage the point could be reached where debt would pose a substantial threat of cash inadequacy.

As management brings its attitudes toward risk to bear on the information produced in a recession cash flow analysis regarding the chance of being out of cash, in the process of setting limits on long-term borrowing, it is most important to distinguish between cash inadequacy as described here and cash insolvency. This is a distinction which is not often made in practice — at least explicitly — and is critical in reaching a sensible decision. Conventional rules of thumb are talked about as if debt in excess of stated amounts posed a serious threat to solvency. This may be true of some companies, but as the example in this chapter shows the only significant threat may be to expenditures which are mandatory only in a policy sense.

In considering the risk that it is willing to bear, a management may quite properly distinguish between cash inadequacy and cash insolvency and be more disposed to bear the former than the latter. Thus, for example, a decision which created a modest chance of having to suspend dividends may be regarded as quite appropriate whereas a decision which created the same degree of chance of becoming insolvent might be rejected. In deciding whether to run a given risk, management is weighing the gains, say from more debt leverage, against the possible "costs." The cost in the sense of going bankrupt may be regarded quite differently from such costs as a loss in efficiency and competitive position, a loss of prestige, or damage to the market for the common stock.

Once again, it should be apparent that unless management has recession cash flow data similar to those which have been generated for the rubber company, it cannot draw this important distinction. The conventional approaches to debt capacity are not in a form which is of any real value in this regard.

THE DETERMINATION OF SPECIFIC DEBT LIMITS

It was indicated in Chapter 7 that a cash flow analysis which focused on the adverse *limits* of variation, rather than on the whole range, had inherent limitations for the assessment of risk. The practical considerations which suggested an analysis in this form have thus imposed restraints on the extent to which the information can be used to assist management in making decisions that affect the corporate risk level. Refined tools of analysis cannot be developed from partial and/or approximate data. Up to this point the questions that have been raised and answered by the data have been of a sort that the data can answer. They may be summarized as follows:

(1) Given a company's past experience and management's present expectations, is there a chance of cash insolvency in the future?

(2) If so, does the evidence point in the direction of a substantial probability of occurrence or merely a remote possibility of occurrence?

(3) How would the amount of debt servicing required by a specific debt proposal or permitted under an established debt limit decision rule affect the prospects of cash insolvency? Assuming that this amount of debt was outstanding, would the risk of cash insolvency be substantial, remote, or "nonexistent"?

(4) Is the rough order of magnitude (substantial vs. remote) attached to the chances of cash insolvency by the recession cash flow analysis generally consistent with the related risk expectations implicit in the company's established debt limits, given management's attitude toward risk bearing? If not, then the *direction* of modification of the debt limit rule is indicated.

(5) Given a disposition on the part of management to place cer-

tain expenditures ahead of debt servicing even though not mandatory in a survival sense (e.g., minimum dividend payments), the
same questions raised above can be answered with respect to cash
inadequacy as distinguished from cash insolvency.

The main limitations of the data become apparent when we pur-
sue the answer to question number (4) above. Suppose, for example, that our company "A" had a debt limit of 20% of capitalization based on the assumption that debt in excess of this posed a
substantial threat to solvency. A review of the evidence of Exhibit 8 shows clearly that this is not the case, at least under any
conventional definition of the word "substantial" and it might well
be so concluded by management. The risk is apparently less than
it was believed to be. This is valuable information and suggests
that a more liberal debt capacity rule would be more consistent
with management's disposition toward risk bearing. The problem
comes, however, in deciding how far to go in this direction.

To solve this problem in a completely satisfactory manner, we
require a consideration of the full range of anticipated experience
along the lines indicated in Chapter 7 and elaborated in Appendix B. What is required is an estimate of the probability of insolvency at various levels of debt servicing so that changes in the
amount of debt outstanding can be translated with some degree of
objectivity into changes in the level of risk.

Whether this lack of information will be a matter of serious concern to management in practice — and whether there will be a
strong incentive to develop a more elaborate analysis — will depend to an important degree on the other dimension of the debt
capacity decision, the attitude toward risk bearing. In this regard,
the field study of corporate practice suggested three different approaches to risk bearing. First, there were those companies, few
in number, that would exclude debt from consideration if there was
any expectation that it posed a threat to solvency, however remote.
For such managements the data of this study are entirely adequate.
They give a clear answer to the question as to whether the event of
cash insolvency lies within management's expectations. If the analysis shows the hazard exists, then of course there will be a rejection
of debt entirely. If the analysis shows positive cash balances at the
extremes of adverse behavior, then the amount of these balances is

an objective measure of the extent to which amounts of debt servicing can be added without creating the chance of insolvency.

Second, there were those companies that showed a disposition to finance through long-term debt instruments so long as the risk of insolvency was "remote." As previously discussed, this approach reflects an essentially negative attitude toward debt leverage — a basic dislike of debt but a willingness to use it in time of financial need (because the equity alternatives are even more distasteful) so long as it did not pose a "serious" threat to solvency. This attitude appeared to be relatively widespread among these large, mature companies which financed primarily out of retained earnings but were from time to time "forced into" debt because of a temporary acceleration of the corporate growth trends.

It is obvious of course that the words used here to describe the acceptable level of risk are relative and may mean different things to different people. The basic attitude that these words reflect does, however, focus attention on the lower or adverse end of the range of possible events. In a crude way the distinction between Most Probable and Maximum Adverse Limits tends to fit this approach. Having separated events within the anticipated normal range of behavior from adverse events which are regarded as having only an "outside chance" of occurrence — and having done so determinant by determinant without any knowledge of how this distinction would ultimately affect net cash flows — management has a rough guide as to where it may wish to draw the line.

Thus management may be disposed to consider additional debt servicing charges so long as they do not pose a threat of insolvency at the Most Probable Adverse Limit of behavior. To go beyond this is clear warning that the level at which cash balances will prove inadequate has moved up into the normal range of events where the probability of occurrence of these events is substantial and where the cumulative probability of events being *at least* as adverse as this, may be expected to grow at an accelerating rate. Thus although there is nothing absolute or magical about the Most Probable Adverse Limit, it does serve as an "early warning" device for management. This interpretation of the limit brings up again a point made earlier in this study that debt capacity rules are customarily a guide as to the point where management ceases to be more or less comfortable with long-term debt and beyond which it becomes actively hostile to it. It is in this sense that the Most Probable Adverse Limit has special meaning.

For Company "A" the evidence would suggest that almost any level of debt which institutional lenders could be persuaded to agree to would be adequately covered at the Most Probable Adverse Limit and would involve a very small risk of cash insolvency. Such evidence might induce the management of Company "A" to depart from conventional debt rules and to take advantage of opportunities for higher and more continuous leveraging of its capital structure. This is, of course, a decision which the management of the company concerned alone can make.

The third approach to risk bearing may be described as a positive approach in which management is deliberately pursuing the potential income advantages of debt by balancing possible gain against possible loss. In terms of the sample of this study, the number of companies that might be so characterized were relatively few. Nevertheless, considering the basic problem presented by debt financing, this approach is the one which will have the greatest rational appeal for those who assume that the primary objective of business is to maximize the return on the shareholders' equity. From this point of view, the data of Exhibits 6 to 8 will do no more than serve as a useful but preliminary test of the appropriateness of existing debt capacity decision rules as previously described. It will not serve as a basis for determining what the decision rule *should* be, even in an approximate form. For this we require the type of analysis suggested by Appendix B, so that management can examine the specific "odds" of insolvency and decide the chance it is willing to take in view of the expected rewards.

When the consideration of how specific restraints on long-term debt are to be formulated is extended to include a consideration of the risks of cash inadequacy as well as cash insolvency, the need for more refined data is likely to appear substantially more widespread and urgent. Among the customary "breed" of financial officers of large corporations there do not appear to be many who are prepared to flirt with insolvency to any significant extent, given a reasonable alternative. On the other hand, if offered proof that what they were really considering was not the risk of insolvency to any significant extent but rather the risk of cash inadequacy — for one or more of several self-imposed fixed minimum expenditures — there would probably be a considerably larger number prepared to take chances if the rewards were high enough. Here also a formal appraisal of the maximum risk consistent with company attitudes and income opportunities calls for some method of quantifying changes in risk for varying levels of fixed cash outflow.

THE INFLUENCE OF MANAGEMENT ACTION ON THE RISK OF CASH INSOLVENCY

Throughout the cash flow analysis of this and the previous chapter, it has been assumed that management's behavior in the future would follow the patterns of the past and would not be modified in the light of new information provided by the analysis. In view of the fact that the occasion for the analysis is a serious re-examination of the risks of cash insolvency and inadequacy, however, and particularly in view of the fact that the results of the analysis may reveal a risk dimension which differs from the previous conceptions of management, it is quite possible that management may take deliberate steps to modify its behavior in the future. One of the functions which may be served by the cash flow analysis is to identify those determinants of cash flow which are subject to managerial control in some degree and those determinants to which cash flows are most sensitive.

This is illustrated in a general way by the results of the several combinations of assumptions given in Exhibits 6 to 9. These exhibits single out for separate consideration (1) the financial condition prior to the recession, (2) the behavior of Sales during the recession, and (3) the behavior of all other determinants of cash flow during the recession. Normally, item number (2), Sales, must be taken as given and management cannot expect to have much influence on this variable except over the long run. (An example of an exception to this would be sudden and substantial diversification of product lines through a merger.) On the other hand, management can do something about the state of the company's finances in anticipation of a possible recession and about its responses once a recession manifests itself.

Considering the financial condition first, Exhibit 8 shows that the effect of varying this assumption while holding the other two dimensions constant is significant. Thus, for example, if Sales and Other Determinants are taken at their Maximum Adverse Limit of behavior, and the assumption as to Financial Condition Preceding Recession is changed from Maximum Adverse to Most Probable Adverse, the recession net cash balance is increased from a negative $3,470,000 in the first year to a positive $3,130,000. This variation in the assumptions represents a considerable range in recession cash flows and net cash position; it suggests that this company could by a deliberate modification of its general financial structure in times of normal business activity alter substantially the chances of cash insolvency in recessions and thus influence the opportunity to assume additional fixed cash outflows within the risk standards acceptable to management.

This situation would not be true of all companies. The opportunity to affect the risk of insolvency in this way depends on such factors as the characteristic proportions among assets, the extent of reliance on spontaneous credit, and so on which vary greatly between industries and even within industries from company to company. Company "A" serves as an example of a situation where the Earnings Coverage standard of debt capacity, by leaving these factors out of consideration, does not give a well-rounded picture of the debt capacity question. Of course, the evidence of variations in recession cash position cited above does not necessarily mean that management can, as a practical matter, modify its financial characteristics to this degree or that it would wish to do so if it could.

To cite an example, a company could in normal times bear down harder on inventory turnover and use the cash so released as a reserve in anticipation of possible recession cash drains. At some point, this could have adverse effects on sales potential or production efficiency and certainly the cash so released could be invested in less liquid but productive assets. These costs have to be weighed against the gains from the added debt leverage made possible by the improved prospects for the company's recession cash position. Thus there is no clear and general answer to the question of whether such action would be advisable. Certainly, however, these aspects of finance must be recognized as interdependent and whatever choice is made must recognize the impact on the risk of insolvency. To the extent that this interdependence has not been explicitly evaluated prior to the cash flow analysis, opportunities for a better balance of objectives may exist.

A factor of equal if not greater potential importance in this respect is the response of management to recession conditions, a response which has been built in to the assumptions regarding the behavior of determinants of cash flow (other than Sales). The figures of Exhibit 8 suggest the importance of variations in this behavior. A change from Maximum to Most Probable Adverse Limits in this factor alone shifts the recession Cash balance for Company "A" in Year One from a negative $3,470,000 to a positive $16,440,000. The process of analysis will have revealed the particular determinants of cash flows which have been most influential in this modification of cash flows and the extent to which the response of these determinants is influenced by managerial behavior.

Having thus identified its opportunities, it is then possible for management to consider possible modifications in its behavior in the interests of improved recession cash flows and focus on those modifications which have the highest pay-off in this respect. For example, in Company "A" the first year of the recession proved to be the most critical one with respect to the risk of insolvency. The second year of the recession was by contrast substantially better. This suggests that steps which would mean a quicker response to the onset of a recession would improve the over-all recession cash flow situation. One of the areas of potential improvement is in the commitment of cash to raw material, work in process, and finished goods inventories. Inventory and production scheduling policies which are generally valid in a period of prosperity and growth can and should be modified in a period of decline, with particular attention being given to the conservation of cash. Often the appropriate modifications are delayed unnecessarily and the cash position is jeopardized because of insensitivity to economic change and rigidity in policy administration. Improved information, better tools of analysis, more rapid communication, or a change in management's scale of values could accelerate the change-over and thus modify the expected behavior of cash flows in recession Year One. Once again, a cost will doubtless be involved but up to a point may be bearable when compared to the reduction in the risk of cash insolvency or inadequacy.

Speaking generally, there is reason to believe that modifications of decision rules, operating procedures, and management responses will be easier to implement in recession than in prosperity — hence there would appear to be more hope for a modification in the expected response of the determinants of cash flow in the recession than in the financial conditions preceding recession. Similarly, there would appear to be greater opportunities in a more severe recession than in a mild one and in a long recession than in a short one. In the last analysis, however, it comes down to the individuals who make up the management team — their capacity to anticipate the turning points and their willingness, as a team, to give priority to cash flow considerations in periods of contraction. If through this teamwork it is possible to tighten up on cash flows so as to quicken desired responses, remove bottlenecks, and minimize unnecessary absorption of cash in idle "pockets," there may be a substantial improvement in the recession cash position. But obviously this does not come merely by changing the assumptions on a cash flow projection sheet, and it may be that the costs of such action are considered to be excessive. Smaller inventories, tighter production schedules, and shortened lead times on management decisions at some point create pressures on efficiency and executive peace of mind which make the hoped-for result of added fixed cash outflow capacity not worth the effort. Undoubtedly the considerable financial slack which is apparent in many companies is directly related to the comfort of management. The tighter the fit, the greater the danger of both management and finances "coming apart at the seams."

In these various ways the assumptions of the analysis must be reviewed. In the process significant opportunities for modifying cash flow behavior and reducing the risk of cash insolvency or increasing the opportunity for assuming fixed cash outflows with safety may be disclosed. Incidentally, this kind of analysis and reconsideration of management practices may be undertaken whether or not debt is contemplated since the hazard of cash insolvency is obviously not limited to companies that borrow.

THE BROADER IMPLICATIONS OF THE CASH FLOW ANALYSIS

It should now be clear to the reader that by dealing with the risks of debt in terms of cash flows, the fact that the mandatory cash outflows are due to a debt contract is actually of minor significance. Exactly the same problem arises in connection with any decision which will result in an increase in the company's fixed cash outflows. The more fundamental question therefore is: Given management's attitude toward risk bearing, *what is the capacity of the company to assume incremental fixed cash outflows?* The same analysis will be employed for a prospective lease contract decision, for example, as for a prospective debt contract decision. Analysts have been troubled by this problem because in trying to force the risk appraisal into the mold of conventional criteria they run into difficulties. Many of these analysts, equating leases to the burden of debt, try to find the balance sheet equivalent according to some capitalization rate and then lump this amount with long-term debt on a Percent of Capitalization basis. There is, however, notable lack of agreement as to how the capitalization rate is to be derived. In the view of the author this process is artificial and unnecessary. Under the process proposed in this study all we need to know is the amount of the annual contractual obligation to pay in dollars of cash outflow. The analysis is then identical with that proposed for debt.

The discussion of cash inadequacy as distinguished from cash insolvency also indicated that, in addition to contractual commitments, there are fixed outflows that are mandatory in a policy sense and that compete in the minds of management for whatever capacity is assumed to exist. Here also the process of analysis is the same with the exception that there may be differences in the willingness to bear the risk as previously explained.

At any point in time, therefore, a going concern has a given set of determinants of cash flow which lead to certain definable expectations as to recession behavior and the chances of insolvency. These will be modified by any action that adds any specified sum to the fixed cash outflows, regardless of the purpose. The process of appraisal of risk magnitudes before and after the action will be essentially the same, and the effect of the action on the risk will be essentially the same, given equivalent dollar amounts of cash outflow over a comparable period of time. *The recession cash flow analysis is therefore seen to be a necessary preliminary to a whole set of financial decisions involving fixed cash outflows, and the opportunity for long-term debt financing clearly cannot be decided independently of other purposes to which a willingness to bear increased risk might be put.*

This statement should not be interpreted to suggest that management does have or should have a concept of the risk magnitude that it is willing to bear which can be defined in advance of knowledge of specific opportunities which would modify the risk. Unless and until management has a measure of the potential rewards from risk bearing, it cannot make a rational decision, and these rewards will obviously vary from one alternative to another. Given two or more alternatives, however (say, increased debt leverage versus a long-term lease contract), involving comparable fixed cash outflows where the anticipated financial rewards are in each case sufficient to induce management to accept the increased risk but where the combined risk would be considered excessive — a choice must obviously be made.

Thus it is seen that it is somewhat artificial to talk of debt capacity as though it is a definable value which remains constant over time, even if the potential rewards from debt leverage can be expected to remain relatively constant. What we are really concerned with is the capacity to assume incremental fixed cash outflows; and to the extent that more attractive uses for this capacity present themselves from time to time, the remaining capacity to assume long-term debt, if any, will vary.

THE RELATION OF DEBT CAPACITY RULES TO GENERAL CORPORATE LIQUIDITY

It is customary for management, particularly financial management, to approach a choice involving a possible modification of the risk of cash insolvency or inadequacy in the knowledge that certain defensive measures would be available if adversity becomes a reality. Many financial managers make sure that their financial structure has a number of built-in "shock absorbers" which provide flexibility if events take a sudden unexpected turn for the worse. Thus bank balances which are more than adequate to meet normal operating needs, marketable securities, and comfortable inventory levels may be thought of as serving this function. In the same way, a knowledge that certain inefficiencies exist in the control of cash flow or in operating procedures affecting cash flow (which, although possibly justified under prosperous conditions, could be tightened if cash flow achieved sufficient priority) will be taken into account when assessing the threat of insolvency.

In many companies one of the primary elements of flexibility, at least in the minds of management, is "unused" debt capacity. The assurance of being able to call on creditors for financial assistance on very short notice when substantial cash needs are presented unexpectedly is an important support of management peace of mind. The limitations of this expectation have been noted in a previous chapter. Insofar as this unexpected need was thought of as that which might occur in a recession period, there are good reasons to doubt the reliability of such a reserve, as suggested in Chapter 4. Bank and insurance company lending is predominantly for the addition of new earning assets, not for the protection of existing assets which are currently losing money. Thus a reserve of debt capacity is meaningful largely if not entirely in terms of unexpected growth opportunities. Carrying this idea a step further, it may even be argued that the use of debt capacity rather than its disuse is the better protection against a recession *if* the funds are invested in such a manner that they can be liquidated during the recession in an amount in excess of the related servicing charges.

There is no question of the importance of the concept of a reserve to management, however, and this is clearly reflected in the debt capacity rules used by many companies which establish a clear margin between the maximum amount of long-term debt which the company will use and that which is available according to the conventional standards used by creditors.

The question arises as to how the proposed recession cash flow analysis would affect the conventional concepts of liquidity and flexibility to the extent that they represent a defense against adversity. The answer depends on the information produced by the analysis and whether it serves to confirm or modify management's previously held expectations as to the magnitude of the risk of insolvency and the behavior of cash flows under recession conditions. If the analysis shows the risk to be substantially less than assumed or reveals defenses against an adverse cash position not previously recognized, then it may be perfectly appropriate for management to act so as to reduce its liquidity and flexibility as previously defined. As a part of this response to new information, management may act to reduce or eliminate unused debt capacity on the grounds that it is prepared to bear whatever risk of insolvency remains after this emergency source is dried up.

If, on the other hand, the analysis merely spells out in detail a pattern of cash flow behavior, the general dimensions of which are known by management, and/or reveals the chance of insolvency as being in the general vicinity of what management had come to expect from less sophisticated evidence, then it is to be expected that the existing elements of liquidity and flexibility will be left alone. To take action which would reduce the proportion of liquid or near-liquid assets, reduce unused debt capacity, or modify the behavior of cash flows under such circumstances would disturb the balance between the disposition to assume risk and the risk itself. It must be assumed that the willingness to bear whatever risk is involved has already taken account of whatever defenses against insolvency exist, and to reduce or eliminate one or more of these defenses will inevitably change the disposition to assume the risk.

Thus the risk inherent in a certain set of financial circumstances may be accepted in part because, for example, it is known that if need be $1,000,000 could be squeezed out of inventory on relatively short notice without impairing the flow of production or sales. To take action which removes this "cushion" is bound to lead management to take compensating action elsewhere, such as to reduce the level of acceptable debt servicing charges (increase the unused debt capacity). This interpretation of management responses should serve to alert the reader to the fact that merely because the cash flow analysis reveals opportunities for making more efficient use of cash, it cannot be assumed that such action can be taken without possible repercussions on the acceptable level of long-term debt. This is a point which is sometimes forgotten by over-zealous advocates of efficiency in cash management.

Summary and Comment

The approach to debt capacity described in this and the preceding chapter has not been presented as a total substitute for existing debt capacity decision rules, even though theoretically at least it could be developed as such. The reader will have noted the qualifications which were presented along with the results of the analysis. Its primary function so far as long-term debt capacity is concerned has been to provide a rational basis for relating the commonly used and highly generalized rules of thumb to the financial circumstances of the individual industry and firm. It provides useful evidence on the critical questions posed on page 207 in a form which debt capacity decision rules in their conventional form cannot begin to resolve. And not the least of its merits, it discusses the impact of debt in the analytical framework best suited to rational analysis — that is, in terms of its impact on the behavior of cash flows.

It is assumed that a business undertaking such an analysis will continue to consider all information which is relevant to the question of appropriate debt limits. This would certainly include information on the debt policies of comparable businesses and the debt capacity standards of existing or potential creditors. Management will seek the counsel of experts in the capital market as it seems appropriate. On the other hand management will no longer be solely dependent on such external sources as the basis for its own financial policy in this regard. It is a simple fact that not only does internal management have the best data for a solution of this problem, potentially at least, but also as custodian of the interests of those who bear the risk the board of directors is the only body properly qualified to say what the appropriate risk posture shall be. The evidence from the field study suggests that some managements have been either unaware of this responsibility or have considered themselves unable to fulfill it. This study has been designed as a contribution to the removal of these misconceptions.

There is no doubt that a number of the financial executives to whom the findings and recommendations of this study are primarily directed will be inclined to resist any change in their present approach to the debt capacity question. For some there will be a natural reluctance to move from simple, clear-cut, and time-honored rules to an involved and time-consuming analysis in which it becomes evident that there are no absolute values. It should be clear, however, that the problem is inherently complex and the use of simpler rules of thumb does not of itself eliminate the complexity but rather tends to gloss over it. It is in the interests of better decision making to move in the direction of a more precise definition of the problem and to attempt to come to grips with the relevant data.

Thus the real question is whether, assuming that the basic data on cash flows are available, the added information is worth the expenditure of time and money to get it. It appears to the author that, considering the relatively crude form of much of present-day debt capacity analysis, the opportunity for unhurried consideration of this area of long-term policy, and the broad implications of a recession cash flow analysis which go far beyond the debt question, there should be little hesitation, particularly on the part of larger corporations with substantial cash flow experience behind them, to take full advantage of the opportunity.   As already noted the analysis can be carried out at different levels of refinement depending on objectives and circumstances, and the results can and should be interpreted in conjunction with the more conventional debt capacity criteria.

A second major objection is likely to be that the question of debt capacity is primarily decided by the creditor and the borrowing corporation must work within limits set for him by those who set the lender's risk standards.   The inference is that the determination of debt capacity by the borrower's independent analysis would be largely if not entirely an academic exercise.   While recognizing that the debt contract is a negotiated instrument and presumes a willing lender as well as a willing borrower, this study has made a strong plea for an independent appraisal by the borrower.   The reasons are primarily that: (1) there is usually a range within which the amount of debt acceptable to the creditor can be negotiated, and (2) again, the recession cash flow analysis of the capacity to bear incremental fixed cash outflows goes far beyond the consideration of long-term debt.

A defense of existing debt-capacity decision rules which is related to the question of creditors' standards is the argument that investors generally think in these terms (the conventional rules of thumb), and to depart from customary standards, regardless of how unrealistic they may be for a particular company, will involve penalties through a lower credit rating or a depressed market price for the common stock.   The answer to this line of argument is essentially the same as that expressed in the preceding paragraph, namely, that the market's standards generally provide for a range of acceptable behavior and the job of management is to position itself within that range to maximum advantage.   Improved information about corporate risks does not imply a violation of practical considerations but rather suggests a more intelligent response to them.

One of the practical problems involved in this type of analysis is that it is made at one point in time and that as time passes added information is received which may modify one's expectations in some respect. In general, our fundamental determinants of cash flow were factors, such as credit terms, customer buying habits, production processes, and the like, which tend to change slowly in regard to their limits of variation. Change does occur, however, and consequently a periodic reconsideration of the assumptions underlying the recession cash flow analysis is essential. There should also be a periodic reconsideration of the attitude toward risk bearing. Such periodic reviews will not only serve as a means of integrating new information but will also be useful as an added check on the judgments made at an earlier period of time.

This obviously means that debt and other policies based on such analysis may change over time. This is quite appropriate to the extent that risk (or management's concept thereof) changes and/or the willingness to bear the risk changes, the latter change being traceable either to changes in individual and group attitudes and circumstances or to changes in the personnel of the stockholders and/or management. If such changes were sudden, substantial, and frequent, the effect on debt policy could be undesirable since it is not an easy matter to expand or contract long-term debt suddenly. But this is not likely to be the case, at least so far as the determinants of cash flow are concerned, because of the many factors involved. The primary factor which could bring about a sudden shift would be a sudden major change in stock ownership or management where views on risk are radically different. Even here, however, changes tend to be gradual in the normal process of turnover of personnel and basic attitudes may remain essentially the same over long periods of time.

Chapters 7 and 8 have been primarily concerned with methodology and with the general interpretation and application of the results of a recession cash flow analysis. We now turn in the final chapter from the general to the specific and from the hypothetical to the actual. In Chapter 9 the recession cash flow analysis is applied to five of the companies included in the field study of debt policy and the results are compared with individual management attitudes and debt capacity decision rules. It should be noted that here also the purpose is primarily to illustrate — not to generalize

about industries or classes of companies. The study has emphasized again and again that the debt burden decision is an individual
one and can only be defined in terms of the individual circumstances of the company in question and by those charged with the
responsibility of taking the "calculated risk."

CHAPTER 9

A Review of the Debt Policies of
Five Companies in the Light of Their
Simulated Recession Cash Flows

INTRODUCTION

The purpose of this chapter is to illustrate the application of a recession cash flow analysis as a means of formulating corporate debt policy and a concept of debt capacity. One company has been chosen from each of the five industries represented in this study and a cash flow analysis has been made as outlined in the two preceding chapters. These analyses were based on the historical evidence of the behavior of the determinants of cash flow and the expectations of management as to the limits of variation in recession periods. Having worked out the net cash flows implied by these expectations, we now proceed to relate these to the stated debt policy of the company. This latter policy also has expectations for the future implicit in its decision rules, particularly as regards debt capacity, and the comparison will be a test of the degree of consistency in management thinking. Since the decision rules with respect to debt capacity have been observed to come largely from sources *outside* the company, it will not be surprising if some such inconsistencies emerge.

In addition to the test of the company's individual debt policies, it will also be informative to apply some of the conventional rules of lenders to observe their implications in the individual case. We

223

now proceed to look at each company in turn. All data have been disguised but the significant relationships have not been disturbed. It is important to emphasize that although the industry of each company is revealed as a matter of interest to the reader, the case must not be construed as representative in any sense.

COMPANY "A" (THE RUBBER INDUSTRY)

The first case to be considered is the company which was used for illustrative purposes in the two preceding chapters. This company is typical of the companies in the sample in that it has been in existence for many years, has demonstrated a capacity to maintain an important place in the industry, and for most of these years has been profitable. In spite of its size, stability, and profitability, however, the company is not disposed to finance by long-term borrowings merely for the income leverage of low, tax-deductible interest rates or the inflationary hedge of a fixed dollar obligation (though these potential advantages are recognized by management). The stated reason for borrowing is, rather, because of the fact that investment needs tend to have an irregular timing beyond the control of management and beyond the capacity of current internally generated funds. Given the option, management has stated that it would prefer to do this financing entirely from retained earnings.

It appears implicit in the statements of the financial management of this company that the company has specific and essentially nonfinancial limits to its investment "horizon" and that the company borrows only to make up deficiencies (hopefully temporary) in the funds generated by operations in excess of the relatively stable dividend payments. It has been suggested by the existing management that borrowing beyond this limit merely to "trade on the equity" would be "senseless" since it would tend to produce idle cash balances which in turn would create pressures for higher dividends, with the ultimate result being to force management to generate investment projects to "use up" the excess cash.

In spite of this refusal to use debt merely for the purpose of lowering the average cost of capital, management does not appear to be afraid of long-term debt in what it considers to be reasonable amounts. Every balance sheet for the past 20 years shows some long-term debt outstanding at the year end. Management volunteers the evidence, now commonly accepted in the industry, that the risks involved in the manufacture of rubber products have declined — for reasons cited earlier in this study. They are proud of the fact that rubber stocks are now to be found among the "blue chips." They feel that this improved stability in earnings is here to stay for the indefinite future. This improvement is, of course, relative — cyclicality remains and five-year forecasts of the cash position of the company are still labeled as "not worth a damn" so far as accuracy is concerned.

The current financial management of Company "A" believes that long-term debt would not be incurred if the total principal amount of such debt exceeded 30% of the total book value of the net tangible assets of the company. (This would be the same as 30% of Total Capitalization.) At the current level of asset book values this would be a debt of approximately $52,000,000. The practical application of this rule of thumb appears to be supported by the record since new debt issues over the past 20 years have generally produced a maximum debt percentage in the 25% to 30% range without ever deliberately exceeding the upper limit. In elaborating on this standard, management has indicated that 30% represents an extreme upper limit and that in practice "you never want to borrow all you can because you must be prepared for the unexpected." Thus 25% would probably be a more meaningful operating limit. Management asserted that when on rare occasions necessity forced the company to borrow close to the 30% "outside limit" it produced a "scared feeling" and a sense of urgency to get the ratio down as quickly as possible.

Given these attitudes toward debt and concepts of debt capacity, we now turn to their implications for recession cash flows. It can be assumed that the scared feeling to which management referred was the prospect of cash insolvency resulting from an unexpected decline in cash inflows. The data developed in the cash flow analysis give us a rough measure of the probability of this event for this company and the effect of any given amount of debt servicing on that probability. These data, given in the preceding chapter, have been reproduced here for convenient reference in Exhibits 10 and 11. Exhibit 10 shows the recession cash balances anticipated at the limits of adverse behavior, considering only those expenditures which are vital to the continuity of current sales and income. This

EXHIBIT 10. CASH SOLVENCY AT THE LIMITS OF ADVERSITY
COMPANY "A" (RUBBER INDUSTRY)

Anticipated Recession Cash Position Associated with Adverse
Limits of Behavior of Determinants of Cash Flow:
Considering Only Those Expenditures Required to Generate
Current Income

			Assuming Recession Experience with respect to:		
	Cumulative Net Cash Balance at End of Recession Year:		*Financial Conditions Preceding Recession*	*Behavior of Determinants of Cash Flow During Recession*	
				Sales Contraction	*Other Determinants*
No.	*One*	*Two*	*Reaches its Adverse Limit described as:*		
1	$(3,470,000)	$(2,090,000)	Maximum	Maximum	Maximum
2	(1,060,000)		Maximum	Most Probable	Maximum
3	3,130,000	14,510,000	Most Probable	Maximum	Maximum
4	3,080,000		Most Probable	Most Probable	Maximum
5	7,530,000	25,930,000	Current Condition	Maximum	Maximum
6	7,640,000		Current Condition	Most Probable	Maximum
7	16,440,000	33,300,000	Maximum	Maximum	Most Probable
8	17,650,000		Maximum	Most Probable	Most Probable
9	19,040,000	40,610,000	Most Probable	Maximum	Most Probable
10	22,000,000		Most Probable	Most Probable	Most Probable
11	27,960,000	55,860,000	Current Condition	Maximum	Most Probable
12	28,440,000		Current Condition	Most Probable	Most Probable

is the basic test of solvency. Exhibit 11 considers the adverse limits of recession cash balances remaining after all minimum expenditures considered by management to be mandatory in a recession
period. Given a possible long-term debt of $43,000,000 to
$52,000,000 (25% to 30% of N.T.A.), this can be translated
into an equivalent dollar amount of annual debt servicing by making some standard assumptions about the terms of the debt. Let it
be assumed that the term is 20 years, the interest rate is 5%, and
the sinking fund is sufficient to retire the debt by maturity in equal
annual payments. This means an annual incremental cash outflow

EXHIBIT 11. CASH ADEQUACY AT THE LIMITS OF ADVERSITY
COMPANY "A" (RUBBER INDUSTRY)

Anticipated Recession Cash Position Associated with Adverse
Limits of Behavior of Determinants of Cash Flow:
Considering All Expenditures Given Priority over Debt Servicing

			Assuming Recession Experience with Respect to:		
			Financial Con-ditions Preceding Recession	Behavior of Determinants of Cash Flow During Recession	
Cumulative Net Cash Balance at End of Recession Year:				*Sales Con-traction*	*Other De-terminants*
No.	*One*	*Two*	Reaches its Adverse Limit described as:		
1	$(15,970,000)	$(22,090,000)	Maximum	Maximum	Maximum
2	(13,560,000)		Maximum	Most Probable	Maximum
3	(6,370,000)	(990,000)	Most Probable	Maximum	Maximum
4	(6,420,000)		Most Probable	Most Probable	Maximum
5	(1,970,000)	10,430,000	Current Condition	Maximum	Maximum
6	(1,860,000)		Current Condition	Most Probable	Maximum
7	3,940,000	13,300,000	Maximum	Maximum	Most Probable
8	5,150,000		Maximum	Most Probable	Most Probable
9	9,540,000	25,110,000	Most Probable	Maximum	Most Probable
10	12,500,000		Most Probable	Most Probable	Most Probable
11	18,460,000	40,360,000	Current Condition	Maximum	Most Probable
12	18,940,000		Current Condition	Most Probable	Most Probable

for debt servicing (interest and sinking fund) of approximately
$4,300,000 to $5,200,000 at its maximum point.

Referring to Exhibit 10 it can be seen that the debt policy described above does not assure "absolute" protection against cash
insolvency since the chance already appears to exist even before
any long-term debt is built in. On the other hand, all the events
represented in this exhibit are at the negative extreme of expected
experience and the remoteness of their probable occurrence must
be taken into account. The implication of the scared feeling at the
30% debt level is that the management of Company "A" believed that it was assuming some risk of cash insolvency at that
point and that the risk was substantial — sufficiently so that a

dominant consideration in making general financial decisions under such circumstances would be the reduction of the outstanding debt.

On examining the details of Exhibit 10, it can be seen that the only circumstances under which there is *any* expectation of insolvency under debt-free conditions is when both the financial conditions preceding the recession *and* the response of the determinants of cash flow during the recession are taken at or close to the "absolute" limit of adverse behavior (Maximum Adverse Limit). If on the other hand the Sales decline is assumed not to exceed the Most Probable Limit and the other determinants are also assumed to be at this Most Probable Adverse Limit, the minimum net cash balance is $22,000,000. It is therefore apparent that the risk of insolvency is confined to the narrow range of circumstances close to the extreme limit of adversity. If attention is confined to what may be called "normal" recession conditions, there appears to be no chance of insolvency. The cushion of cash available under Most Probable Adverse circumstances in the near future is even greater, being $28,440,000.

A 30% of capitalization debt limit begins to have some meaning in the light of this evidence. It is apparent that an additional cash outflow of $5,200,000 would not be enough to create the chance of insolvency under Most Probable Adverse Limits. Thus even with 30% debt the risk of insolvency is still confined to the remote, low-probability fringe of adversity. The change has not been enough to move the event of insolvency within the range of normal recession experience. On the other hand, there does remain some chance of insolvency and this is inevitably increased (though very modestly) by the addition of this amount of fixed cash outflows.

Another way of viewing the rule in the light of Exhibit 10 is to observe the most adverse combination of assumptions under which a debt burden of $5,200,000 could be carried without insolvency. We see that this is somewhere between set (4) and set (5) — that is, where the recession behavior of the determinants of cash flow including Sales was at the Maximum Adverse Limit but the financial conditions prior to the recession no more unfavorable than they are at present (No. 5) or, considering the slightly more adverse set, where the conditions preceding the recession and the Sales decline were at Most Probable Adverse Limits (No. 4). Eight of the twelve sets of adverse events produce a minimum recession cash balance adequate to cover such a fixed charge.

Of major significance to the interpretation of the data is the question of the sensitivity of cash flows to the various determinants and in particular to those which are subject to some management control. In this regard we may wish to rule out the Sales contraction as being beyond any short-run influence by management. It will be observed, incidentally, that in this case the difference between the Maximum and Most Probable Sales declines did not produce a significant variation in net cash flow. It will also be observed that the variations in the determinants of cash flow other than Sales tended to be the critical consideration since the six most adverse sets of assumptions all included the assumption that this factor was at its Maximum Adverse Limit. The most adverse cash balance when this factor was at the Most Probable Adverse Limit was $16,440,000. This suggests that there may be opportunities for a modification of management responses to the onset of a recession period which could have a significant bearing on the chances of insolvency. If further examination of the cash flow data confirmed this, it could have an important bearing on how the management would view particular debt limits such as the 30% rule under discussion.

This evidence of the comparatively remote chance of insolvency for this company at this point in time does not, of course, represent a condemnation of management's 30% rule in and of itself. It does, however, suggest a possible misconception of risk magnitudes on the part of present management. If we can assume that its primary concern is for protection against insolvency, and can take at face value the evidence of real anxiety for the continuity of the company if debt exceeds 30%, the only basis upon which this can be explained as rational behavior is if management is of a highly conservative character and extremely sensitive to small changes in risk. Management alone — being aware of its own subjective feelings about the voluntary assumption of risk — can decide if the existing rule, considered in the light of this new information, is out of line.

So far we have related the 30% debt limit to the risk of cash insolvency. There is also the question of the risk of cash inadequacy. This turns our attention to Exhibit 11 where recession cash balances must provide not only for expenditures essential to current Sales and Income generation but also for those minimum expenditures which in management's judgment must be maintained good times and bad, in the best long-term interests of the company. Thus they would be given priority over debt servicing in any capitalization decision. In this case these have been identified as a certain minimum capital expenditure and a minimum dividend payment.

It can be seen from the exhibit that the chances of being unable to meet these minimum management objectives at the anticipated limits of adversity are significantly greater than the chance of insolvency. Only four of the twelve sets of assumptions would provide any substantial cushion of cash on hand, assuming that debt in the amount of 30% of capitalization was incurred. Debt of this magnitude is not very far from the level where the chance of cash inadequacy as previously defined would fall within the Probable range of experience — within the limits of a normal recession as management views it.

On the other hand, it is a fact that the anticipated cash balance for Most Probable Adverse Limits is $12,500,000 as compared with the annual burden of 30% debt of $5,200,000 — slightly in excess of a 2:1 margin. Thus it can be asserted that the risk of cash inadequacy also has a comparatively low probability, being confined to a range of events beyond normal recession experience.

One interesting way of looking at the data is to ask what level would debt have to achieve before the threat of insolvency or inadequacy was brought within the range of anticipated normal, average, or typical recession experience. Before answering this question for this company, it should be emphasized that this is *not* an answer to the question as to what the debt level *should* be. Considering solvency first, it is apparent that with a $19,000,000 cushion at the Most Probable Limit the company could assume virtually any amount of debt that would be made available to it without bringing the chance of insolvency within the range of anticipated normal recession experience. Considering cash inadequacy, it can be seen that the company could go up to 60% debt before the event came within the range of normal recession experience.

The reaction of the practical businessman is likely to be that this is meaningless since creditors of the type with which this company would associate are not going to lend anywhere near 60% of the company's capitalization. This is true. But *if* the management was disposed to take risks of this magnitude and *if* it was disposed to utilize some of the capacity to assume the incremental fixed cash outflows which appear to be permissible at this level of risk for the purpose of debt leverage, then the data serve the useful purpose of indicating that the company should not be hesitant to assume the maximum amount of debt which such creditors will make available to them and to do so on a continuous basis.

In this regard it is interesting to look at the cash flow data in relation to the standards of safety of Company "A" 's sources of debt capital. As previously indicated, the evidence on lenders tended to be somewhat generalized but it is significant to consider the concepts of debt capacity held by the particular lenders with which an individual company has become associated. In the case of Company "A" attention focuses on an insurance company, an investment banking house, and a bond rating agency. Considering the insurance company first, it should be noted that it was customary for all sophisticated financial analysts to qualify heavily any statements of general practice and to emphasize the overriding importance of judgment in the individual case. With this major qualification the representative of this insurance company with whom Company "A" had negotiated was prepared to suggest that a company in an industry such as the rubber industry should have an average earnings coverage ratio of at least two times debt servicing. This was a ratio of average net earnings after depreciation and taxes but before bond interest to bond interest plus sinking fund payments at their maximum point.

Applying this standard to Company "A," we come up with a maximum annual cash outflow for debt servicing of $7,700,000. It will be noted that this is significantly above the company's own 25% to 30% limit but well below the level suggested by a risk-bearing concept designed to protect against adverse events beyond the Most Probable Limits of variation, especially if solvency is the primary concern. It is interesting to note that this insurance company volunteered the observation that a 30% to 35% debt limit standard was commonly accepted in the insurance industry but that the company itself did not adhere to this standard. As can be seen here, the earnings coverage standard applied to Company "A" would be somewhat more liberal than a 35% of N.T.A. upper limit (which would have an equivalent annual burden of $6,100,000).

Company "A" 's investment banking connections indicated that so far as they were concerned this was a case where the company set its own debt policy without the benefit of advice from them. This implied that the company was operating within what they considered to be appropriate limits. Discussion and documentary evidence on other roughly comparable situations, however, indicated that the investment banker would view a 30% to 35% of Capitalization as an upper limit on long-term debt. In the case of Company "A" this rule could be somewhat in conflict with a second standard used by this same investment banker which was that earnings coverage should be at least 2 to 3 times debt servicing. However, these standards are very close to being identical with those suggested by the insurance company.

Finally, from the point of view of bond ratings, evidence suggests that the company would have to hold its debt close to or below 20% of capitalization if it hoped to qualify for an Aa or Aaa rating. The rating is, of course, in the last analysis an agency judgment based on wide experience and the evaluation of many factors of which the debt proportion is only one. The above statistic, however, is considered to be a very common characteristic of top-rated bonds. For bonds in the "A" category the debt proportions may be higher. Here the Percent of Capitalization may be as high as 40% or even 50% but these percentages are uncommon. Recognizing that an "A" rating is considered by most large and mature companies as the lower limit of respectability for their bonds, this suggests a debt limit somewhere in the 20% to 40% range.

From this information it would appear that the standard of debt capacity set by the management of Company "A" is somewhat more conservative than its sources of debt capital would be inclined to impose. At the same time even the standards of the lenders are comfortably within the burden magnitudes suggested by the data for the Most Probable Adverse Limit of recession experience. The conclusion is that both borrower and lender have consciously or unconsciously adopted a debt policy designed to protect against adverse events which have a remote probability of occurrence. The impression of the author is that in this case both the lenders and the borrower have overestimated the risks associated with debt of the magnitude indicated.

One application of this analysis would be to propose for management's consideration a lifting of its operating debt limit from 25% to 35%. This would mean additional borrowings of $18,000,000. The incremental cost of this debt could be measured against the incremental cost of an equivalent amount of equity capital and the two compared with the expected return from the investment of these funds. In considering the anticipated impact on the earnings of the existing stockholders, it must be recognized that as long-term debt approaches the limit of the lender's "willingness to lend" the point may come when he considers the risk of the investment to have been increased and therefore expects a compensating increase in the interest rate. Evidence of this would be a change in the rating of the company's bonds to the next lower category — say from A to Baa. This was not contemplated in the change proposed for Company "A," at least so far as public offerings are concerned. If it was likely to occur as a result of moving from 25% to 35% debt, however, then the incremental cost of the new debt would be not only the expected interest charges on the $18,000,000 but also the premium which would have to be paid on the outstanding debt ($43,000,000) when it was refinanced. At some point this could inhibit incremental borrowing on the cost consideration alone. It should not be inferred, however, that there is a direct and automatic relationship between interest rates and debt proportions. Observation suggests that there are different "bands" or ranges of debt proportions within which the interest rate remains the same. If this is so, then there may be a real incentive in seeking out the upper limits of these ranges, assuming of course that they are within the limits of risk bearing for borrower and lender.

COMPANY "B" (THE BAKING INDUSTRY)

The company labeled Company "B" is one of the older and larger baking companies operating on a national scale. The record of the past 20 years shows that this company has not made extensive use of long-term debt. Management's comment on this record is that this has been due, not to a reluctance to borrow, but rather to the fact that funds from this source were not needed on a continuous and substantial basis. Such has indeed been the case if management is prepared to take as given (1) an investment horizon limited to the baking industry and to an objective of maintaining a certain competitive position within that industry, (2) the comparatively gradual process of change in product and in the technology of the production process, (3) the unusual stability in the demand for the product and the modest long-term rate of growth, (4) the established level of earnings retention, with sales and earnings subject to comparatively modest dips in periods of recession. The critical variables are, of course, the investment horizon, profitability, and the retention of earnings and, given a long-term balance here and no real disposition to change, there is obviously no major role for debt except occasionally to meet a temporary imbalance produced by a peaking of current investment in physical facilities.

In view of the assertion by management that it was not opposed to some long-term debt, it must be assumed that these policies were dictated by considerations other than the limitation of financial risk. At the same time, there was evidence that management considered this to be a comfortable state of affairs and was reluctant to make it less so through substantial additions of debt. "Besides," management said, "debt involves an added cost." This indicated a cost-free concept of retained earnings. Management also suggested that there was a natural human inertia which worked against dealing with an unfamiliar segment of the capital market for the first time.

There were two circumstances under which management had given active consideration to the use of long-term debt. One was to provide funds to acquire an operating company and the other was to assist in the retirement of a preferred stock. Both of these uses turned out to be of limited significance, however. Debt was found to be unacceptable in acquisitions since almost invariably the owners of the acquired company preferred an exchange of stock for tax reasons. With respect to the retirement of preferred, debt becomes a temporary means of providing the substantial sum for paying off the preferred shareholders and is then retired itself through retained earnings; so as previously indicated, the ultimate result is to replace preferred equity by common equity.

Under these circumstances the question of the limits of debt capacity is somewhat academic. The management did profess, how-

ever, to have done some thinking about this question in view of the chance that "someday" they might want to do some substantial debt financing. What they came up with was the conventional 30% of capitalization rule with the commonly used qualification that some reserve of debt capacity should always be preserved against an unexpected adverse turn in the company's affairs. There was the added proviso that they would not want to have a bond rating below an A. These two rules of thumb would appear to be consistent. The 30% was stated as being derived from "the 50% rule" for public utilities by making an adjustment for the risk differential. There was no evidence of any objective test for this risk differential. Apparently the company officers concerned had merely accepted on faith the widely held financial folklore on the subject.

As in the case of Company "A," we now consider Company "B" 's operating rules on debt capacity in the light of an analysis of cash flows under extreme recession assumptions. The data are shown in Exhibits 12 and 13.

It will be noted that, on balance, Company "B" shows up more favorably than Company "A." Considering the test for solvency first, Exhibit 12, it is seen that under conditions of an all equity capitalization the chances of insolvency within the limits of management's expectations are zero. Further, under the worst possible combination of events the company still is left with a positive minimum recession cash balance of $4,900,000. This obviously presumes that the recession will not last longer than one year, an expectation which has been confirmed by the experience of the past 20 years.

An interesting point of contrast between "A" and "B" is the way in which the different sets of assumptions affect cash flow. In Company "A" the dominant influence in the cash flow experience was the variation in the determinants during the recession experience — the six most favorable sets included the Most Probable Adverse assumption in this respect. In the case of Company "B" it will be noted that the differential between Maximum Adverse and Current values with respect to the conditions preceding the recession more than offset the improvement from Maximum Adverse to Most Probable Adverse Limit for the recession variations in the determinants so that the ranking was changed in the middle range of outcomes. The point here is simply that the dominant influences in

EXHIBIT 12. CASH SOLVENCY AT THE LIMITS OF ADVERSITY
COMPANY "B" (BAKING INDUSTRY)

Anticipated Recession Cash Position Associated with Adverse
Limits of Behavior of Determinants of Cash Flow:
Considering Only Those Expenditures Required to Generate
Current Income

		Assuming Recession Experience with respect to:		
	Cumulative Net Cash Balance at End of Recession Year	*Financial Conditions Preceding Recession*	*Behavior of Determinants of Cash Flow During Recession*	
			Sales Contraction	*Other Determinants*
No.	*One*	*Reaches its Adverse Limit described as:*		
1	$4,900,000	Maximum	Maximum	Maximum
2	6,200,000	Maximum	Most Probable	Maximum
3	11,900,000	Most Probable	Maximum	Maximum
4	12,800,000	Most Probable	Most Probable	Maximum
5	11,300,000	Maximum	Maximum	Most Probable
6	12,100,000	Maximum	Most Probable	Most Probable
7	13,300,000	Current Condition	Maximum	Maximum
8	14,300,000	Current Condition	Most Probable	Maximum
9	17,100,000	Most Probable	Maximum	Most Probable
10	18,500,000	Most Probable	Most Probable	Most Probable
11	18,500,000	Current Condition	Maximum	Most Probable
12	19,900,000	Current Condition	Most Probable	Most Probable

cash flow will change from one company to another and that there is no set pattern of behavior. Consequently, the focus of any corrective or risk-averting action will vary from one company to another.

Company "B" 's 30% of capitalization rule can be translated into an approximate annual fixed cash outflow by using the same assumptions as were employed in Company "A." Rationally, one might expect the terms to be somewhat more lenient in this case but such changes will not have any appreciable effect on the outcome unless they involve a substantial change in the period over which the debt is repaid. Interest rate variations in this range of

EXHIBIT 13. CASH ADEQUACY AT THE LIMITS OF ADVERSITY
COMPANY "B" (BAKING INDUSTRY)

Anticipated Recession Cash Position Associated with Adverse
Limits of Behavior of Determinants of Cash Flow:
Considering All Expenditures Given Priority over Debt Servicing

		Assuming Recession Experience with respect to:		
	Cumulative Net Cash Balance at End of Recession Year:	*Financial Conditions Preceding Recession*	*Behavior of Determinants of Cash Flow During Recession*	
			Sales Contraction	*Other Determinants*
No.	*One*	*Reaches its Adverse Limit described as:*		
1	$(5,000,000)	Maximum	Maximum	Maximum
2	(3,700,000)	Maximum	Most Probable	Maximum
3	3,500,000	Most Probable	Maximum	Maximum
4	4,400,000	Most Probable	Most Probable	Maximum
5	1,400,000	Maximum	Maximum	Most Probable
6	2,200,000	Maximum	Most Probable	Most Probable
7	5,700,000	Current Condition	Maximum	Maximum
8	6,700,000	Current Condition	Most Probable	Maximum
9	8,700,000	Most Probable	Maximum	Most Probable
10	10,100,000	Most Probable	Most Probable	Most Probable
11	10,900,000	Current Condition	Maximum	Most Probable
12	12,300,000	Current Condition	Most Probable	Most Probable

risk will be of minor significance. For Company "B" a 30% debt would mean an annual burden of roughly $7,000,000, assuming 5% interest and full retirement over 20 years.

Exhibit 12 shows that this debt capacity rule involves no risk of insolvency whatsoever in the immediate future (see data related to Current conditions). Indeed, it is apparent that if there is no sudden and radical change in the current financial structure, the company could stand a great deal more debt without any apparent hazard of cash insolvency. Considering the more distant future, which would necessarily be required in any policy of continuous borrowing, a 30% debt rule would involve only a very slight chance of insolvency. Actually it would only be under conditions of a coincidence of the Maximum Adverse values of all determinants of cash flow that insolvency would occur. The next most adverse set of conditions, (No. 2), in which Sales have been taken at the Most Probable Limit of contraction comes very close to providing the necessary coverage ($6,200,000 compared to the required $7,000,000), and the third most adverse set provides an excess cash balance of $4,900,000.

Thus in Company "B," even more so than in Company "A," the evidence on expected minimum recession cash balances appears to be inconsistent with management's explanation of its debt capacity criterion, especially in view of the stated need for a cushion of unused debt capacity to protect against the uncertainties of the future. The only rational way of reconciling these pieces of evidence, assuming that solvency was in fact the point of primary concern, is to characterize management as having virtually ruled out of consideration any incremental financial risks associated with long-term debt. In this case, however, this does not fit the characterization of itself which management presented.

The cash flow analysis for Company "B" suggests that the only substantial internal risk involved in a long-term financing policy which restricts debt to 30% of the capitalization is the risk of whatever penalties are to be associated with an abrupt interruption of dividend payments or capital expenditures. Exhibit 13 shows that when the test of cash adequacy is considered, which, of course, includes payments that are considered mandatory for policy reasons, the range of adverse events under which a 30% debt load would appear "safe" is significantly narrowed. The only Maximum Adverse behavior which could be assumed with complete peace of mind is the Sales contraction. With respect to the other variables the company would be "betting" on experience being no more adverse than the Most Probable Adverse Limit of behavior. Of course, this is still a relatively modest risk considering the whole scale of possible events, and with the exception of the two most adverse sets of assumptions *some* debt would appear to be permissible without threatening cash adequacy in recessions. Considering the immediate future, where the current financial conditions dominate, the data indicate that the company could have up to 24% of its capitalization in long-term debt without threatening minimum recession expenditures.

In interpreting Exhibit 13, it is significant to note that the duration of the recession has an important bearing on the outcome. Because of the assumption that the recession would not last more than one year for this company in this industry, it was not considered practicable to expect any major cutback in dividends and capital expenditures even though management would be disposed to consider it. The problem is in part the inevitable lag in management's reaction to the decline and in part the desire to have such action gradual rather than abrupt. As a consequence the data in Exhibit 13 for Company "B" assumed that the dividend was not reduced at all ($5,800,000 per year) and capital expenditures were reduced by only 50% (the recession capital expenditures ranging between $1,800,000 and $4,100,000).

In the absence of a lender whose particular standards may be applied to this company, it will be of interest to apply one of the more generally accepted tests of debt capacity in use by investment analysts for publicly issued bonds. Company "B" is in a position to issue such bonds if it so chooses, and this test will tell us what would be an acceptable maximum of debt for a bond of minimum investment quality. Undoubtedly one of the best known and widely accepted sources of investment concepts and standards is Graham and Dodd's *Security Analysis.*[1] For industrial bonds of fixed-investment quality, Graham and Dodd propose certain standards for the relation of earnings to total debt charges (earnings coverage). These are summarized as follows:

(1) Average before-tax earnings for a period of from 7 to 10 years should equal at least 7 *times* the total fixed charges of the debt.

(2) Alternatively, the before-tax earnings of the poorest year should equal at least 5 *times* total fixed charges.

(3) A supplementary rule is that the Average available income before taxes should be at least 20 *per cent* of the total funded debt.

Applying rule No. 1 to Company "B" (on a 7-year average earnings basis) we find that the maximum permissible total annual debt servicing charges would be approximately $6,000,000. The sec-

[1] B. Graham and D. L. Dodd, *Security Analysis.* New York, McGraw-Hill Book Co., 3d edition, 1951, pp. 320–321.

ond rule would indicate a figure of $7,800,000 — more liberal because of the small fluctuations in the earnings of this company over the years. The third rule would suggest a figure for annual charges of roughly $10,000,000 if the bonds did not have a Sinking Fund, $20,000,000 of annual charges with a full Sinking Fund (on the basis of previous assumptions as to terms). Since this latter is only a supplementary rule and is substantially more liberal in this case, it will be disregarded in favor of the first two which will be governing. Considering these rules, it is seen that the earnings coverage standards for fixed income securities brackets the figure produced by a 30% rule and at its lower level is significantly more conservative. Once again we find a standard which falls in the 25% to 35% of capitalization range, adding further support to the idea that this is a widely accepted working guide for industrials for both borrowers and lenders. Once again the standard shows up as a highly conservative one, the associated risks of which appear very small indeed. It does suggest, however, that *if the management of Company "B" was so disposed* it might push its debt limit up to 35% with only a very modest risk involved and without jeopardizing the investment quality and interest rate of the securities they would be offering to the investing public.

COMPANY "C" (CHEMICALS)

The chief financial officer of Company "C" was unusually articulate in expressing his views on the use of long-term debt and debt capacity, and it will add much to the significance of the data on this company to report these views in considerable detail. First, it should be indicated that at one time this company had taken considerable pride in a "clean balance sheet." Changes in the industry and in management's attitudes toward growth, however, gave rise to recognized needs which were substantially in excess of the then currently generated funds. This is an industry in which investment requirements tend to come in big "bites." As a consequence "the company had to get used to the idea" of going to the capital market for funds.

At the same time there was a reluctance to go to an issue of common stock because of the short-run adverse impact on market price and earnings per share. A debt issue was considered distinctly preferable because of its relatively low cost and the presumed absence of these adverse market effects. In the abstract at least the company was prepared to face an issue of common, but it was considered likely only if the company experienced a period (say 5 years) of sustained and substantial need for funds and had pushed its debt to what was considered an appropriate limit. So far this had not occurred and there was no immediate prospect of it in the future. If and when it did, management indicated a preference for a convertible debenture so that the impact on the market for the common would be delayed and would come at a time of a firm upward movement in price.

With regard to debt capacity it is interesting that this was one of the very few borrowing companies whose financial officers thought of debt limits in an earnings coverage frame of reference. At the time of the study, long-term debt was close to being at its all-time high which was approximately 29% of capitalization. A consideration of debt capacity was expressed in terms of assumed increases of 50% and 100% above the present level and whether the approximated earnings coverage at these levels was judged adequate. It was observed that at the 100% increase level the net earnings of the recent past (before taxes) would cover expected debt charges by roughly 5 times, and this was judged to be adequate but probably an outside limit from the company's point of view. The financial officer conjectured that if debt of this magnitude was put to a vote of the Board, there would be active debate and a close vote but it would probably get by.

Thus while the feeling was that the company could stand long-term debt in these amounts (58% of capitalization), it would be wise not to push it that far and a 50% increase (43% of capitalization) would be a safer and sounder operating limit. Several considerations entered into this, apart from the very practical one of getting assured support from the Board. One of these was the usual plea for a cushion of unused borrowing power against times when money may be needed and stock hard and/or expensive to market. A respectable bond rating — at least A — was given high priority in setting debt limits. There was the consideration of the corporate image and the preservation of the corporate entity. A company "as large and mature as ours cannot afford to go for broke." The company had a number of built-in fixed charges — "real and psychological," as the financial officer expressed it. One of the tests applied against the upper limit of debt was a comparison of the annual amount of the debt servicing to annual expenditures for research and development. At this point the debt servicing was approaching equality with R & D expenditures and this suggested the unwelcome prospect of having to cut back on the latter at some time in the unforeseen future.

On the other side, management recognized a good deal of flexibility in the cash position. While dividends had become essentially a fixed charge, the management would not reject the idea of a cutback in "an emergency." Capital expenditures could be drastically cut back if necessary though the company would prefer not to have to cut them below two-thirds of the depreciation charges in a recession. But they could "hack these expenditures to pieces" if necessary.

In summary, the management of Company "C" borrowed on a long-term basis because it found it could not generate enough for its need internally. While it would like to retire this debt, it was not seriously concerned about the risks of continuous borrowing so long as they were kept within "reasonable" bounds. The company record indicated that debt had never exceeded 30% of capitalization ($10,500,000 of annual charges). The desirable operating limit was set at about 45% ($15,500,000 of annual charges) and the maximum debt which the company "could handle" was set at approximately 60% ($21,000,000 of annual charges). These figures for annual debt service charge equivalents are based on the terms assumed in previous examples. In fact, there is real reason to expect that the interest rate might increase substantially if the company actually tried to push to a 60% debt level. No allowance has been made here for this refinement, however, in view of the approximate nature of the data.

When compared with previous industrial debt capacity standards, these decision rules appear to imply a significantly greater disposition to assume risk. It is particularly interesting, therefore, to check these rules against the recession cash flow analysis for Company "C." Exhibit 14 shows the results of the test for cash solvency under a 100% equity capitalization. According to standard procedure, the Maximum Adverse sales contraction represented the worst recession experience of the past 20 years which, as can be seen, did not exceed a two-year duration. The reader will probably be impressed by the remarkably strong cash position of the company under Maximum Adverse assumptions. According to the expectations built into the analysis, the company could carry the maximum debt servicing under existing decision rules (60% of capitalization) and would still have a comfortable margin of safety at the depths of the recession. There is apparently no threat to solvency at all under existing corporate debt limits, and the judgment of management that these represent "safe" limits appears to have strong confirmation even though it represents a major departure from the conventional concepts of appropriate debt capacity in industrial businesses. Instead of being evidence of bold and venturesome management, company debt policy is once again shown to be highly conservative in respect to corporate cash solvency.

The test of cash adequacy, given in Exhibit 15, presents a different picture. For this company there were three major expenditures, minimum levels of which management wished to give priority over debt servicing: capital expenditures, dividends on common stock, and research and development expenditures. Under maximum adverse assumptions these minimum outlays totalled $52,100,000. Thus when these are taken into account the comfortable cushion of recession cash balances seen in Exhibit 14 rapidly disappears. It is apparent that Company "C" does not have "absolute" assurance of cash adequacy as it did of cash solvency and that in adopting even its minimum debt capacity rule it is running some risk of having to interrupt these self-imposed mandatory expenditures. On the other hand, the risk is still relatively modest. Only the three most adverse sets of assumptions, Nos. 1, 2, and 7, do not provide adequate coverage for the company's lower debt capacity rule (30% of capitalization, $10,500,000 of debt servicing charges), and this is the rule that the company has applied in practice up to this time. Four of the twelve sets of adverse assumptions would not provide adequate cash balances under what was described as the desirable operating limit (45% of capitalization). Only the four most favorable sets of assumptions would provide the desired coverage with a 60% rule.

What this analysis has done for Company "C" is to clearly identify the *nature* of the risk inherent in the company's current debt capacity rules and give a rough measure of its magnitude. Whether

EXHIBIT 14. CASH SOLVENCY AT THE LIMITS OF ADVERSITY
COMPANY "C" (CHEMICAL INDUSTRY)

Anticipated Recession Cash Position Associated with Adverse
Limits of Behavior of Determinants of Cash Flow:
Considering Only Those Expenditures Required to Generate
Current Income

			Assuming Recession Experience with respect to:		
	Cumulative Net Cash Balance at End of Recession Year:		*Financial Conditions Preceding Recession*	*Behavior of Determinants of Cash Flow During Recession*	
				Sales Contraction	*Other Determinants*
No.	*One*	*Two*	*Reaches its Adverse Limit described as:*		
1	$41,000,000	$74,000,000	Maximum	Maximum	Maximum
2	42,300,000		Maximum	Most Probable	Maximum
3	48,800,000	92,000,000	Most Probable	Maximum	Maximum
4	50,200,000		Most Probable	Most Probable	Maximum
5	54,000,000	103,000,000	Current Condition	Maximum	Maximum
6	55,400,000		Current Condition	Most Probable	Maximum
7	61,600,000	109,500,000	Maximum	Maximum	Most Probable
8	63,600,000		Maximum	Most Probable	Most Probable
9	71,300,000	129,200,000	Most Probable	Maximum	Most Probable
10	73,300,000		Most Probable	Most Probable	Most Probable
11	76,500,000	140,500,000	Current Condition	Maximum	Most Probable
12	78,500,000		Current Condition	Most Probable	Most Probable

management would choose to modify its debt capacity rule in the light of this information depends on whether this new information confirmed or contradicted previous conceptions.

In view of the fact that the cash flow analysis lends support to the idea that debt servicing substantially in excess of what would be permitted under conventional rules of thumb could be carried without threat of insolvency, the case of Company "C" raises the interesting question of how far the company could or should go in exploiting debt leverage capacity. When it is remembered that debt amounting to 60% of capitalization is considered close to the upper limit for the best public utilities, there is strong reason to expect

EXHIBIT 15. CASH ADEQUACY AT THE LIMITS OF ADVERSITY
COMPANY "C" (CHEMICAL INDUSTRY)

Anticipated Recession Cash Position Associated with Adverse
Limits of Behavior of Determinants of Cash Flow:
Considering All Expenditures Given Priority over Debt Servicing

			Assuming Recession Experience with Respect to:		
	Cumulative Net Cash Balance at End of Recession Year:		*Financial Conditions Preceding Recession*	*Behavior of Determinants of Cash Flow During Recession*	
				Sales Contraction	*Other Determinants*
No.	*One*	*Two*	*Reaches its Adverse Limit described as:*		
1	$(11,100,000)	$(6,500,000)	Maximum	Maximum	Maximum
2	(9,800,000)		Maximum	Most Probable	Maximum
3	15,200,000	30,000,000	Most Probable	Maximum	Maximum
4	16,800,000		Most Probable	Most Probable	Maximum
5	18,300,000	38,900,000	Current Condition	Maximum	Maximum
6	19,700,000		Current Condition	Most Probable	Maximum
7	9,500,000	29,000,000	Maximum	Maximum	Most Probable
8	11,500,000		Maximum	Most Probable	Most Probable
9	37,700,000	67,200,000	Most Probable	Maximum	Most Probable
10	39,700,000		Most Probable	Most Probable	Most Probable
11	40,800,000	76,400,000	Current Condition	Maximum	Most Probable
12	42,800,000		Current Condition	Most Probable	Most Probable

that it would not be accepted by investors or if it was, that there
would be a substantial down-grading of the credit rating and a cor-
responding rise in the interest rate. This could quite possibly rule
out debt in these proportions on an incremental cost basis since the
interest premium would ultimately apply to all outstanding debt.

This would then appear to be a situation in which the company's
attention would turn to alternative uses of the substantial capacity
to assume incremental fixed cash outflows. Among these might be
found leasing opportunities which to date have not been equated by
the general capital market to the burden of debt in their effect on
corporate risk (though this analysis indicates that they should).
The unused capacity would also have implications for the long-

term budgeting of capital expenditures, research and development expenditures, recession employment and inventory policy, and so on. Thus the fact that practical market considerations may deny to this company the use of debt in amounts which it may consider quite safe does not invalidate the evidence on fixed cash outflow capacity nor does it negate its usefulness for other areas of corporate financial policy.

The primary source of capital market opinion on the debt capacity of Company "C" was the investment banking house which had been advising the management on long-term financing problems. Officers of this company indicated that their general policy was to urge borrowers to seek the maximum freedom from restrictions on new long-term loan contracts on the grounds that debt is likely to be the primary or only source of funds in an emergency. For this reason they also urged that a reserve of debt capacity be provided against such an eventuality. In the case of Company "C" the latest debt contract did not contain any covenant concerning limits on future borrowing, which suggested that the lenders believed the amount was comfortably within acceptable debt capacity. This implies a standard somewhat more liberal than that employed in the two companies previously discussed. The investment banker who had been involved in the latest negotiation indicated that within his company opinions would differ somewhat as to what would be an appropriate maximum debt for an industrial company in a "highly competitive industry" such as this. The more conservative were represented as probably having a 20% to 25% of capitalization standard and the more liberal a 40% standard. It was pointed out that in the chemical industry balance sheet ratios tended to be misleading because of rapid write-offs of substantial fixed assets which gave debt the appearance of being more burdensome than it really was. For this reason earnings were suggested as a more reliable guide.

From this it would seem that the lending side of the capital market might be disposed to consider debt in amounts up to 40% of the capitalization of Company "C" without major concern. As we have noted, however, this apparently liberal standard turns out to be well covered by expected recession cash flows so far as solvency was concerned.

One of the interesting questions which is raised but not answered by this study centers on the extent to which there are common cash flow characteristics among companies within the same industry group which derive from the nature of the industry. To the extent that there are such, and they are important in determining the recession behavior — relative to management and policy factors — there is an opportunity for industry-by-industry studies to identify these characteristics. The author believes this to be an area for fruitful research. For example, there is some evidence that the remarkable recession net cash flows for Company "C" may be somewhat characteristic of the chemical industry, the product, and the productive process. The substantial and relatively liquid current assets, the unusually low short-term liabilities, the strong net earnings record even after very substantial write-offs of fixed asset values, the character of the need for physical facilities, the importance of research and development — these and other factors are not confined to this one company.

On the assumption that there may be a better-than-average capacity to bear fixed cash outflows in the chemical industry, it is of interest to consider briefly the debt policies of the other three chemical companies included in the study. Did they, too, have a debt capacity standard which like Company "C" was, in theory at least, in the 40% to 60% of capitalization range? The answer is clearly in the negative. One of the remaining three had a definite policy against long-term debt and did not borrow on a long-term basis even for temporary needs. The ostensible reason was that the industry was "too risky" to justify it. There is reason to conclude even in the absence of a cash flow analysis that this position reflected an ultra-conservative viewpoint. The author is strongly convinced that this company could carry a significant amount of debt and still be relatively "risk-free" under Maximum Adverse assumptions.

The second company of the remaining three stated: "In this industry we go by the rule of thumb that debt should not exceed 30% of the total capitalization." The same company also stressed the dynamic nature of the industry, the need to maintain substantial research and development expenditures, and the need to have a reserve of borrowing power in the event either of sudden adversity due to product obsolescence or of sudden opportunity due to a research break-through. Within these limits the company borrowed freely on a relatively continuous basis.

The remaining chemical company had a somewhat more aggressive debt policy. Here it was stated that "some members of top management would consider a 30% limit too low." On the other hand, because a reserve of borrowing power was considered essential: "When debt gets up into the 30% to 40% range we begin to wonder about our reserve." It is interesting to note here that the company's concern with risk was *not* a fear of jeopardizing cash solvency — which was considered quite safe at these levels — but rather the chance of having to disrupt important company policies involving continuous expenditures of funds. This coincides with the observations on Company "C."

COMPANY "D" (ETHICAL DRUGS)

The situation of Company "D" is in several respects significantly different from that in the three companies previously discussed. Perhaps the most significant is the fact that it is operating in an industry which appears to be unusually resistant to the adverse effects of general recession periods. During the past 20 years Company "D" has never experienced an actual sales decline. The worst that has happened is that during a single year sales failed to increase. As a consequence this was used as the assumption for the Maximum Adverse Sales experience. Under the circumstances a Most Probable value for adverse sales experience was omitted from the calculations. Another feature found among a number of companies in this industry was a relatively strong profit experience, substantial internally generated and retained funds which made possible a considerable degree of freedom from the capital market in spite of sustained growth, and a strong cash position.

In spite of these and other features which on balance suggest hopeful prospects for recession cash flows, the sample of companies studied in this industry turned out to be generally shy of long-term debt. At the time of the study Company "D" had still to approach its first major long-term debt decision. This is undoubtedly due in part to the fact that it has generated so much of its funds internally. However, this is not the whole story. The managements of some of these companies do not appear fully convinced as yet that the industry is ready to join the ranks with public utilities and retail food chains in being substantially free from major sales contractions in recession periods. A very strong financial conservatism prevails. This attitude tends to be supported by the arguments for holding debt capacity in reserve against the hoped-for major product "break-throughs" which in a research-minded industry are always just around the corner. There are also the risk elements other than recessions which in this industry turn out to be of greater concern and which tend to downgrade the significance of a recession-oriented cash flow analysis as a tool of debt policy. The primary fear here is of sudden product obsolescence and unexpected adverse market reactions. Reason would suggest, however, that this risk may be currently overrated as the industry has matured and the companies have grown in size and diversification of products.

In any event these were all elements of the thinking of financial management in Company "D." At the same time, while the company did not need debt leverage as a means of presenting an acceptable return on the equity investment, the financial people were giving serious thought to what their policies should be in the event that debt funds were needed. In this thinking they appeared to be somewhat in advance of the Board's thinking and probably would have to do some "selling" and compromising to gain acceptance of the debt proportions they were considering. As a result of some fairly extensive analysis of the company's financial position and the probable effects on earnings per common share of different alternatives, the financial management came up with a debt capacity of $21,000,000 to $31,500,000. Using the previous approximation of the debt terms this would mean annual fixed outflows of $2,000,000 to $3,000,000. As a Percent of Capitalization this would be a maximum of 18%.

Exhibit 16 gives the data on the solvency test for Company "D." It shows that under any possible combination of adverse circumstances which may be deduced from past experience there is no possibility that this company would face cash insolvency in a recession period. The lowest cash balance anticipated is $18,700,000. This is primarily the result of the very strong cash position which this company has preserved over many years. Under the first two sets of assumptions there would be an excess of current cash outflow over inflow but these amounts ($5,500,000 net outflow under No. 1 and $2,700,000 net outflow under No. 2) are dwarfed by the reserve of cash and marketable securities.

It is apparent therefore that so far as the threat of insolvency in

Exhibit 16. Cash Solvency at the Limits of Adversity
Company "D" (Drug Industry)

Anticipated Recession Cash Position Associated with Adverse
Limits of Behavior of Determinants of Cash Flow:
Considering Only Those Expenditures Required to Generate
Current Income

Assuming Recession Experience with respect to:

	Cumulative Net Cash Balance at End of Recession Year:	Financial Conditions Preceding Recession	Behavior of Determinants of Cash Flow During Recession	
			Sales Contraction	Other Determinants
No.	One	Reaches its Adverse Limit described as:		
1	$19,700,000	Maximum	Maximum	Maximum
2	26,700,000	Most Probable	Maximum	Maximum
3	34,600,000	Current Condition	Maximum	Maximum
4	44,300,000	Maximum	Maximum	Most Probable
5	51,000,000	Most Probable	Maximum	Most Probable
6	54,100,000	Current Condition	Maximum	Most Probable

recession periods is concerned, the company's present debt policy which would hold debt servicing to a maximum of $3,000,000 is far more conservative than it needs to be for complete protection. Turning to Exhibit 17, the test of cash adequacy, the data show a possibility of cash inadequacy, even under a 100% equity capital structure. The sharp differences between Exhibits 16 and 17 are due to comparatively heavy minimum expenditure levels for capital investment, dividends, and research and the fact that on a one-year basis little can be done to cut back sharply from prosperity levels. It must be noted, however, that under the current debt capacity concept of management the threat of cash inadequacy exists only under one set of assumptions — when all determinants behave in the Maximum Adverse manner. It can therefore be stated with some confidence that the risk of cash inadequacy arising from recession conditions is very small and at worst would reduce the total of these expenditures for dividends, research, and new investment from $25,400,000 to $19,700,000.

In the light of this information, such a policy could still be justified on the grounds of ultra conservatism on the part of manage-

EXHIBIT 17. CASH ADEQUACY AT THE LIMITS OF ADVERSITY
COMPANY "D" (DRUG INDUSTRY)

Anticipated Recession Cash Position Associated with Adverse
Limits of Behavior of Determinants of Cash Flow:
Considering All Expenditures Given Priority over Debt Servicing

		Assuming Recession Experience with respect to:		
		Financial Conditions Preceding Recession	Behavior of Determinants of Cash Flow During Recession	
	Cumulative Net Cash Balance at End of Recession Year:		Sales Contraction	Other Determinants
No.	*One*	*Reaches its Adverse Limit described as:*		
1	$(5,700,000)	Maximum	Maximum	Maximum
2	5,000,000	Most Probable	Maximum	Maximum
3	9,200,000	Current Condition	Maximum	Maximum
4	18,900,000	Maximum	Maximum	Most Probable
5	29,300,000	Most Probable	Maximum	Most Probable
6	28,700,000	Current Condition	Maximum	Most Probable

ment with respect to the voluntary assumption of financial risks, although probably most managements would reject such "timidity" if recession behavior was the only consideration. As previously suggested there are other considerations. There is no doubt that management in this industry is very conscious of the possibility of sudden shifts in sales volume and competitive position as new products hit the market. It is a young industry characterized by phenomenal growth and rapid and unpredictable shifts in product acceptance. So far as debt is concerned this has the double-edged effect of making management sensitive to avoidable fixed cash drains and anxious to preserve the capacity to lay their hands on external funds quickly to capitalize on the next "break-through."

As already suggested, the author has gained the impression that the risks in this regard may be overrated in the large diversified ethical drug manufacturer of the type which Company "D" represents. Even if taken at face value, however, there is still a decision to be made as to how far this will be allowed to restrain the use of debt leverage. In any rational decision the opportunity for raising the level of corporate earnings, or, stated negatively, the opportunity cost of failing to do so by this means must be taken into account.   One aspect of the analysis which this situation does emphasize is constant alertness for significant changes in the underlying assumptions with respect to the determinants of cash flow and a need for periodic re-examination of the data.

COMPANY "E" (MACHINE TOOLS)

The last company to be considered is situated in the machine tool industry.   As such it has been exposed to several relatively sharp periods of sales contraction during the past 20 years.   This is an experience which on the surface at least presents a far more severe test of cash solvency than that of the other four companies illustrated in this chapter.   The severity is experienced not only with respect to the extent of the contraction (it may be substantially in excess of 50% of the sales of the preceding peak period) but also with respect to the duration.   As will be seen in the data for Company "E," the Maximum Sales contraction is assumed to last six years from the peak to the low point of the succeeding trough.

On the other hand, there are several circumstances which tend to mitigate the effects of the sales decline.   These have been mentioned previously but will be reviewed here.   One of the more important is the simple fact that the managements of these companies are used to such recessions, accept them as a part of life, and make plans on the assumption that they will continue in the future.   One of the variables of cash flow responses discussed in the previous cases is the lag in management's response to the onset of a recession — the lag in recognizing what is happening in the first instance and the delay in moving to conserve cash even when it is recognized.   These lags tend to be at a minimum in the machine tool industry.   Management and labor know what happens to the demand for durable capital goods if there is a major dip in the general level of economic activity.   There is no great problem of selling the importance of cash conservation to the management team.   In addition, there is the very real advantage of having advance warning of as much as one to two years before the pressures on cash flow actually emerge.   As previously indicated this is due to the characteristic of the industry of being in a substantial under-capacity position in prosperity which produces a heavy backlog of firm orders. It is the disappearance of this backlog that heralds the coming slump in cash inflows.

The recession cash flow is also aided by the fact that in most such businesses the backbone of sales is production to the customer's specification, and since the customers generally stand behind their orders and are good credit risks, much of the large inventories and accounts receivable shown on the books in the period immediately preceding the recession can be counted on to produce cash in the bank when the working capital cycle runs its course. The effect of this is that, unless the recession is prolonged beyond three or four years, the problem of the machine tool company is not how to preserve cash solvency but rather what to do with excess cash.

The major recession problem of the machine tool company, therefore, is not that of forecasting the cash flow characteristics of the downswing — these are fairly clear. It is rather one of the forecasting the timing of the upswing — since the recession may last two years or it may last six. If the recession is prolonged at these very low sales levels, then real problems of solvency may arise. Under the circumstances these companies are accustomed to bold action on the cash flows over which management exercises discretionary power. The capital expenditures and dividend payments which other companies feel so solicitous about they will cut abruptly, to zero if necessary, and apparently survive the experience without a crippling reaction.

This does not mean, however, that they will deliberately add to the likelihood of requiring such action without very careful consideration. In general these companies are very reluctant to add to contractual cash outflows and tend to preserve a strong cash position through periods of prosperity. They are also reluctant to add to their slow-turning assets (plant and equipment) even though strong competitive pressures may exist. Company "E" is typical in this respect. Its general policy is that it should not borrow on a long-term basis for "bricks and mortar." It considers short-term debt money to be appropriate for cyclical expansion of working capital since there is a high degree of confidence in the capacity to liquidate such assets in the normal course of business when a recession occurs. The only sound basis for long-term debt is considered to be for "one shot" investment opportunities (in particular, acquisitions of going concerns) where the payout is considered comparatively certain.   The potential cash difficulties of recessions are also considered to be a possible reason for debt, but this is likely to be on a short-term basis.

Since the company has not in recent years found any desirable opportunities to acquire subsidiaries for cash, the above set of attitudes actually adds up to a general policy of no long-term debt. This may now be considered in the light of recession cash flow data given in Exhibits 18 and 19.   Certain things immediately stand out. One of these is the considerable difference in duration (though not so much in severity of decline) between the assumed Maximum Adverse sales decline and the Most Probable Adverse experience. Another is the wide range of combinations of adverse events over which substantial negative annual cash flows are apparent.   A third characteristic is that these negative flows are largely to be found in the prolonged recession and that the first couple of years tend to be years of substantial cash inflows in spite of sharp cuts in sales volume.

Exhibit 18 gives the data on the test for solvency at the anticipated limits of adverse recession cash flow behavior.   It can be seen that the Maximum Adverse sales contraction which is assumed to extend over a six-year period produces insolvency under five of the six sets of assumptions — in the first set by the third year. In the sixth set where other factors are held to their Most Probable Adverse Limit a positive cash balance still remains by the sixth year.   In view of the fact that in the sixth year there was a net cash outflow of $5,500,000, however, there is a real possibility that the company would have run out of cash before recovery once again reached the point where net cash inflows occurred.   Thus for all practical purposes the analysis shows that the Maximum Adverse decline would produce insolvency over the whole range of assumptions — and this, of course, with a 100% equity capitalization.

The Most Probable Sales contraction produces significantly different results, not so much because the contraction is less (the assumed contraction here is a 55% decline from the preceding peak level) but primarily because it is assumed to last only two years. It can be seen that even under Maximum Adverse sales performance the company is still solvent at the end of two years — over the entire range of assumptions.   This situation has some interesting implications. One conclusion to be drawn is that the "best" recession from a cash flow point of view appears to be one that is sharp enough and long enough to permit a substantial liquidation of current assets and the firm establishment of a cash conservation psychology among members of the management team — but not so long as to use up the cash resources so released. Under any set of assumptions the first two years are "safe," and this is an advantage in the sense that it gives management time to plan its recession strategy and convert these plans into action. Under these circumstances modification of managerial policies and procedures as a defense against insolvency makes more sense than in the case of previous examples where the recession could well be over before such action could be implemented effectively.

Perhaps the most significant implication of the data, however, is the challenge that it presents to management's attitude to risk bearing. The data tell us that within the range of "normal" recession experience there is no threat of insolvency. This is borne out in part by experience in this industry where the usual problem in recession is not how to get enough cash to pay the bills but what to do with idle cash. There is an outside chance of a prolonged recession, however, and if this occurs there is a significant chance that the company will face insolvency. Thus the question for management is how to react to the event of low probability but extremely adverse effects.

In this situation the evidence on the test of cash adequacy (Exhibit 19) should be added. What this exhibit shows is that even within the range of Most Probable Sales contraction there is a chance of not having the cash to meet those expenditures which management considers essential to the long-term interests of the company. On the other hand, it can be seen that four of the six sets of assumptions do provide for these expenditures without exhausting cash balances and if all variables are taken at their Most Probable limit the cash balance does not get below $11,700,000.

It should be noted that since Company "E" had a "one shot" approach to debt (for certain limited purposes) the assumptions relating to the Current financial conditions are particularly significant (Nos. 3, 4, 9, 10). If a company borrows at any point in time with the definite objective of repaying it as rapidly as possible, then the financial conditions existing at that time are particularly signif-

EXHIBIT 18. CASH SOLVENCY AT THE LIMITS OF ADVERSITY
COMPANY "E" (MACHINE TOOLS INDUSTRY)
Anticipated Recession Cash Position Associated with Adverse Limits of
Behavior of Determinants of Cash Flow:
Considering Only Those Expenditures Required to Generate Current Income

No.	Cumulative Net Cash Balance at End of Recession Year:						Assuming Recession Experience with respect to:		
								Behavior of Determinants of Cash Flow During Recession	
	One	Two	Three	Four	Five	Six	Financial Conditions Preceding Recession Reaches its Adverse Limit described as:	Sales Contraction	Other Determinants
1	$5,500,000	$900,000	$(5,300,000)	$(11,700,000)	$(18,100,000)	$(25,700,000)	Maximum	Maximum	Maximum
2	8,000,000	5,900,000	1,500,000	(4,000,000)	(9,700,000)	(16,400,000)	Maximum	Maximum	Most Probable
3	12,400,000	13,100,000	7,400,000	1,200,000	(5,000,000)	(12,100,000)	Current Condition	Maximum	Maximum
4	16,700,000	19,200,000	15,800,000	10,500,000	5,000,000	(1,400,000)	Current Condition	Maximum	Most Probable
5	14,200,000	17,600,000	13,700,000	8,200,000	2,000,000	(4,400,000)	Most Probable	Maximum	Maximum

6	19,100,000	24,200,000	22,400,000	18,700,000	14,100,000	8,600,000	Most Probable	Maximum	Most Probable
7	6,200,000	1,600,000					Maximum	Most Probable	Maximum
8	8,700,000	6,600,000					Maximum	Most Probable	Most Probable
9	13,000,000	13,700,000					Current Condition	Most Probable	Maximum
10	17,400,000	19,900,000					Current Condition	Most Probable	Most Probable
11	14,500,000	18,200,000					Most Probable	Most Probable	Maximum
12	19,500,000	24,600,000					Most Probable	Most Probable	Most Probable

EXHIBIT 19. CASH ADEQUACY AT THE LIMITS OF ADVERSITY
COMPANY "E" (MACHINE TOOLS INDUSTRY)

Anticipated Recession Cash Position Associated with Adverse Limits of
Behavior of Determinants of Cash Flow:
Considering All Expenditures Given Priority over Debt Servicing

| | Cumulative Net Cash Balance at End of Recession Year: | | | | | | Assuming Recession Experience with respect to: | | |
| | | | | | | | | Behavior of Determinants of Cash Flow During Recession | |
No.	One	Two	Three	Four	Five	Six	Financial Conditions Preceding Recession	Sales Contraction	Other Determinants
							Reaches its Adverse Limit described as:		
1	$(4,600,000)	$(11,900,000)	$(20,100,000)	$(28,500,000)	$(36,000,000)	$(44,700,000)	Maximum	Maximum	Maximum
2	(2,100,000)	(6,900,000)	(13,300,000)	(20,800,000)	(27,600,000)	(35,400,000)	Maximum	Maximum	Most Probable
3	5,300,000	3,300,000	(4,400,000)	(12,600,000)	(19,900,000)	(28,100,000)	Current Condition	Maximum	Maximum
4	9,600,000	9,400,000	4,000,000	(3,300,000)	(9,900,000)	(17,400,000)	Current Condition	Maximum	Most Probable
5	6,400,000	7,100,000	1,200,000	(6,300,000)	(13,600,000)	(21,100,000)	Most Probable	Maximum	Maximum

6	11,300,000	13,700,000	9,900,000	4,200,000	(1,500,000)	(8,100,000)	Most Probable	Maximum	Most Probable
7	(3,800,000)	(11,100,000)					Maximum	Most Probable	Maximum
8	(1,400,000)	(6,200,000)					Maximum	Most Probable	Most Probable
9	6,900,000	4,900,000					Current Condition	Most Probable	Maximum
10	10,300,000	10,100,000					Current Condition	Most Probable	Most Probable
11	6,700,000	7,700,000					Most Probable	Most Probable	Maximum
12	11,700,000	14,100,000					Most Probable	Most Probable	Most Probable

icant as compared to what they might be ten years hence. In the case of Company "E," this may make an important difference in the conclusions reached since if the debt is floated at a time of favorable financial circumstances and is repaid rapidly, it may be virtually free of any threat of insolvency. Under the Current conditions of Exhibits 18 and 19, there is a comfortable margin with the Most Probable Sales contraction (even considering cash adequacy), and under a Maximum contraction assumption insolvency does not occur unless the recession lasts for five years. This is not "absolute" protection but may be a risk that management is prepared to accept quite readily.

In view of this evidence it is interesting to note that Company "E" did, at one point during the past 20 years, become involved in a long-term borrowing arrangement. The circumstances were such that the company felt "forced" into it against its clear-cut attitudes to the contrary. An expansion of plant seemed necessary, and accumulated resources plus a stock issue (considered to be the maximum amount readily marketable at the time) were not sufficient to cover the estimated outlay. A term loan was therefore arranged which placed debt on the balance sheet to the extent of approximately 15% of capitalization. The hope was that this would be paid down substantially before a recession occurred.

Unfortunately a serious and prolonged recession occurred while a substantial portion of the debt was still outstanding. It proved to be a very difficult experience. Capital expenditures and dividend payments were quickly cut back and eventually approached the zero level. It is interesting to note that the whole method of financial reporting to management was changed so as to group expenditures by levels of urgency and establish priorities among groups. The situation was reviewed at frequent intervals, and management repeatedly faced the difficult decision as to whether to continue certain expenditures (e.g., sales promotion and engineering development) in the long-term interests of the company or cut them back to conserve cash. In cash flow terms, postponement of action meant that some cash was irretrievably lost. This decision obviously hinged in large degree on the current cash position and the expectations for the timing of an upturn.

In spite of the severity of this experience, however, the company's cash solvency was never seriously threatened. At the very depths of the recession the financial officer was faced with the paradoxical situation of having idle cash to invest in some sort of short-term securities. On the other hand, this fact should not obscure a full awareness of these considerations: (1) that the particular combination of circumstances in this recession was not the Maximum Adverse, (2) that in order to preserve solvency drastic action had to be taken which jeopardized certain policies and activities which had an important bearing on the future of the company, (3) that management took such action reluctantly and with misgivings, and (4) that the period was one of considerable frustration and discomfort for management — an experience the probability of which they would not deliberately increase in the future. The debt servicing charges were, relatively speaking, a "drop in the bucket" but enough so that the then financial officer resolved to avoid them in the future. One thing was abundantly clear. Long-term debt would not be incurred by this management team merely to gain the leverage effect on income. The penalties for misjudgment were considered too high to justify the use of this source except under pressure of an imperative need for funds which could not be satisfied in any other way.

In reviewing the loan to Company "E" from the lender's viewpoint it is clear that the institution concerned considered the loan to be somewhat marginal. Actually the borrower had sounded out the possibility of a loan from other lending institutions before approaching this one but had concluded that the chances of a loan were best here because the institution had a reputation for "flexibility." The lender indicated that while as a general rule it considered 30% of capitalization as an appropriate upper limit of long-term debt for industrial companies, there were exceptions ranging up and down from this standard. This lender, as well as others contacted relative to other machine tool companies, held a firm belief that the machine tool industry was unusually risky and therefore the rule of thumb did not apply here. As we have shown, the balance sheet ratio frame of reference for debt limits does not provide any useful guides as to how to make allowance for variations in risk except to move up or down from some customary reference point such as 30% of capitalization. In this case the loan was at the 15% level which appeared to provide a comfortable margin. At the same time, the loan contract contained a covenant prohibiting any funded debt in excess of that provided for in the contract. Such a provision is usually strong evidence that the borrower has pushed hard on the limits of its borrowing with that particular lender. The more conventional restraint on future borrowing at least provides for some increase if and when equity increases to maintain some desired proportion.

We therefore conclude that both borrower and lender saw this loan as being unusually risky. The data suggest that this was certainly the most risky of the five companies considered. On the other hand, it is to be noted that the real risk lay at the Maximum extreme. If the Most Probable limits are used, the threat appears not as one of possible cash insolvency but rather as a threat to certain expenditures which are mandatory only in the policy sense.

SUMMARY AND CONCLUSIONS

In this final section of the study there will be no attempt to reproduce all the principal observations and conclusions on corporate debt policy. The purpose is rather to re-emphasize certain of the results of the study, particularly those relating to the application of the proposed analytical approach to decisions on debt capacity. Having now considered the results of such an analysis in five companies, certain useful generalizations may be drawn. These are as follows:

(1) The primary usefulness of this analysis for debt policy decisions in established companies lies in the basis it provides for identifying the implications and assumptions of decision rules in use by the company and its sources of long-term debt capital. It is believed that the examples amply demonstrate the possibility of significant inconsistencies between the expected behavior of recession cash flows based on an orderly analysis of past experience within the individual company and the expected behavior of cash flows which is implicit in standards of debt capacity inherited from predecessors, proposed by creditors, or drawn from the folklore of corporate finance.

(2) The examples suggest that for some mature and generally successful companies the customary debt capacity rules of thumb imply a concern for events of extremely remote probability and an extreme conservatism. Further, this evidence appears

at variance with the apparent expressed beliefs of management and lenders as to the risks involved as the accepted limits are approached.

There are two possible interpretations of these observations. One is that the risks of debt financing within conventional borrowing limits are substantially over-estimated by management. The alternative interpretation would be that management tends to be highly conservative with respect to financial risks. If the latter is the case, then there is a question of consistency with regard to risk bearing since these same companies appear to be far more aggressive in assuming the risks of new product development, expansion of markets, inventory accumulation — all of which hold potential hazards for cash solvency just as debt does. Whichever interpretation is correct, there is strong evidence that misjudgment may be present. The matter is worthy of serious attention.

(3) It has been further indicated that for some companies the risk of actual cash insolvency appears practically nonexistent and that the primary risk, to the extent that it exists, is the risk of interfering with expenditures which are mandatory only in a policy sense. On the other hand, much of the general attitude toward the risk of debt appears to rest on a fear of insolvency. If the nature of the risk can be identified through a recession cash flow analysis, it may serve to change the disposition to assume the risk, particularly when the adverse event appears to have a remote probability of occurrence.

(4) The examples point up the major differences which exist in the recession cash flow patterns of companies within the industrial group, a group which is generally assumed to have a common range of debt-bearing capacity. This evidence underlines the need for an approach to the question of debt policy that takes individual company and industry characteristics into account. A single standard such as the widely accepted 30% of capitalization rule is clearly inappropriate as an operating guide to debt policy in the borrowing corporation. The only defense for such a rule is that it seems to assure a high degree of safety for the lender with a loan portfolio dominated by mature and profitable and relatively stable companies.

(5) The obvious importance and complexity of total cash flows as

the dominant consideration in debt capacity further illustrates the inadequacies of simple balance sheet or income statement ratios as a basis for reaching decisions on debt policy in the individual firm. They are at best a convenient but crude way of summarizing a decision rule that should be derived by other means.

(6) It has been demonstrated that the effect of variations in the amount of debt, within the usual range of consideration, on the chances of cash insolvency may be minor in comparison with the effect of variations in management policies, practices, procedures, and responses. A valuable by-product of the analysis is information on those factors to which cash flows are particularly sensitive and the extent of the sensitivity.

(7) None of the foregoing is to be construed as implying that all or any of these companies could or should assume more long-term debt. The furthest one can go in this direction is to say that an objective appraisal of the expected behavior of the determinants of cash flow in recession periods and an assessment of the probabilities of cash insolvency under varying combinations of events may reveal existing debt policies to be more conservative than they were intended to be. But improved information on these dimensions of risk will not alone change policy. Management generally operates on the basis of certain assumptions as to the nature of the adverse event and its likelihood of occurrence and of a general awareness of various buffers or cushions against adversity which exist in excessive cash balances, cash float, marketable inventories, unused debt capacity, and the like. These all form a part of the total concept of an acceptable debt capacity standard. Merely to confirm these assumptions or dimensions of the problem will not change policy though it is still a useful thing to do. Policy may change only if there is a substantial revision of assumptions or new knowledge is added about the dimensions of total cash flows. Even then the policy may not change. The new understanding may simply be used as a further contribution to management's peace of mind.

(8) Finally, the reader is reminded once again that increased debt financing is only one way of utilizing the capacity to assume incremental fixed cash outflows which a cash flow analysis,

when matched with attitudes toward risk bearing, may reveal. Debt must be set in the perspective of total financial policy and its potential advantages weighed against the alternative uses of this limited resource. In view of the nature of some of these alternative uses, the ultimate allocation is likely to be based on nonfinancial as well as financial considerations.

APPENDICES

APPENDIX A

Company-by-Company Record of the Means
by Which Funds Were Provided in Years When
Total Funds Applied Exceeded Internally Generated Funds Plus Funds Released from Other Assets

Company Code No.	Years of Deficiency		Supplied Internally by		Supplied Externally by		
	Date	Amt. as % Total Need	Reduction in Liquid Reserve	Reduction in Dividend	Issue of Common	Issue of Preferred	New Debt
1	1941	11%		×			
	1942	12		×			
	1944	62	×				
	1945	5	×				
	1946	8	×				
	1949	37	×	×			
	1950	7	×				
	1951	78	×	×			
	1955	3	×	×			
2	1939	31%	×				
	1941	28					×
	1945	60	×	×			
	1946	81	×				×
	1947	67					×
	1951	65		×			×
	1954	9	×				
	1955	9				×	
	1956	21					×

Company Code No.	Years of Deficiency		Supplied Internally by		Supplied Externally by		
	Date	Amt. as % Total Need	Reduction in Liquid Reserve	Reduction in Dividend	Issue of Common	Issue of Preferred	New Debt
3	1941	9%	×				
	1947	10	×				
	1949	18	×	×			
	1951	8	×				×
	1958	6	×				
4	1941	12%	×				
	1942	8	×	×			
	1946	20	×				
	1948	8	×				
	1950	4	×				
	1951	29	×	×			
	1952	4					×
	1954	14	×				
	1955	30	×				
	1956	9	×				
	1957	6	×				
5	1946	9%	×				
	1947	34	×				
	1948	39	×				
	1952	61	×				×
	1953	34					×
	1954	60	×		×		
	1956	28	×				
	1957	8	×				
6	1940	16%	×				
	1946	42	×				
	1947	30	×				
	1951	25	×				
	1956	2	×				
7	1939	8%			×		
	1940	18	×				
	1941	45	×		×	×	
	1942	25	×	×			
	1944	19			×		
	1945	11	×				
	1947	17	×				
	1951	35				×	
	1952	16	×				
	1956	1	×				
	1957	3	×				
	1958	21	×				

Com- pany Code No.	Date	Amt. as % Total Need	Reduction in Liquid Reserve	Reduction in Divi- dend	Issue of Common	Issue of Preferred	New Debt
8	1941	57%			X	X	
	1944	30	X				
	1946	46			X	X	
	1947	16					X
	1948	10					X
	1949	20				X	
	1951	51		X		X	
	1952	60	X				
	1953	9			X	X	
	1954	3	X				
	1957	8	X				
	1958	14	X				
9	1939	17%	X	X			
	1941	37					X
	1942	49					X
	1944	9					X
	1945	2	X				
	1947	3	X				
	1948	6	X				
	1951	15	X				
	1952	44					X
	1955	6	X				
	1956	5	X				
	1957	4	X		X		
10	1939	2%	X				
	1944	12	X				
	1946	33	X				
	1947	31					X
	1948	16					X
	1950	10	X				
	1952	37	X				
	1954	27	X				
	1955	18	X				
	1956	18	X				
	1957	32	X				

Column group headers: *Years of Deficiency* (Date, Amt. as % Total Need); *Supplied Internally by* (Reduction in Liquid Reserve, Reduction in Dividend); *Supplied Externally by* (Issue of Common, Issue of Preferred, New Debt).

Company Code No.	Years of Deficiency		Supplied Internally by		Supplied Externally by		
	Date	Amt. as % Total Need	Reduction in Liquid Reserve	Reduction in Dividend	Issue of Common	Issue of Preferred	New Debt
11	1941	55%	X				X
	1943	78	X				
	1944	15	X	X			
	1945	35	X				
	1946	61	X	X			X
	1950	50	X				
	1953	13	X				
	1954	38			X		
	1955	73	X	X			X
	1957	40	X	X			
12	1941	4%	X	X			
	1942	49		X			X
	1946	46	X				
	1950	36	X				
	1954	5	X				
	1955	67	X				
	1958	90	X	X			
13	1941	26%	X	X			
	1945	6	X				
	1946	2	X				
	1947	25	X	X			
	1949	14	X	X			
	1951	6	X				
	1953	29	X				
	1954	1		X			
	1955	39	X				X
	1956	50					X
14	1939	27%	X	X			
	1941	33	X				
	1946	21					X
	1948	1	X				
	1949	25					X
	1950	26	X				
	1952	58					X
	1953	53	X			X	
	1954	31	X	X			

Company Code No.	Date	Amt. as % Total Need	Reduction in Liquid Reserve	Reduction in Dividend	Issue of Common	Issue of Preferred	New Debt
			Supplied Internally by		*Supplied Externally by*		
15	1940	25%	X				
	1941	3					X
	1944	38	X				
	1945	36		X			X
	1946	62	X				X
	1947	64		X		X	X
	1951	28	X	X			X
	1952	42					X
	1953	42	X				X
	1954	26				X	
	1956	28	X		X		
	1957	37	X		X		
	1958	38	X				
16	1940	59%	X				
	1941	23	X				
	1943	58				X	
	1944	44					X
	1946	16				X	X
	1947	2	X				
	1948	64					X
	1951	50	X				X
	1952	26			X		X
	1953	43	X				X
	1954	46			X	X	
	1955	41				X	
	1956	68					X
	1957	58					X
17	1940	20%	X				
	1941	30	X				X
	1942	33		X			X
	1943	53	X				
	1946	14	X				
	1947	56					X
	1948	10	X				
	1950	40	X				X
	1951	50		X			X
	1952	58	X				
	1955	46		X	X		X
	1956	17	X				X
	1957	6	X				

Company Code No.	Date	Amt. as % Total Need	Supplied Internally by		Supplied Externally by		
			Reduction in Liquid Reserve	Reduction in Dividend	Issue of Common	Issue of Preferred	New Debt
	Since 1950						
18	1951	57%	×				
	1952	34					×
	1953	76					×
	1954	43					×
	1955	34					×
	1956	39	×				
	1957	62					×
	1958	51		×			×
	Since 1950						
19	1951	12%					×
	1952	63		×			×
	Since 1951						
20	1952	17%	×				
	1954	18	×				

APPENDIX B

A Probability Approach to the Evaluation of

Corporate Debt Capacity

Chapter 7 contained a brief outline of a comprehensive approach to the analysis of the risk of cash insolvency in the individual firm (pages 171 to 176). For those readers who found this too abbreviated for a clear understanding of what was being proposed, this appendix adds a somewhat more elaborate statement. The reader must be warned, however, that the appendix is intended as an aid to understanding the general concept and not a step-by-step description of an operational procedure. In practice the procedure would require a combination of the skills of the financial analyst and the statistician coupled with the judgment of experienced management.

As already indicated in Chapter 7, there are a number of analytical problems which must be resolved as a part of the over-all process including the identification of the elements of change in net cash flows, the description of patterns of recession behavior relating to both independent and interdependent variation, and the problem of the timing of change as well as the magnitudes. What we are particularly concerned with here is how the analysis would differ and how the results would differ if we had information not only on the *limits* of variation but also on the behavior within these limits. We are also interested in the character of the information required.

Going back to an example used in the text of Chapter 7, suppose the recession sales contraction from peak to trough is expected to be within the range of −4% to −32%. In the analysis of adverse limits we focused on contractions at or near the −32% value. Now we consider the whole range. The question is one of whether it is possible to make meaningful statements about the chances of a recession reaching the various levels of contraction described within these limits. The obvious answer is to refer to past experience and hopefully to come up with evidence that, for example, there have been twice as many recessions which reached the −10% level as there were those which reached −20%. This leads to certain expectations about the chances of similar contractions in the future. If there was a large amount of such data, we might come up with a frequency distribution such as that described in Chart 5, page 187, in which precise distinctions could be drawn over the entire range. As has been noted in Chapter 7, however, meaningful historical data on recession experience may be severely limited.

Operating within a realistic framework as to available data, it is necessary to consider alternative approaches which are not totally dependent on historical frequency curves. It might simply be assumed that the probabilities were more or less "normally" distributed around some measure of central tendency, such as the mode, with the latter value estimated on the basis of whatever evidence is available. There is, however, considerable practical appeal in the approach which turns to experienced management for its subjective judgments on the distribution of probabilities.[1] It is presumed that mature business judgment represents wisdom gained from experience, separating and retaining that which has enduring significance and discarding the irrelevant and the transitory. Certainly, the opinions of management will reveal the nature of the evidence upon which it will be willing to base its decisions, and this is the ultimate test of the validity of data for decision-making purposes.

Following this approach the expected range of experience could be divided into significant intervals — significant in the sense that they would be large enough for management to draw meaningful distinctions about the chances of the recession reaching these levels of contraction. Then, drawing on all its resources of information, understanding, and good judgment, management would proceed to make an estimate (or "best guess" if the reader prefers) in quanti-

[1] For a full treatment of this subject see: R. Schlaifer, *Probability and Statistics for Business Decisions* (New York, McGraw-Hill Book Co., Inc., 1959).

tative terms of the chances of the recession falling within these intervals as in the following example:

Range Number	Range of Percentage Contraction of Sales	Estimated Chances of Recession Being at Least as Severe as Range of Contraction Shown
1	1–10%	$\frac{10}{10}$ (certain)
2	11–20%	$\frac{9}{10}$
3	21–30%	$\frac{4}{10}$
4	30–40%	$\frac{1}{10}$

These ranges taken together may be assumed to describe all relevant possibilities. It gives us the information upon which a curve describing all eventualities within that range in terms of their specific probabilities of occurrence can be based. For the sake of a simple example we will assume that there are only four possible events which are the mid points of the above ranges. Thus probabilities would appear as follows:

Event	Sales Contraction Corresponding to Mid Point of Ranges	Probability of Occurrence
1	5%	$1 - \frac{9}{10} = .1$
2	15%	$\frac{9}{10} - \frac{4}{10} = .5$
3	25%	$\frac{4}{10} - \frac{1}{10} = .3$
4	35%	$\frac{1}{10} = .1$
All Events Combined:		$\overline{1.0}$ (Certain)

It must be emphasized that for this or any other determinant management would subdivide the range and assign probabilities only to the extent that such distinctions could be made with confidence. Since this way of going about the problem is most meaningful for illustrative purposes, it will be continued throughout this appendix.

Given the information in the above table on the recession behavior of Sales, we can proceed to consider the variation in Collections from Sales (C_s) by bringing in the other major determinant of C_s, the Average Collection Period (ACP). If it happens that the recession behavior of ACP is expected to be completely independent of S, a table of values for ACP similar to that for S would be set up and probabilities assigned. The next step would then be to set up a table of all possible values of C_s resulting from all possible combinations of S and ACP, with the probability of each value for C_s being the product of the separate probabilities of the related values of S and ACP.

It is more likely to be the case, however, that Sales and the Average Collection Period are at least partially correlated so that the greater the Sales contraction, the greater the anticipated lengthening of the Collection Period. This will be particularly likely in a prolonged general recession. In this case the assignment of probabilities becomes somewhat more complex. Let us continue the hypothetical example by making the assumption that the anticipated recession experience with Collections of Accounts Receivable may be described as follows:

Range Number	Number of Days by Which Collection Period Is Expected to Lengthen	Possible Events Described by Mid Point of Range	
		Event No.	Lengthening of Collection Period
1	1–10 days	5	+ 5 days
2	11–20	6	+15
3	21–30	7	+25
4	31–40	8	+35
5	41–50	9	+45

The values for Collections from Sales (C_s) will be obtained by calculating all possible combinations of Events 1–4 (for S) with Events 5–9 (for ACP), given some assumption about the initial level of Sales and the initial Collection Period. Suppose that the recession lasts one year, Sales immediately prior to the recession were running at an annual rate of $20,000,000, and the beginning Collection Period was 35 days. Then, for example, a combination of Events 1 and 5 would give Collections in the recession year of $18,800,000. All other possible combinations and the related figure for collections under these simple assumptions are shown in Table B-1. Note that some combinations are considered impossible, such as the combination of Events 1 and 9 or 4 and 5, since the contraction in Sales and the length of the Collection Period are considered to be positively correlated.

The working out of the probabilities for the various values of C_s would be as follows. We have already assigned "odds" among the

TABLE B–1. TABLE SHOWING ALL POSSIBLE VALUES
FOR COLLECTION FROM SALES (C_s) GIVEN
PREVIOUS ASSUMPTIONS REGARDING S AND ACP

(1) Anticipated Collection Experience No.	(2) Assumption for Change in Sales (S)	(3) Assumption for Change in Average Collection Period (ACP)	(4) Related Collections (C_s)	(5) Probability of Occurrence*
1	− 5%	+ 5 days	$18,800,000	.050
2	"	+15	18,300,000	.035
3	"	+25	17,700,000	.015
4	"	+35	17,200,000	0
5	"	+45	16,700,000	0
6	−15%	+ 5 days	17,000,000	.100
7	"	+15	16,600,000	.150
8	"	+25	16,100,000	.150
9	"	+35	15,600,000	.100
10	"	+45	15,100,000	0
11	−25%	+ 5 days	15,200,000	0
12	"	+15	14,800,000	.060
13	"	+25	14,400,000	.090
14	"	+35	14,000,000	.090
15	"	+45	13,500,000	.060
16	−35%	+ 5 days	13,500,000	0
17	"	+15	13,100,000	0
18	"	+25	12,700,000	.015
19	"	+35	12,400,000	.035
20	"	+45	12,000,000	.050

Combined Probability: 1.000

* This joint probability is obtained by *multiplying* the conditional probability of the event in column (3) by the marginal probability of the event in column (2).

four possible values for the Sales contraction. We now proceed to estimate the chances of ACP lengthening by, say, 5 days (Event 5), *given* a Sales contraction of, say, 5% (Event 1). This is called the Conditional Probability of ACP relative to S. Thus management might judge that if S declines only 5% in the one-year recession, the chances of the Collection Period lengthening by 5 days are .5; by 15 days — .35; by 25 days — .15; by 35 days — 0; and by 45 days — 0. In other words, if the Sales decline is this small, the Collection Period is not expected to go beyond 60 days (35 + 25) under any circumstances, and the highest probability is assigned to the shortest Collection Period. The same process would be repeated for Sales contractions of 15%, 25%, and 35% and the conditional probabilities of the various values for *ACP* might appear as follows:

Sales	Conditional Probabilities of ACP, given S				
Contractions	+5 days	+15	+25	+35	+45
− 5%	.5	.35	.15	0	0
−15%	.20	.30	.30	.20	0
−25%	0	.20	.30	.30	.20
−35%	0	0	.15	.35	.5

We are now in a position to come up with a set of *joint* probabilities for each value of C_s since we have the (marginal) probability of the related *S* and the conditional probability of the related *ACP*, given *S*. For example, for the value of C_s which combines Events 1 and 5, the probability of a Sales contraction of 5% was given as .1, and the conditional probability of *ACP* lengthening by 5 days, given a 5% contraction, was shown as .5. The joint probability of these two events is (.1 × .5) or *.05*. It is in this manner that the probabilities given in the last column of Table B-1 were obtained.

Perhaps it should be repeated here that the purpose of this appendix is not to lay out in detail the mechanics of the financial and statistical processes for achieving the desired results. The purpose is rather to illustrate the general nature of the process and the kinds of data required so that the reader can better understand the end product of the analysis. As indicated previously, where several variables are involved and there is a considerable degree of interdependence among these variables, a careful statement of the full range of recession behavior and of the joint probabilities of all possible combinations of events can become a task which only an experienced statistician can resolve.

The important point, however, is that there is a method for resolving the problem which has been illustrated in simple form in the foregoing examples. Having now derived a full range of values for C_s and the related probabilities of occurrence, these values could then be combined with all possible values of Other Revenue (*OR*) to produce a full range of values for Cash Inflow — again with the related probabilities assigned to them. By a similar process the range of possible values for Cash Outflow would be produced and the combination of the various values of *CI* and *CO* would produce values for Net Cash Flow (*NCF*). It can be readily seen that with 14 possible values for C_s and anything like the same number of values for the other variables, the number of possible combinations (and, therefore, possible values for *NCF*) would become very large — in the tens of thousands possibly. At some point, therefore, if this analysis was carried to any real degree of refinement there would be a strong argument for using mathematical formulas or for programming the values on an electronic computer.

Associated with each possible value for *NCF* will be an estimate of its probability of occurrence. As in the case of C_s, the probability of any given *NCF* occurring in the future is determined by calculating the joint probabilities of the values of the several determinants which have combined to produce this particular result. It will be seen that if there are any significant number of determinants with several possible values for each, the probability of any *single* value for *NCF* may be small.

The net result of all this computation is to produce the following:

(1) a list of all possible values for Net Cash Flow,

(2) an itemized list of the specific assumptions regarding the determinants of Cash Flow associated with each of these values,

(3) a list of the estimated probability of occurrence of each of these values of Net Cash Flow during a future recession period.

The next question is: How is this to be used? The skeptical, practical-minded business reader may be disposed to doubt the usefulness of thousands of finely graduated values for *NCF* and the related and equally finely graduated probability estimates. If, however, the original subdivisions within the expected range of values for each determinant were significant enough to draw realistic estimates of probable occurrence, as originally assumed, then these data can be of great significance. *It is a fundamental principle of this approach as a practical business tool that refinement will be carried only so far as it is meaningful to management.*

The author proposes that the data on *NCF* be used in the following manner. All possible groupings of the variables which determine NCF will be ranked in order of decreasing adversity, with the most adverse coming first on the list and the most favorable (to cash flows) coming last. For example, in our list of values for C_8, value No. 1 was the most favorable and No. 20 the most adverse. Suppose Other Revenue (OR) had five possible values numbered from No. 21 to No. 25, Expenditure No. 1 (E_1) had nine values numbered from No. 26 to No. 34, E_2 had eight values numbered from No. 35 to No. 42, and so on. In each case the convention is to have the most adverse value associated with the highest number. Thus the most adverse combination would be No. 20 for C_8, No. 25 for OR, No. 34 for E_1, No. 42 for E_2, and so on. This combination and the related NCF would come first on the list.

This ranking of values for NCF is illustrated in Table B-2. In this hypothetical example it will be seen that the most adverse of assumptions for NCF produce a substantial negative Net Cash Flow. It will be seen that at some point on the list of values of NCF arranged, as stated before, in order of decreasing adversity of assumptions NCF is assumed to become positive. This value is adjusted in the adjoining column for that portion of the initial cash balances (CB_0) which was considered available as an offset to NCF in periods of recession without jeopardizing continued operations. The last two columns show a hypothetical probability associated with each value of NCF and the cumulative probability of the event that Net Cash Flows will be at or below the level indicated.

Thus arranged, Table B-2 shows an orderly summarization of the full range of recession cash experience and the associated chances of reaching different levels of adversity. For the management preoccupied with the event of insolvency, it now has an objective measure of the chances that this event will occur. It is shown by the cumulative probability at that level where the grouping of the assumptions with respect to the determinants of NCF shifts the Recession Net Cash Position from a negative to a positive value (where the value in column 9 becomes zero). This is the probability that events will be as adverse as or more adverse than those assumed at this point. If the cumulative probability at this point is, say, .05, then we can say that the chances of cash insolvency for this company in the best judgment of management are one in twenty.

At the same time there are potential penalties (risks) associated

TABLE B–2. TABLE INDICATING RECESSION NET CASH FLOWS ASSOCIATED WITH ALL POSSIBLE GROUPINGS OF DETERMINANTS ARRANGED IN ORDER OF DECREASING ADVERSITY

Possible Variations of NCF	Possible Groupings of Assumptions with Respect to Determinants						Associated Net Cash Flow in Dollars	Recession Net Cash Position, Given: $CB_0 = \$500,000$	Probability of Occurrence	
	Inflow		Outflow						Single NCF	Cumulative
	C_s	OR	E_1	E_2	E_3 →	E_n				
1	No. 20	No. 25	No. 34	No. 42	No. 49		$(1,565,000)	$(1,065,000)	.00002	.00002
2	No. 20	No. 25	No. 34	No. 42	No. 48		(1,530,000)	(1,030,000)	.00004	.00006
3	No. 20	No. 25	No. 34	No. 42	No. 47		(1,505,000)	(1,005,000)	.00008	.00014
4	No. 20	No. 25	No. 34	No. 42	No. 46		(1,476,000)	(976,000)	.00015	.00029
	At some point between #4 and #867 negative values for NCF would diminish to zero and then become positive.									
867	No. 14	No. 23	No. 30	No. 38	No. 48		$ 950,000	$ 1,450,000	.02310	.09835
868	No. 14	No. 23	No. 29	No. 38	No. 48		990,000	1,490,000	.02561	.12396
869	No. 14	No. 23	No. 28	No. 38	No. 48		1,065,000	1,565,000	.02940	.15336
	No. 1	No. 21	No. 26	No. 35	No. 43		$ 3,950,000	$ 4,450,000	.00008	1.00000

with various contractions in the company's Cash position short of the extreme event of insolvency, such as the suspension of dividend payments, cutbacks in capital investments, or interference with other company policies involving the continuous expenditures of funds. Here also the data give a measure of the chances of reaching levels at which such action would become unavoidable in order to protect the company's cash position.

In utilizing this information company management must bring to bear the second dimension of the risk problem — the disposition or willingness to bear risk. Having set up a framework in which the magnitude of the risk has been described, those who are to bear the risk (or their authorized representatives) must exercise judgment in terms of personal, subjective feelings about the level of risk which, given a choice, they will be prepared to assume. Naturally this choice will take into account the expected rewards from such risk-taking. One of the keys to success in risk analysis (and one of the most difficult to come by) lies in keeping separate the measurement of risk from attitudes toward risk bearing until each has been given separate identity, at which time they can be brought together to make the desired decision.

With respect to attitudes toward risk bearing, there are studies in existence which have attempted to describe individual preferences ("utility") in a rigorous and quantitative form. In theory at least there is an opportunity for relating a generalized description of management attitudes to the above description of the risk phenomenon to which these attitudes relate.[2] What the practical potential is here the author is not prepared to say. It is not necessary, however, to become involved in utility analysis to demonstrate the way in which these attitudes might be brought to bear on the data in a practical, usable form. For example, it would be reasonable to ask management for an approximate measure of the chances of insolvency which it is prepared to assume in the interests of maximizing profits. The response might be in the following form: "We are prepared to assume the chance of becoming insolvent so long as the odds are no greater than one in fifty" (or one in ten or any other such value). There is, of course, no reason why this measure of willingness to bear risk should coincide with the chances of insol-

[2] See F. and V. Lutz, *The Theory of Investment of the Firm* (Princeton University Press, 1951), Chapter XV, pp. 179–192.

vency related to the current condition and capital structure of the company as reflected in the cash flow data (illustrated as being one in twenty). It would be an odd coincidence if it did.

Suppose the management of our hypothetical company defined its position as a willingness to "ignore" the more adverse of all possible events so long as their chances of occurrence are no greater than one in ten. We now return to Table B-2 and go down the cumulative probability column until we come to the level where a combination of events of an equal or greater adversity have a cumulative probability of .1. It will be seen that if management chooses to "gamble" that the adverse events at and above this line will not occur during some relevant future period, then the *worst* Recession Cash Position within the anticipated range of experience will be a positive balance of *$1,490,000. This value then becomes the measure of the capacity to assume incremental fixed cash outflows.* Assuming that events are no worse than this, the company could stand an additional cash outflow of this magnitude without exceeding minimum cash resources during periods of recession. Again the reader is reminded that management may wish to use this capacity in ways other than the servicing of debt, but *if there are no competing uses this becomes the measure of debt capacity so far as this company and this management are concerned at this point in time.* This value for maximum debt servicing charges can readily be converted into principal amounts of debt given expectations as to the terms of the debt contract to be used.

In a similar manner management could approach its willingness to bear risks of lesser magnitude than that of insolvency. The willingness to run the risk of being "out of cash" for any specific purpose or set of purposes could be given an approximate objective value and the table of cash flows could be modified to suit the conditions. Thus management might, as indicated in Chapter 8, wish to give priority to a certain minimum dividend payment, level of capital expenditures, etc. The net cash flows could readily be recalculated with these outflows added in. The result would be a new break-even point with a higher probability of occurrence. Management's estimate of the chances of being out of cash which it is willing to assume could then be applied directly to the table and any capacity to bear additional fixed outflows could be determined.

Selected Readings Related to the Subject of

Corporate Debt Capacity

The following bibliography will serve the dual purpose of giving the reader added perspective and of providing an opportunity for the author to acknowledge the contribution to this study which has been made by the authors of previous writings in this field. It is intended to be representative rather than exhaustive and includes what the author considers to be the most helpful publications on this subject to date.

GENERAL FINANCE TEXTBOOKS AND HANDBOOKS

(1) *Corporate Treasurer's and Controller's Encyclopedia.* Edited by Lillian Doris. Prentice-Hall, Inc., four volumes, 1958. Volume II, Chapter 11, written by John F. Childs.
(2) *Essays on Business Finance.* 3rd Edition. Ann Arbor, Masterco Press, 1957. Chapter 7.
(3) *Financial Handbook.* 3rd Edition. Edited by J. I. Bogen. Ronald Press, 1950. Section 11.
(4) Guthmann, H. G., and Dougall, H. E. *Corporate Financial Policy.* Prentice-Hall, Inc. 3rd Edition, 1955. Chapters 7, 10, 12; especially pp. 215–226.
(5) Hunt, P., Williams, C. M., and Donaldson, G. *Basic Business Finance.* Revised Edition. Richard D. Irwin, 1961. Chapters 15 & 16.
(6) Johnson, R. W. *Financial Management.* Allyn and Bacon, 1959. Chapters 7 & 14.

SPECIFIC REFERENCES ON DEBT CAPACITY AND RISK

(1) Durand, D. "Costs of Debt and Equity Funds for Business: Trends and Problems of Measurement" in *Conference on Re-*

search in Business Finance. National Bureau of Economic Research, New York, 1952.

(2) Durand, D. "The Cost of Capital in an Imperfect Market: A Reply to Modigliani and Miller" in *The American Economic Review,* June 1959.

(3) Fisher, L. "Determinants of Risk Premiums on Corporate Bonds" in *Journal of Political Economy,* June 1959.

(4) Jacoby, N. H., and Weston, J. F. "Factors Influencing Managerial Decisions in Determining Forms of Business Financing: An Exploratory Study" in *Conference on Research in Business Finance.* National Bureau of Economic Research, 1952.

(5) Johnson, R. W. "Subordinated Debentures: Debt that Serves as Equity" in *Journal of Finance,* March 1955.

(6) Lutz, F. & V. *The Theory of Investment of the Firm.* Princeton University Press, 1951. Especially Chapters XIV–XVI.

(7) *Management of Corporate Capital.* Edited by Ezra Solomon. Graduate School of Business, University of Chicago, published by Free Press, Glencoe, Illinois, 1959.

(8) Modigliani, F., and Miller, M. H. "The Cost of Capital, Corporation Finance and the Theory of Investment " in *American Economic Review,* June 1958.

(9) Schwartz, E. "Theory of the Capital Structure of the Firm" in *Journal of Finance,* March 1959.

(10) Silberman, C. E. "How Much Can Business Borrow" in *Readings in Finance from Fortune.* Edited by J. F. Weston.

(11) Smith, D. T. *Effects of Taxation: Corporate Financial Policy.* Harvard Business School, Division of Research, 1952.

(12) Walter, J. E. "The Use of Borrowed Funds" in *Journal of Business,* April 1955.

(13) Walter, J. E. "A Discriminant Function for Earnings-Price Ratios of Large Industrial Corporations" in *Review of Economics and Statistics,* February 1959.

(14) Weston, J. F. "Norms for Debt Levels" in *Journal of Finance,* May 1954.

(15) Winn, W. J., and Hess, A. "The Value of the Call Privilege" in *Journal of Finance,* May 1959.

DEBT FROM THE INVESTOR'S VIEWPOINT

(1) *Business Loans of American Commercial Banks.* Edited by B. H. Beckhart. Ronald Press, 1959. Chapter 9, written by George S. Moore.

(2) Graham, B., and Dodd, D. L. *Security Analysis.* McGraw-Hill. 3rd Edition, 1951. Especially Part III.

(3) Hickman, W. B. *Corporate Bond Quality and Investor Experience.* National Bureau of Economic Research, Princeton University Press, 1958.

HISTORICAL DATA ON DEBT AND ITS INTERPRETATION

(1) Chudson, W. A. *The Pattern of Corporate Financial Structure.* Studies in Business Financing, National Bureau of Economic Research, 1945.
(2) Hickman, W. B. *The Volume of Corporate Bond Financing since 1900.* Princeton University Press, 1953.
(3) *Quarterly Financial Reports for Manufacturing Corporations.* Securities and Exchange Commission.
(4) Shapiro, E. "The Post War Market for Corporate Securities: 1946–1955" in *Journal of Finance,* May 1959.

INDEX

Accounts Payable (AP), 164
Accounts Receivable (AR), 164
Accrued Expenses (AE), 164
Adverse Limits of Recession Cash
  Flow Behavior, 178ff, 185,
  191, 228
Analysts, External and Internal,
  163, 180, 183, 194
Annual Cash Drain, 150
Application of Funds Pattern, 47
Asset-Debt Ratios (Net Tangible
  Assets/Total Long-Term
  Debt), 130
Assets, Composition of, 151, 212

Baking and Biscuit Industry, 12,
  17, 34, 119, 233–240
Balance Sheet Standard, 149ff
Balloon Repayment, 108, 150
Bank Balance, 216f
Bond Rating, 116, 232, 235
Borrowing,
  Arguments Against, 80
  Characteristics, 23
  Continuous, 138ff
  Cushion, 241
  Guides, 116
  Incentives, 68, 70f, 75ff
  Limits, 5
  Purpose, 140
  "Rules of Thumb," 100ff
  Standards, from Lenders, 114

Capital,
  Expenditures, 73, 153, 204
  Requirements, 9
Capital Budget Proposals, 53f

Cash,
  Budgeting, 160
  Commitment, 213
  Dividends per Share, 56
  Excess, Idle, 253, 255
  Expenditure Description, 162
  Expenditure, Nondiscretionary
    (E_n), 163
  Fixed Outflows, 87, 214ff, 245,
    264
  Future Obligations, 11
  Inflow, Outflow, 5, 7, 162, 167,
    180, 202
  Insolvency, 7, 126, 142, 159,
    174, 184, 202, 206, 263
  Position Flexibility, 242
  Risk of Inadequacy, 7, 158,
    202, 206, 210, 229f, 250
  Solvency, 83, 87, 150, 242f,
    254ff
  Test of Adequacy, 238, 245,
    255
Cash Balances Position (CB),
  165, 174, 180ff, 198
Cash Flow, 15f, 72, 132, 137,
  159, 161–164, 260
  Analysis, 9, 153, 156ff, 181,
    195, 202, 211, 235, 264
  Change, 165
  Determinants, 161, 165, 211,
    215, 221
  Dimensions (Three Basic Di-
    mensions), 188f
  From Accounting Data, 166
  Industry Characteristics, 246f
  Influences, 235

289

Cash Flow (*cont.*)
  Limits of Variation, 207
  Pattern, 143
  Payments, Mandatory, Discretionary, 132, 159, 214
  Sensitivity to Determinants, 229
  Throwoff, 106
  Total, 263
Cash Forecast, 71, 119, 131, 160
  Cash Budget Form, 72, 160
Cash Generation Standard, 74
Chemicals Industry, 12, 18, 240–248
Collection from Sales (C_s), 163, 178
Collection Period, 178f
Commercial Banks (Investment Banks), 10
Common Stock, 49, 56, 58, 240
Company "A," Rubber Industry, 193ff, 224–233
Company "B," Baking Industry, 115, 233–240
Company "C," Chemical Industry, 115, 240–248
Company "D," Ethical Drugs Industry, 248–252
Company "E," Machine Tools Industry, 252–262
Comparative Approach to Magnitude of Risk, 90ff
Contract, Typical, 139
  Covenants, 11, 109, 116f, 130
Control of Decision Making, 82
Convertible Debentures, 241
Corporate Debt Policy, 93, 223
Cost Concepts (Actual Outlays, Foregone Income), 60
Cost of Goods Sold, 162, 241
Credit,
  Revolving Short-Term, 10f

Short-Term, 153
Spontaneous, 10, 212
Standing, Rating, 87, 245
Creditor, Importance of, 220
Current Internal Generation of Funds, 39
Cushion, of Asset Values, 149, 218
  Of Unused Borrowing Power, 241

Data,
  Choice, 87
  Limitations, 208
Debt,
  Adverse Effects, 81
  Amount, 93, 107, 264
  Approaches,
    Rapid Payback, 106
    Single Project, 105
  Capacity, 116, 223, 234
    Analysis, 119
    Determination, 133
    Lender-Borrower Standards, 135
    Preservation, 84f
    Reserve, 202, 246, 249
    Rules, 216f
    Standards, Criteria, 111, 118, 124, 144, 146, 148, 150, 152ff
    "Unused," 217
  Capital, Need for, 75
    Availability of, 139
  Characteristics, 3, 138
  Contracts, 11, 109, 116f, 130, 139
  Criterion, 150
  Financing, 104, 145, 215
  Forms, 9, 110
  Income Advantage, 4, 68ff, 140
  Independent Standard, 118

Issue, Advantages, 240
Leverage, 68, 140, 251f
    Capacity, 244f
    vs. Cost, 212
    Limits, 207
    Payment, "Patient Money," 12
    Policy, 42, 140
    Rating Status, 87
    Restraint Covenants, 109, 116f, 130, 261
    Rules of Thumb, 262
    Servicing Charges, 107f, 126, 242
    Source of Funds, 70, 76
    Standard, 100ff, 124, 145ff, 154
    Vis-à-vis Equity, 71
Debt-Equity Alternative, Ratio, 4, 8, 142, 151
Debt Limit Covenant, 130, 261
Debt Limit Decision, 146
Decision Rules, 94–107, 148
    Comparative Approach, 90ff
    Modification of, 213
Default, 11
Determinants of
    Cash Flow, 161, 165, 168, 176, 221, 229
    Independent Variation, 168f, 185f
    Interdependence of, 178f
    Recession Behavior, 168
    Need for Capital Funds, 39
Dividends,
    Cash (Per Share Criterion), 56, 74
    Payments, 28, 153
    Payout, 42, 61
    Policy, 43

Earnings,
    Economic Considerations vis-à-vis Company Policy, 54

Per Share (EPS), 56f, 70
Performance Test, 53f
Projections, 58
Standard, 61
Earnings Coverage Standard for Debt Capacity (Income Statement Standard), 103ff, 151ff, 161, 239, 241
Equity Base, 56
Ethical Drugs Industry, 12, 18, 248–252
Executive Stock Option Plans, 58
Expenditures,
    Discretionary, 203
    Fixed, Mandatory, 11, 74f, 159, 241
    Plant and Equipment, 29
    Policy, vis-à-vis Debt Leverage Opportunity, 203
    Profits, for, 74
Experience Criterion, 90, 112, 135, 137, 147, 160, 169, 262

Field Research, Industries Used, 12
Finances, Structure, 52, 180, 211
Financial Requirements, 29
Financial Theory, 60, 99
Forecasting, Financial (Fund Flows), 89
Frequency Distribution (of Sales Contraction), 172
Fund,
    Flows, 57, 89
    Requirements, 32, 53
Funds,
    External Sources, 37, 48ff, 56
    Internally Generated, 36, 69
    Investment Rate, 41
    Meaning, 27
    Need for, 27, 34, 71, 147
    Opportunity for Profit, 71
    Rate of Application, 55

Funds (*cont.*)
Rate of Investment, 40
Total Applied, 28
Funds from Operations, 41
Future Financing, 99

Graham and Dodd (*Security Analysis*), 239
Growth Rate,
Long-Term, 42ff, 52, 55
Paced, 42

Income, Maximization, 140
Income Statement Standard (Earnings Coverage), 103ff, 151ff, 161, 239, 241
Industry, Characteristics, 170
General Practice, 126
Inter, Intra-Industry Comparisons, 91
Insolvency,
Avoiding, 189
Expectation of, 228
Interest Rate, 233, 236, 242, 245
Internal Rate of Return, 62
Inventory Levels, 162, 164
Investment,
Analyst, 239
Banking, 11, 116, 232, 246
Characteristics, 32
Decisions,
Cost Free Concept of Retained Earnings, 61f
Internal Opportunity Cost Standard, 61f, 74
Familiar, 30, 67
Horizon, 224f, 234
In Other Assets, 29f
"One Shot" Opportunity, 254
Opportunities, 145
Pace, 42
Rate of Funds, 40

Return on, 53
Standards, 67
Average Cost of Capital Standard, 74
Voluntary, Mandatory, 62
Irregular Investment Expenditures, 35

Lease Contract Decision, 215
Lender, 8, 23, 75, 79, 129ff
Borrower Differences, 134
Risk Standard, 128ff, 261
Standards, 114
Leverage,
Continuous, 138f
Debt, 68, 140, 209, 251, 261f
Opportunity vis-à-vis Expenditures, 203
Limits of Adversity, 7, 185, 209, 228
Limits to Corporate Needs, Built-in, Self-Imposed, 31
Liquid Reserves, Internal Source of Funds, 47
Minimum Liquid Asset Balance, 182f
Liquidation, 149
Liquidity (Defense Against Adversity), 217
Long-Term Debt, 10, 141, 218, 234
Long-Term Expansion, Growth, 42ff

Machine Tool Industry, 12, 16, 34, 91, 105
"Maintenance of Working Capital Provision," 11
Management,
Attitudes toward
Adversity, 264
Debt Policy, 81, 136, 141

Investment, 75
Risk, Uncertainty, 87, 201
Shareholders, 70
Use of External Funds, 51, 56
Use of Long-Term Debt, 68, 203
Conservatism, 262
Decision, 3, 180, 216
Discretion, 42, 168, 180, 253, 263
Importance of, 82, 87, 146, 211ff, 219
Response to Recession, 213, 252, 255
Marginal Approach to Capital Budgeting, 54
Market Price, Price-Earnings Ratio (Per-Share Criterion), 56ff, 246
Maximum Favorable Limit (of Sales Contraction), 171
Adverse Limits, 171, 185, 209
Methodology, 157, 175
Minimum Earnings Standard, 74
Moody's Industrials, 87

Need for Funds, 27, 34, 75, 147
Negotiation, 131
Net Cash Balances (CB), 162
Net Cash Flows (NCF), 162f, 165, 177ff, 185
Determinants of, 188f
Relation to Recession, 137, 163
Net Cash Throw-Off, 195
Net Earnings, 152
Net Income (NI), 152ff
Net Tangible Assets/Total Long-Term Debt Standard, 116, 130
No-Debt Policy, 94, 200, 254
Noncash Expenses, 152
"Normal Earnings," 152

"One Shot" Approach to Debt Financing, 104, 254
"One Shot" Approach to Investment Opportunity, 253
Open-Ended, Continuous Debt Financing, 104
Opportunity Cost, 60, 65
Internal Opportunity Cost Standard, 61f, 74
Other Receipts in Cash Form (OR), 163
Overlapping Loan Agreement, 139

"Patient Money," 12
Patterns of Application of Fund Requirements, 32, 47f
Payback Criterion (Debt Limit Rule), 58
Payroll Expenditures (P_a), 163
Percent of Capitalization Rule for Debt Limit (Balance Sheet Standard), 100ff, 127, 149, 225, 236ff, 246ff, 261ff
Pilot Companies, 12, 20
Plant and Equipment Expenditures, 29f
Policy Dictated Expenditures (Discretionary), 203
Preferred Stock, 63ff, 234
Prepayment, 77, 106, 108
Present Value, 57, 84
Price-Earnings Ratio, 56, 58
Prime Rate, 87, 97
Principal Repayment, 107, 150
Private Enterprise Characteristics, 125
Probability Distribution of Insolvency, 172, 208
Profit Maximization = Cost Minimization, 97

Rate of Application of Funds, 52
Rate of Return Standards, 62
Rating by Bond Agencies, 98
Rational Behavior Pattern, 126
Raw Materials Expenditures (RM), 163
Recession
  Behavior, 168, 188, 211, 215, 262
  Cash Balances, 188ff
  Cash Flow Analysis, 198, 215ff, 220, 223, 235
  Duration, Severity, 137, 239
  Experience, 165
  Net Cash Flow, 163, 176, 202, 225
  Repayment Period, 106f
  Response, 252
Reserves, Liquid, 47, 182f
Retained Earnings, 54, 58
  Cost Free Concept, 61f
Return on Investment (Expected), 53
Revolving Credit, 11f
Risk, 6, 86
  Analysis (Comprehensive Method), 171
  Appraisal, 4, 131ff, 147f, 154, 164, 215
  Fragmented Approach, 142ff
  Control, 93, 107ff
  Of Debt in Terms of Cash Flow, 214
  Decision (Gain vs. Cost), 129, 206
  Magnitude, 124, 146, 158
  Measurement, 9, 211
  Standard, 134
Risk-Bearing Approaches, 208–210
Rubber Industry, 12, 19, 34, 90, 146, 203

Sales (S), 165ff, 211
  And Cash Receipts, 153
  Collection, 153, 164, 178
  Contraction, 187
  Maximum Adverse Behavior, 178
  Performance, 229, 254
Sample Characteristics and Selection, 14, 20, 22, 23
Securities, Marketable, 47
Securities and Exchange Commission (SEC), 21
Shareholders, 56, 61, 67, 128
"Shock Absorbers" (Built Into Financial Structure), 216
Sinking Fund, 64, 152, 240
Solvency Test, 235, 249, 254
Sources
  of Capital, 11, 64
  of Funds, External, 36f, 46, 48, 56, 76ff
  Internal, 36, 67
"Spontaneous Credit," 10
Statistical Approach to Cash Flow Analysis, 172ff
Status in Debt Rating, 87
Stock Exchange, New York, 21
Stock Market, 127
Subjective Decisions, 147, 158
Subsidiaries, 49, 105, 143, 234

Tax Shield (as Incentive to Borrow), 68, 70f
Term Loan, 10, 150
Theory, Financial, 60, 99
Timing of Sales Contraction, 177
Total Funds Applied, 28
Trading on Equity, 60f

Uncertainty, 4, 85ff
Unlimited Debt Policy, 95
Utility Scale (Willingness to Bear Risk), 187